The Cultural Legacy of German Colonial Rule

The Cultural Legacy of German Colonial Rule

Edited by
Klaus Mühlhahn

DE GRUYTER
OLDENBOURG

This volume was subsidized by a generous fund from Einstein Foundation Berlin.

Einstein Stiftung Berlin
Einstein Foundation Berlin

ISBN 978-3-11-064673-3
e-ISBN (PDF) 978-3-11-052562-5
e-ISBN (EPUB) 978-3-11-052572-4

Library of Congress Cataloging-in-Publication Data
A CIP catalog record for this book has been applied for at the Library of Congress.

Bibliographic information published by the Deutsche Nationalbibliothek
The Deutsche Nationalbibliothek lists this publication in the Deutsche Nationalbibliografie; detailed bibliographic data are available on the Internet at http://dnb.dnb.de.

© 2019 Walter de Gruyter GmbH, Berlin/Boston
This volume is text- and page-identical with the hardback published in 2017.
Einbandabbildung: „Gerader Streckenabschnitt der Ugandabahn, Britisch-Ostafrika",
© Deutsches Historisches Museum, Berlin
Druck und Bindung: CPI books GmbH, Leck
♾ Gedruckt auf säurefreiem Papier
Printed in Germany

www.degruyter.com

Table of Contents

Klaus Mühlhahn and Frederike Schneider-Vielsäcker
Preface —— VII

Frederick Cooper
Colonies, Empires, Nations: A Twentieth Century History —— 1

Britta Schilling
Material Memories of Empire: Coming to Terms with German Colonialism —— 23

Nina Berman
***Schaffe, schaffe, Häusle baue:* German Entrepreneurs and Settlers on the Kenyan Coast since the 1960s —— 51**

Patrice Nganang
Writing under Colonial Rule —— 73

Dotsé Yigbe
Is Togo a permanent Model Colony? —— 97

Werner Hillebrecht
Monuments – and what else? The Controversial Legacy of German Colonialism in Namibia —— 113

Yixu Lü
Colonial Qingdao through Chinese eyes —— 127

Malama Meleisea and Penelope Schoeffel
Germany in Samoa: Before and After Colonisation —— 143

Craig Alan Volker
The legacy of the German language in Papua New Guinea —— 167

Klaus Mühlhahn and Frederike Schneider-Vielsäcker
Preface

This volume addresses central questions about the historical memory and cultural heritage of German colonial history. Discussing it from various perspectives are ten scholars from formerly colonized societies in Africa, Asia and Oceania as well as European and American scholars working in the fields of colonial history. For a long period, German colonial history did not receive significant attention in the field of historical studies. While historians in other countries such as France and Great Britain began discussing their colonial legacy during decolonization, in contrast, West German postwar society as a whole, including its leading intellectuals, writers and academics, were more involved in their own history during World War II and the Holocaust. After a few publications in the 1960s and 1970s, West German historians became interested in German colonialism in the 1980s. In the beginning, most studies shared a focus on political history, diplomatic history, the role of the Christian missions, migration, and the economic dimensions of colonialism and imperialism.[1] In addition, some literary scholars began to rediscover the literature of colonialist fiction and non-fiction.[2] However, East German scholars were more interested in German colonialism and historical research had already begun in the 1950s. Nevertheless, their distinct view was informed by Marxist theory. Therefore, fascism was understood in the larger framework of capitalism, while colonialism as well as imperialism were viewed as manifestations of capitalism.

The hesitation of historians to write about German colonial history has been pronounced because of the German colonial empire's short and fleeting duration. German colonial history lasted only for thirty years from 1884 to 1919. Many historians and the public seemed to believe that such a brief history did

---

[1] See, among other titles, Horst Gründer, *Geschichte der deutschen Kolonien* (Paderborn: Schöningh, 1985); Klaus J. Bade et al., *Imperialismus und Kolonialmission: Kaiserliches Deutschland und koloniales Imperium* (Wiesbaden: Steiner, 1982); Jürgen Osterhammel, *China und die Weltgesellschaft: Vom 18. Jahrhundert bis in unsere Zeit* (Munich: Beck, 1989); Francesca Schinzinger, *Die Kolonien und das Deutsche Reich: Die wirtschaftliche Bedeutung der deutschen Besitzungen in Übersee* (Wiesbaden: Franz Steiner 1984).
[2] See Joachim Warmbold, *"Ein Stückchen neudeutsche Erd'..."*: *Deutsche Kolonial-Literatur. Aspekte ihrer Geschichte, Eigenart und Wirkung, dargestellt am Beispiel Afrikas* (Frankfurt am Main: Haag + Herchen, 1982); Sibylle Benninghoff-Lühl, *Deutsche Kolonialromane, 1884–1914, in ihrem Entstehungs- und Wirkungszusammenhang* (Bremen: Im Selbstverlag, Übersee-Museum Bremen, 1983); Wolfgang Bader and János Riesz, *Literatur und Kolonialismus* (Frankfurt am Main: Lang, 1983).

not warrant a deeper and more nuanced historical investigation. Hence, German historians refused to follow their British and French counterparts to rethink their national histories by taking a so-called "imperial turn." German colonialism was conceived as a marginal and inconsequential phenomenon, amounting at best to the addition of historical anecdotes. These viewpoints were asserted by eminent historians. Jürgen Osterhammel once concluded that, "the social histories above all of Great Britain, Portugal, and the Netherlands, and in some respects of Russia and France, have to remain incomplete or incomprehensible once divorced from their imperial-colonial context,"[3] suggesting that in Germany, separation can more easily be made. David Blackbourn concurred: "One could hardly argue that the German colonies possessed the same centrality for domestic political debate as the far larger empires of the British and French."[4]

After something of a lull in the 1980s, interest among both academics and the wider intellectual public in German colonial history has recently been thriving, largely in response to the fallout from globalization. But while younger historians in Germany have started to produce new and well-researched histories of German colonialism that confront the whole spectrum of the colonial world from everyday culture to racist politics, the main terminology seems to have changed. Most historians now shy away from concepts of imperialism or colonialism, preferring the differently inflected and somewhat cleaned-up language of "empire."[5] During the 1960s "imperialism" and "colonialism" were used to highlight the coercive domination and exploitative relations imposed by metropolitan countries on the more vulnerable parts of the world, above all in the period of high-imperialism and intensified expansion between the 1880s and the First World War. The current understanding of empire however often recedes to the sphere of international politics such as foreign policy making, national security concerns, geopolitical strategy, international monetary policy, trade agreements, international policing, and the deployment of military force.

In the wake of the burgeoning interest in cultural history, new scholarship has shown that there was an impressive dissemination of colonial ideas into all possible areas of popular culture and everyday working-class life during the period. The thrust of this new historiography has challenged the idiosyncrasy

---

[3] Jürgen Osterhammel, "Transnationale Gesellschaftsgeschichte: Erweiterung oder Alternative?," *Geschichte und Gesellschaft* 27, no. 3 (2001): 468.
[4] David Blackbourn, "Das Kaiserreich transnational. Eine Skizze," in *Das Kaiserreich transnational: Deutschland in der Welt 1871–1914*, ed. Sebastian Conrad and Jürgen Osterhammel (Göttingen: Vandenhoeck und Ruprecht, 2004), 321–22.
[5] Bradley Naranch, introduction to *German Colonialism in a Global Age*, ed. Bradley Naranch and Geoff Eley (Durham, London: Duke University Press, 2014), 1.

or insignificance of empire for ordinary life, but rather highlighted its all-prevailing presence. In other words, research on the topic of popular involvement in imperialism came to opposite conclusions than the research on the thinness of empire in German history. This dichotomy, between an approach stressing the relative shallowness of colonialism's impact inside the home society and one arguing for its cultural impact, marks most of the relevant historical research. Even the recent embrace of "transnational" in German history has only reaffirmed this dichotomy, because the colonies are now seen as an example among many others of Germany's growing interconnectedness in a larger set of global links. It seems, that the transnational perspective has often implicitly downplayed the significance of colonial histories.

All the recent studies have mostly focused on German actors and experiences. Few European scholars have systematically studied colonial subjects and their agency. As Jürgen Zimmerer has reminded us: "Analysing and explaining the dreams of the colonizers is not sufficient for understanding colonialism. It tells us nothing, for example, about the colonized, let alone telling the story from their perspective."[6] As a result of these factors scholarship on German colonialism lacked, and continues to lack perspectives that pay attention to a wider range of social, economic, and political interactions and entanglements between Europeans and the local people, the intellectual history of formerly colonized areas, the agency of colonized individuals and societies, and the configurations of postcolonial developments.

Building on the book "German Colonialism Revisited African, Asian, and Oceanic Experiences" edited by Nina Berman, Klaus Mühlhahn, and Patrice Nganang (2014), this volume is designed to contribute to and expand the ongoing discussion of German colonialism with a fresh focus on the agency of those affected by German colonialism in Africa, Asia and Oceania. This book is a compilation of the multidisciplinary research that has been presented at the symposium "The Legacy of German Colonial Rule", which was hosted by the German Historical Museum Berlin and the Freie Universität Berlin on May 25 to 27, 2016. By focusing on the history of contact, interaction, exchange and mutual influence, this volume aims to intervene in current debates on transnational and intercultural processes and to highlight the ways in which the colonial period is embedded in larger processes of globalization, in particular the global expansion of capitalism, technology, and the western legal framework, but without ig-

---

6 Jürgen Zimmerer, "Forum: The German Colonial Imagination," *German History* 26, no. 2 (2008): 253.

noring the agency of local people. The following chapters reveal the results of this approach.

In his introduction, *Frederick Cooper* explores the relation of world history and political imaginaries such as colonies, empires and nations in the twentieth century. He suggests that German colonialism can only be fully conceived when thinking about the relationship of different forms of the state in this period. Cooper's general approach shows that the history of empires and the history of nation-states have shaped the political landscape of the world in a more complex relationship and created a more diverse set of alternatives than a dichotomy of colonial empires versus nation-states. His thought-provoking essay pushes readers towards new ways of thinking outside the conventional framework in which they are located and urges them to consider differences among people without objectifying them.

Next, *Britta Schilling* provides a glimpse into colonial traces in Germany after 1918 as well as into material memories of colonial times in Namibia. She raises the question whether there has been a coming to terms with the colonial past in Germany. Schilling's survey points out that family memories of four generations such as ethnographic items, hunting trophies, photographs and diaries have been preserved even beyond 1945, and therefore form an essential part of German colonial memory—although private memories rarely appear at the surface of national narratives. Regarding postcolonial heritage in former colonies, as the case of Namibia displays, German architecture is still one of the most visible traces of memory of the colonial past.

Nina Berman's case study delves deep into German economic activities on the Kenyan coast since the 1960s, which can be seen as long-term continuities of the colonial history in East Africa. Her ethnographic fieldwork—conducted during five years from 2009 to 2014—outlines the exceptional impact of German entrepreneurs and investors on infrastructure and social relations, in particular, on the distribution of landownership. These developments build largely on the inequalities created during the colonial period. Berman unfolds lesser-known dimensions of globalization that include an increasing north-to-south migration and new forms of cross-cultural hierarchies and collaborations.

The literary works of Cameroonian writers during colonial rule are the subject of *Patrice Nganang*'s close analysis. His essay focuses on the *Sang'aam*, the memoirs of Ibrahim Njoya (1860–1933), king of the Bamum people, composed between 1911 and 1933. Various examples from the text display the discontent Njoya felt about his position inside the colonial system and the trying situation of his people, namely the transformation of the king into a salaried auxiliary of the French colonial administration and of the population into wage earners, a process already initiated by German colonial masters.

Dotsé Yigbe looks into the origins of Togo's fondness for Germany and the establishment of nostalgic colonial associations such as the Deutsch-Togo-Bund. Considering the hardship Togolese people had to face during the colonial era, his essay asks how Togo developed positive attitudes towards its former colonial power. Yigbe identifies cultural associations and movements which campaign for the reunification of the two parts of East-Togo and West-Togo as an indicator for the German colonial legacy—a legacy that is in this case transnational.

Werner Hillebrecht discusses the far-reaching cultural and economic impacts of German colonialism in Namibia. As an example for the paradoxical memorial culture of Namibia, he examines the touristic value of the Rider Monument in unison with the controversial meaning for indigenous people. Hillebrecht further assesses the irreversible negative effects of land ownership patterns introduced under German colonial rule. He concludes his essay by defining the legacy of German colonial rule in Namibia as destructive and criticizing the absence of visible reminders for indigenous war victims.

Representations of the former German colony Qingdao in Chinese writings are examined by *Lü Yixu*. Her investigation connects the perception of Qingdao in Chinese texts from various genres with German conceptions. This approach reconstructs how the colonized describe Qingdao's past in order to determine whether the split between the colonized and the colonizers is still visible or whether it has changed in any way. Lü reveals that for the Germans, despite all political and social changes in Qingdao, the "ideal colony" remains the most dominant trope. However, Chinese perceptions are more differentiated. On the one hand Chinese writers voice indignation and feelings of national disgrace. On the other hand, visible traces of colonial times are regarded as part of their own identity by present-day Qingdao dwellers.

Malama Meleisea and *Penelope Schoeffel* offer insights about the resonances of the German involvement in Samoa's history which they trace back to the mid-nineteenth century. Their essay points to the visible heritage of German colonial rule: first, the state owns the former German land holdings which is contributing to the modern economic development of Samoa; second, a German colonial style building was in use as headquarters of three administrations and is now being protected with plans to become a museum and cultural center; and third, the German legacy lives on in the names of prominent Samoan families.

Craig Alan Volker's survey, which concludes the volume, concentrates on the visibility of the German language in Papua New Guinea in four historical periods, from 1884 to the present. By using language as a cultural marker and indicator of the legacy of German colonialism, his aim is to provide evidence for the so-called colonial amnesia for the case of Papua New Guinea. Volker demonstrates that although traces of German colonial rule are ever-present in today's everyday life, the legacy is not part of intellectual reflection—it is rarely systematically discussed. In fact, names of German origin are now conceived of as local names, and Tok Pisin[7] as well as Chinese, but not German, are the linguistic legacies of the German colonial past.

Together this set of papers demonstrates that the legacy of colonialism continues to define the relations between Europe and the formerly colonized world. This ambivalent legacy continues to play out in subtle but important ways in the international political arena, in mutual images, in invisible hierarchies and social traditions. Hence, the history and consequences of colonialism cannot be neatly categorized. People in Europe may shrug at the heritage connected to the colonial past. The past is unfortunate, and even regrettable, but one that is the past. Nevertheless, for people in the former colonies this is obviously different, and the legacy is still very much alive and relevant. Academics, think-tank people, and policy makers in the post-colonial world still have the colonial past in the back of their minds and in the fabrics of their societies when confronting the West today. At the very least, this is a compelling reason why the history of colonialism still matters today.

---

[7] The creole language Tok Pisin is the official language of Papua New Guinea and spoken throughout the country. It developed from Melanesian Pidgin English and consists of English and Melanesian elements, but also shows influence of German.

Frederick Cooper
Colonies, Empires, Nations: A Twentieth Century History

In the early twentieth century, elites in the most powerful states believed that they were part of a world order—an imperial order based on a hierarchy of civilizations, of superior and inferior peoples. This order did not last. By the 1950s and 1960s, political leaders and scholars believed that they were shaping a new world order based on the rejection of colonial empire, the right of all peoples to live in their own nation-state, and the notion as embodied in the United Nations, that all states should be considered equivalent. Now, in the early twenty-first century, that order is proving itself incapable of providing a stable and generally acceptable mode of governance.

In Syria, a government no longer protects the nation, but destroys cities and citizens to preserve the power of a ruling clique, producing thousands of refugees who leave their country to seek protection elsewhere. A smaller group of young men abandon the country of their citizenship to join the Islamic State that sees itself as returning to a form of polity dating to the seventh century, the Caliphate. Conflict in Iraq, Israel-Palestine, and Libya, as well as Syria and Lebanon, suggest that the dismemberment of the Ottoman empire nearly a century ago has yet to be digested. In many instances, the breakup of colonial empires from the 1950s to the 1970s did not, put in place structures capable of finding a progressive place in the world economy.[1] The most powerful states— the United States, China, the Russian Federation, and the member states of the European Union—remain marked by the experience of empire, not in a distant past but in their twentieth century histories.

The grand narrative of world history that takes us, over the last two centuries in some versions, from a world of empires to a world of nation-states, leaves us with many uncertainties about the world that has emerged, and a misleading understanding of all that happened along the way. Different sorts of political imag-

---

[1] Social scientists, in the era of decolonization, tried to demonstrate how an order built on nation-states, under the watchful eyes of already great powers, could make for predictable and peaceful international relations. On international relations and the attempts to tame the decolonizing world, see Carl E. Pletsch, "The Three Worlds, or the Division of Social Science Labor, Circa 1950–1975," *Comparative Studies in Society and History* 23 (1981): 565–90 and Nicolas Guilhot, "The Realist Gambit: Postwar American Political Science and the Birth of IR Theory," *International Political Sociology*, 2, (2008), 281–304.

inaries have been in play throughout the twentieth century.² The story of German colonialism is a part of this picture, but my goal in this article is more general: to suggest ways of thinking about the relationship of different forms of the state in the twentieth century.

In the early twentieth century, the major actors in European politics—Great Britain, France, Germany, Russia, Austro-Hungary, and the Ottomans consisted of combinations of territories, colonies, protectorates, dominions, and spheres of interest. Different sorts of empires had to deal with each other.³ Not that national sentiments weren't widespread—and sometimes deep—but whatever sentiments people had they faced the reality of a world dominated by polities that did not limit their reach to "one people."

The new state of Germany called itself a Reich, termed its ruler Kaiser (Caesar), incorporated French, Danish, and Polish speakers but refrained from incorporating the German speakers of the Austro-Hungarian Empire despite its defeat in the Austro-Prussian War.⁴ Japan, ventured into Korea starting from the 1870s, took over Taiwan in 1894–95, and defeated Russia in 1905. It both followed a European pattern of empire-building and claimed to be doing empire its own way, acting as an Asian big-brother.⁵ Qing China was weakened but remained too big for European powers to swallow. The US had its venture in overseas colonialism in 1898, complicating its continental empire-building that had been going on throughout the nineteenth century.⁶

---

2 One form of imaginary—but not the only one—is described in Benedict Anderson, *Imagined Communities: Reflections on the Origin and Spread of Nationalism* (London: Verso, 1983). See also Ernest Gellner, *Nations and Nationalism* (Ithaca NY: Cornell University Press, 1983); Eric Hobsbawm, *Nations and Nationalism since 1780: Programme, Myth, Reality* (Cambridge: Cambridge University Press, 1990); Geoff Eley and Ronald Suny, eds., *Becoming National: A Reader* (New York: Oxford University Press, 1996)

3 These different types of empires are brought together in the studies in Jörn Leonhard and Ulrike von Hirschhausen, eds., *Comparing Empires* (Gottingen: Vandenhoeck anbd Ruprecht, 2011). For an interpretation of the place of empires in the long-durée of history—including recent history—see Jane Burbank and Frederick Cooper, *Empires in World History: Power and the Politics of Difference* (Princeton: Princeton University Press, 2010).

4 Philipp Ther, "Imperial Instead of National History: Positioning Modern German History on the Map of European Empires," in Alexei Miller and Alfred Rieber, eds. *Imperial Rule* (Budapest and New York: Central European University Press, 2004), 47–68.

5 Ryūta Itagaki, Satoshi Mizutani, and Hideaki Tobe, "Japanese Empire," in Philippa Levine and John Marriott, eds., *The Ashgate Companion to Modern Imperial Histories*. (Farnham, England: Ashgate, 2012), 273–99.

6 Charles Maier, *Among Empires: American Ascendancy and Its Predecessors* (Cambridge MA: Harvard University Press, 2006).

Some scholars have attempted to reconcile the age of empires with the age of nations by positing that colonization was really the work of "big states" that saw colonies as wholly subordinate rather than parts of a composite, unlike the empires of old.[7] But the structures were more complicated than that and their interactions more complicated still. Power in the early twentieth century was concentrated in a tiny number of states with an imperial reach, some expanding, some hanging on, some with a more "national" conception of themselves than others, all acting in relation to each other and to the diverse populations that they held in a variety of unequal relationships. A few leaders, including Bismarck, thought that an inter-empire order was possible: agreements among the "civilized" on how to regulate competition with each other and carve up the rest of the world. A section of elites in Europe tried to distinguish between a bad colonialism, like that of King Leopold II of Belgium, and a respectable version. Ideologues promoted a vision of masculine authority, bourgeois self-restraint, and stable racial and gender hierarchies in which all peoples of the world would have their place.[8]

The scramble to colonize Africa was an inter-empire story, less a necessity to seize resources or markets than an effort to preempt other imperial powers from monopolizing them. European powers invested little outside of islands of settler plantations or mining operations. Systematically remaking economy and society in Africa in a European image—or systematically exploiting it—was beyond the capacity of colonizing powers. Empire in Africa was power on the cheap.

Colonial empires, like empires of old, needed intermediaries. In most of Africa, outside of areas of white settlement, the very chiefs and kings whose supposed tyranny and backwardness was invoked to justify colonization reappeared as the incarnation of African traditional authority on which colonial regimes depended. African elites were both manipulated by colonial officials and manipulated officials themselves, skewing patriarchal and clientage relations to their interests.[9] Colonies of the major European powers, even in the most extreme case

---

[7] References to a "second" or even a "third" British empire, to a new imperialism or a new French empire in the late 19th century assume that empires became nation-states and then acquired empires and that history can neatly be divided into epochs—both artificial views of historical processes. In *Empires in World History*, Burbank and I suggest that thinking of shifting repertoires of rule is a better way of understanding change over time.

[8] Ann Laura Stoler, *Carnal Knowledge and Imperial Power: Race and the Intimate in Colonial Rule* (Berkeley: University of California Press, 2002); Lora Wildenthal, *German Women for Empire, 1884–1945* (Durham: Duke University Press, 2001); Ann McClintock, *Imperial Leather: Race, Gender and Sexuality in the Colonial Contest* (Routledge, 1995).

[9] John Lonsdale and Bruce Berman, "Coping with the Contradictions: The Development of the Colonial State in Kenya," *Journal of African History* 20 (1979): 487–506; Sara Berry, "Hegemony

of technological difference and racial prejudice, could not help acting like older empires—through vertical channels of power passing through intermediaries.

And what of the state in Europe itself? The concept of popular sovereignty had been in play since the eighteenth century, but who the people were and where sovereignty lay remained uncertain in 1900. The multi-ethnic empires of Europe survived the nineteenth century. The dual monarchy in Austria-Hungary, the Ottoman Empire's experiment in generalized citizenship and briefly in parliamentary governance, and the Russian Duma were among the innovations in sovereignty regimes within empires.[10] The French state had been ruled by an emperor or king for all but a few years of the period 1789 to 1871, but then it revived the republican vision of 1789. Citizens were all equal with no mediating status groups. Except that women could not vote and most people in the rapidly expanding overseas empire were declared to be "French" but not citizens.

Throughout Europe, activists and intellectuals were questioning the structure of states, sometimes their very existence. Feminism, liberalism, socialism, and anarchism all challenged governments, whether they leaned to the imperial or the national end of the spectrum. Elites were trying both to co-opt and restrict the entry of males of the working and peasant classes into politics. Germany and the Scandinavian states took the lead in making the state "social," although the Bismarckian state was hardly democratic.[11]

The Tsarist regime had its colonising and Russianizing tendencies in the Siberian, Caucasian, and Central Asian empire, parallel to those of western powers, but it couldn't go too far, for Eurasian sovereignty entailed recognizing the role of Islamic and other religious figures.[12] In early twentieth century

---

on a Shoestring: Indirect Rule and Access to Agricultural Land," *Africa* 62 (1992): 327–55; A. E. Afigbo, *The Warrant Chiefs: Indirect Rule in Southeastern Nigeria, 1891–1929* (London: Longman, 1972); Charles Ambler, *Kenyan Communities in the Age of Imperialism: the Central Region in the Late Nineteenth Century* (New Haven: Yale University Press, 1988).

10 Pieter M. Judson, *Guardians of the Nation: Activists on the Language Frontier of Imperial Austria* (Cambridge, Mass.: Harvard University Press, 2006); Michelle Campos, *Ottoman Brothers: Muslims, Christians, and Jews in Early-Twentieth Century Palestine* (Stanford: Stanford University Press, 2011); Robert Geraci, *Window on the East: National and Imperial Identities in Late Tsarist Russia* (Ithaca: Cornell University Press, 2001).

11 Peter Baldwin, *The Politics of Social Solidarity Class Bases of the European Welfare State, 1875–1975* (Cambridge: Cambridge University Press, 1992). Not only did many of the important political movements of the day cross national lines, but a considerable range of political leaders argued specifically for principles and institutions that were international in scope. Glenda Sluga, *Internationalism in the Age of Nationalism* (Philadelphia: University of Pennsylvania Press, 2013)

12 Jane Burbank, Mark von Hagen, and Anatolyi Remnev, eds. *Russian Empire: Space, People, Power, 1700–1930* (Bloomington: Indiana University Press, 2007); Robert Crews, *For Prophet and*

China, a national movement was developing, sometimes trying to brand the Manchu elite that had ruled the empire since 1644 as "foreign" and linking their cause with movements in colonial world against the rule of outsiders and also connecting to the Chinese diaspora.[13] But China's republicans had to contend with patrimonial elements—warlords and their followers—in different parts of the Republic they established in 1912. States were moving in different directions in 1914—not necessarily toward consolidating themselves as "nations."

World War I was a war among empires, and its consequences are sometimes seen as a move from empire to a world of self-determining nation-states. But only if one reads history backwards. The empires of the losers—the Ottoman, Austro-Hungarian, and German—and the Tsarist empire as well—did not die natural deaths. "National" self-determination in Europe could only be national because of what a British statesman who advocated such policies, Lord Curzon, called the "unmixing of people" and we, today, call ethnic cleansing. Making states homogenous in eastern and central Europe wasn't a spontaneous activity of ordinary people. It was carried out by state elites, with the backing of Britain, France, and the US.[14]

Self-determination was for white people. Japan's plea for a statement condemning racism was turned down. To be sure, activists in India, China, Korea, and Africa read Woodrow Wilson's words as if they applied to them, but they soon found that they did not.[15] The breakup of the Ottoman Empire led to waves of ethnic cleansing: Greeks expelled from Turkey, Turks from Greece. Revolts were repressed with enormous violence by Britain in Iraq in the 1920s and Palestine in the 1930s. The powers were at the time able to stuff the genii of citizenship and self-determination back into imperial bottles. Colonial governments

---

Tsar: Islam and Empire in Russia and Central Asia (Cambridge, Mass.: Harvard University Press, 2006); Jane Burbank, "Eurasian Sovereignty: The Case of Kazan," *Problems of Post-Communism* 62 (2015): 1–25.

13 Rebecca Karl, *Staging the World: Chinese Nationalism at the Turn of the Twentieth Century* (Durham: Duke University Press, 2002).

14 This phrase comes from the British statesman Lord Curzon. See Rogers Brubaker, *Nationalism Reframed: Nationhood and the National Question* in the New Europe (Cambridge: Cambridge University Press, 1996) and Philipp Ther, *The Dark Side of Nation-States: Ethnic Cleansing in Modern Europe* (London: Berghahn, 2014).

15 Erez Manela, *The Wilsonian Moment: Self-determination and the International Origins of Anticolonial Nationalism* (New York: Oxford University Press, 2007); Margaret Macmillan, *Paris 1919: Six Months that Changed the World* (New York: Random House, 2003).

asserted their capacity to maintain the distinct cultures of their subjects, protecting them from inappropriate European models of citizenship and civilization.[16]

Pieces of the losers' empires, particularly in the Middle East and Africa, were distributed to the winners. The League of Nations's mandate system made German and Ottoman territories into yet another part of the imperial repertoires of Britain and France. The League did more to internationalize colonialism than to undermine it.[17]

The aftermath of war witnessed not only the continuity of older models of colonial empire, but also the rise of new models of empire—the Soviet and the Nazi. The USSR built on imperial Russia's multinational mode of empire by recognizing national republics each subordinated to an autocratic center. It now termed itself a "union." Each republic was governed by elites from the predominant "national" group, all of whom came up through the Communist Party.[18] The United States did not have a Colonial Ministry, but it had its repertoire of power at a distance, including a few colonies. But it preferred invasions and occupations to colonizations.[19]

The spectrum of imperial politics of difference includes the Nazis, but the line from the atrocities of German Africa to the Shoah is not straight.[20] Neither

---

16 Alice Conklin, *A Mission to Civilize: The Republican Idea of Empire in France and West Africa, 1895–1930* (Stanford: Stanford University Press, 1997). On inter-empire conflict as a framework for history in the first half of the twentieth century, see Burbank and Cooper, *Empires in World History*.

17 Susan Pedersen, *The Guardians: The League of Nations and the Crisis of Empire* (Oxford: Oxford University Press, 2015). The League's supervision of mandates cut two ways: it made the practice of rulers in the mandates subject to discussion (with some possibilities for subjects to petition the League) but reinforced the position of the dominant powers as arbiters of how their power was exercised.

18 Francine Hirsch, *Empire of Nations: Ethnographic Knowledge and the Making of the Soviet Union* (Ithaca: Cornell University Press, 2005); Terry Martin, *The Affirmative Action Empire: Nations and Nationalism in the Soviet Union, 1923–1939* (Ithaca: Cornell University Press, 2001).

19 Paul Kramer implies that politics in the US was too racist to be properly colonial. A powerful faction of its elite did not want to incorporate black or yellow people into an American polity, even as inferiors. *The Blood of Government: Race, Empire, the United States, and the Philippines* (Chapel Hill: University of North Carolina Press, 2006). Adam Tooze adds another factor: the US was becoming the most powerful power of all, but its elite was preoccupied with maintaining itself in the face of social conflicts—over class and race in particular—that had been building up in previous decades and was reluctant to take an active role in forging a new kind of inter-state order. *The Deluge: The Great War and the Remaking of Global Order, 1916–1931* (London: Penguin, 2014).

20 Birthe Kundrus, "Colonialism, Imperialism, National Socialism: How Imperial Was the Third Reich?" in Bradley Naranch and Geoff Eley, eds., *German Colonialism in a Global Age* (Durham: Duke University Press, 2014), 330–46; Sebastian Conrad, *Globalization and the Nation in Impe-*

anti-Semitism nor colonial racism was unique to pre-war Germany. What is singular about German colonial experience was that it lost its colonies without losing its sense of imperial entitlement.[21] Unimpeded by the limitations of governing actual people in the colonies, resenting the loss of imperial stature, Nazi ideologues developed their conception of a new Reich founded on racial superiority, heaping contempt on international law and norms, rejecting the cosmopolitan culture that was characteristic of pre-war Germany.[22] With their conquests, the Nazis developed a repertoire of power different from past empires. Although in France and other countries to the west, Nazis co-opted racially acceptable intermediaries, they did not do so in eastern Europe. Slavs were to be treated as slave laborers or murdered.[23] The Nazis were defeated by other powers with an imperial reach and more capacity to bring diverse material and human resources into the conflict.

The effects of the Second World War were quite different from those of the first. This time, the winners in Europe were almost as devastated—in human losses, destruction of cities, and financial ruin—as the losers. The humiliating defeat that Japan had earlier inflicted on Britain, the Netherlands, the US, and France in southeast Asia shook the confidence elites had in the domination of the white man, while Hitler gave racism a bad name. Labor unrest was challenging colonial regimes in the regions *most* integrated into imperial economies, making clear that colonial control could not be restored by pretending that Afri-

---

rial Germany (Cambridge: Cambridge University Press, 2010); Pascal Grosse, "What Does German Colonialism Have to Do with National Socialism?" in Eric Ames, Marcia Klotz, and Lora Wildenthal, eds., *Germany's Colonial Pasts* (Lincoln: University of Nebraska Press, 2005), 115–34; Isabelle Hull, *Absolute Destruction: Military Culture and the Practices of War in Imperial Germany* (Ithaca: Cornell University Press, 2004). George Steinmetz points out that German colonial practices differed substantially from colony to colony. *The Devil's Handwriting: Precoloniality and the German Colonial State in Qingdao, Samoa and Southwest Africa* (Chicago: University of Chicago Press, 2007).

21 Marcia Klotz, "The Weimar Republic: A Postcolonial State in a Still-Colonial World," in Ames, Klotz, and Wildenthal, 135–47

22 Carl Schmitt's political theories were less an analysis of states as they actually existed than an imagined inversion of the ways in which rival empires constructed their power, an anti-universalist, anti-individual vision, opposed to international law, presuming the uniformity of a people. For a valuable analysis, see Jan-Werner Müller, *A Dangerous Mind: Carl Schmitt in Post-War European Thought* (New Haven: Yale University Press, 2003).

23 Mark Mazower, *Hitler's Empire: Nazi Rule in Occupied Europe* (London: Allen Lane, 2008); Wendy Lower, *Nazi Empire-Building and the Holocaust in Ukraine* (Chapel Hill: University of North Carolina Press, 2005).

cans could continue to live in their tribes.[24] But it would still require hindsight to conclude that the only alternative to the imperial past that was emerging at midcentury was the nation-state.

The national perspective was seized in 1945 in Indonesia and Vietnam, where Japanese conquests had forced the Dutch and the French to try—in vain —to recolonize lost territories. In neither case was a nationalist movement fully united.[25] India had the longest history of a nationalist movement, but when Britain ceded power in 1947, the nations that were created—India and Pakistan—were not the single nation that nationalists had previously imagined.[26]

A different sort of claim emerged in the Pan-African Conference of 1945. African, West Indian, American, and other activists of African origin condemned colonial rule around the world and demanded self-determination. But if the conference agreed that black people throughout the world should govern themselves, they could not decide what institutions would do so. Similarly, movements such as that of the *ulema* in Algeria saw themselves as part of an Islamic world.[27] Liberation could be imagined, in mid-twentieth century, outside of the context of a territorial state.

Less familiar is the story of imperial and post-imperial federalism.[28] Empire and federation both assemble different people; both can look at sovereign power in layered terms, on an emperor as king of kings, on a federal and federated governments each holding defined powers.[29] Imperial rulers thought that federal structures within them—the French in Indochina, the Dutch in the East Indies,

---

[24] Frederick Cooper, *Decolonization and African Society: The Labor Question in French and British Africa* (Cambridge: Cambridge University Press, 1996).

[25] Pierre Brocheux and Daniel Hémery, *Indochine: la colonisation ambiguë, 1858–1954* (Paris: Editions la Découverte, 1995).

[26] See for example Yasmin Khan, *The Great Partition: The Making of India and Pakistan* (New Haven: Yale University Press, 2008). For an account of India's relation to empire that emphasizes questions of gender, see Mrinalini Sinha, *Specters of Mother India: The Global Restructuring of an Empire* (Durham NC: Duke University Press, 2006).

[27] James McDougall, *History and the Culture of Nationalism in Algeria* (Cambridge: Cambridge University Press, 2006).

[28] On the concept of federalism, see Jean Cohen, "Federation," *Political Concepts: A Critical Lexicon*, www.politicalconcepts.org/2011/federation. Theorists and activists distinguish federation from confederation; the former organized by a constitution, the latter by treaties, recognizing the national nature of the component parts. As Cohen points out, the distinction is less than neat, since both are relational concepts entailing a sharing of power at different levels.

[29] The United States emerged as a federal system largely because most of the leaders of the 13 colonies were convinced (and they were not easy to convince) that only by uniting could they survive in a world dominated by empires. David Hendrickson, *Peace Pact: The Lost World of the American Founding* (Lawrence: University Press of Kansas, 2003).

the British in Central Africa and Malaya—might give regional elites a stake in empire and allow for economic coordination.[30] But imperial federalism looked only to narrow, regional elites.

Federalism also appealed to leaders in Africa, who sought not only political voice in their own affairs, but a chance at economic and social political progress that neither colonial empire nor the independence of small and poor nation-states offered. Political leaders in French Africa laid claim to all the rights of the French citizen, a degree of autonomy for their territories, and an equal voice alongside European France in the politics of the overall unit, now renamed the French Union. Their minimum demand, the extension of citizenship rights to all inhabitants of overseas France, was won in the Constitution of 1946.[31]

Senegalese politician Léopold Senghor argued that Africans should balance "horizontal solidarity" and "vertical solidarity," horizontal meaning Africans relating to each other, and vertical meaning Africans with France. Horizontal solidarity by itself offered only unity in poverty. Vertical connections by themselves risked reproducing colonialism, but the two together posed a claim on the superior resources from a position of collective strength. The level of control that Paris could retain as well as how far the Africans could get in claiming political and social equality were the burning themes of politics in sub-Saharan French Africa in the 1950s.

When France began talking in the late 1940s about some kind of European Union, it wanted to include its overseas territories; otherwise, France would be splitting itself in half. The roots of Europe today actually lie in what was then called "Eurafrica," as France sought to combine federal relations with its former colonies with confedederal relations with Germany, Italy, and other European states. Eurafrica would open up a large market and spread the burdens of development finance to European partners, despite the risk of diluting French sovereignty.

---

30 Imperial federalism was related to an earlier movement for a "Greater Britain," a world-wide movement of white, culturally British elites—from Canada to Australia to South Africa to the British Isles—reaffirming their common membership in a British collectivity. See Duncan Bell, *The Idea of Greater Britain: Empire and the Future of World Order, 1860–1900* (Princeton: Princeton University Press, 2007); Daniel Gorman, *Imperial Citizenship: Empire and the Question of Belonging* (Manchester University Press, 2007). On the federal idea and empire during and after World War II, see Michael Collins, "Decolonisation and the 'Federal Moment'," *Diplomacy and Statecraft* 24 (2013): 21–40; Jennifer Foray, *Visions of Empire in the Nazi-Occupied Netherlands* (Cambridge: Cambridge University Press, 2012).
31 Frederick Cooper, *Citizenship between Empire and Nation: Remaking France and French Africa, 1945–1960* (Princeton: Princeton University Press, 2014); Gary Wilder, *Freedom Time: Negritude, Decolonization, and the Future of the World* (Durham: Duke University Press, 2015).

Senghor saw both advantages and dangers in Eurafrica, proclaiming that Africa would not serve as the wedding china that France offered to Germany on the occasion of their marriage. Africans had to have a full voice in governing Eurafrica. In the end, the unwillingness of potential members of the European Economic Community to pay the burdens or accept France's privileged relationship with its former colonies doomed Eurafrica.[32] The European Economic Community would indeed be European.

In French West Africa, political and social movements had turned citizenship into a claim-making language: for social and economic equality, equal pay for equal work, schooling for all, equal benefits for army veterans. By 1956, French officials realized that giving autonomy over internal affairs to African elected governments was the only way to distance the French government from demands centered on the French standard of living. For Africans, this measure turned out to be a Faustian bargain, for it devolved power to the individual territory—and to leaders who acquired real power of patronage and resources that they were loath to give up. By 1960, France and French Africa backed into independence in the form of nation-states that had up to that point been at best a second choice.[33]

Even Kwame Nkrumah's Ghana—the most famous example of the nationalist road to power—turns out to be more complicated. In the 1950s, leaders of the colony's largest ethnic group were calling for their own independence on the same grounds as Nkrumah was claiming independence from the British for the entire colony. The movement was repressed by Nkrumah's transitional government,[34] but he was looking in the other direction: beyond national independence, for the creation of a "United States of Africa." As more African countries became independent, the quest for African solidarity turned from a pan-Africanism of people into a pan-Africanism of states—and largely a mutual protection society of heads of state.[35]

---

[32] Guia Migani, *La France et l'Afrique sub-saharienne, 1957–1963: Histoire d'une décolonisation entre idéaux eurafricains et politique de puissance* (Brussels: PIE Peter Lang, 2008); Muriam Haleh Davis, "Producing Eurafrica: Development, Agriculture and Race in Algeria, 1958–1965," Ph.D. Dissertation, New York University, 2015.

[33] Cooper, *Citizenship between Empire and Nation*; Todd Shepard, *The Invention of Decolonization: The Algerian War and the Remaking of France* (Ithaca: Cornell University Press, 2006).

[34] Jean Marie Allman, *The Quills of the Porcupine: Asante Nationalism in an Emergent Ghana* (Madison: University of Wisconsin Press, 1993).

[35] South Africa occupied a particular place in this process, increasingly defined in relation to an international order in which African self-government was becoming the norm, see Ryan Irwin, *Gordian Knot: Apartheid and the Unmaking of the Liberal World Order* (New York: Oxford University Press, 2012).

Although leaders of new states have attempted, starting at the Bandung meeting of 1955, to work together independently of either the Soviet Union or the United States, the reality of decolonization was that it reflected the divisions that colonization by different powers had created.[36] Fragile states with poor resources had strong incentives to find rich patrons and to play them off against each other. This juggling of rich-poor relations—involving states as well as transnational corporations—in the context of Cold War rivalries, shaped world politics after the 1960s, more so than either neo-colonial relations with former colonizers or Third World solidarity.[37]

Formally, decolonization replaced the hierarchy of an imperial world order with the equivalence of nation-states. Conflict would still take place but it would be within each state—and hence no-one else's business—or among states, which international relations experts thought they understood. The United Nations recognized equivalence, even if the Security Council expressed the notion that some nations were more equal than others. The distinction between "developed" and "developing" nations maintained a sort of hierarchy but assumed it to be self-liquidating; those on top would help those on the bottom along the road to equality

The US played a more active role in reorganizing the international system after World War II than it had after World War I. The US was content to see a small number of powerful empires be replaced by a large number of nation-states, which would be more open to American economic, cultural, and political influence, although Cold War rivalry combined with the advent of relatively autonomous state actors introduced a great deal of uncertainty.

Encased in their borders, the governing elites of the poorest states play a zero-sum game with their rivals to control the resource that matters most, sovereignty, and with it access to foreign aid, contracts with multinationals, clients within the territory and patrons outside it.. Contrary to the advocates of free markets, success stories like South Korea and Taiwan owe much to highly interventionist states. Contrary to advocates of a radical break with global capitalism, states that sought a revolutionary path—Mozambique, Benin, let alone North Korea—succeeded more in alienating their own populations than in finding routes to prosperity.

---

36 Christopher Lee, ed., *Making a World After Empire: The Bandung Moment and Its Aftermaths* (Athens: Ohio University Press, 2010); Robert Vitalis, "The Midnight Ride of Kwame Nkrumah and Other Fables of Bandung (Ban-doong)," *Humanity* summer 2013: 261–88.
37 On the overlap of decolonization and Cold War, see Odd Arne Westad, *The Global Cold War: Third World Interventions and the Making of Our Times* (Cambridge: Cambridge University Press, 2007).

Looking at trajectories out of colonial empire should give perspective to something taken for granted today. Why should Malians' access to piped water or higher education be determined by the resources within its borders? The history that created impoverished African states was not a uniquely African history. For a time, French Africans made claims to resources as French citizens; now they ask for foreign aid. It was a historical process culminating in the national form of the state that divided much of the world into donors and supplicants, complicated by Cold War rivalries and continually changing recipes for "development."[38]

Since colonial empires ceased to be taken-for-granted constituents of the world order, we have lived with a tension between values that many hold to be universal and the specific value attached to the self-determining nation-state. The Universal Declaration of Human Rights of 1948 listed social and economic rights alongside freedom from arbitrary punishment and free speech, although including such rights in the Declaration was controversial. Anti-colonial movements in the 1950s staged their campaigns not just in the name of self-determination, but in the name of social and economic justice, in the face of colonial exploitation.[39] But after colonies achieved independence, their rulers generally insisted that social and economic justice were internal matters, and outsiders had no business telling rulers of independent states how they should treat their citizens.

Decolonization in the form of territorially bounded nation-states, inheriting weak institutions for the collection of revenue and the provision of social services, with narrow channels of communication and low levels of education, has led to zero-sum battles for control over the resource that mattered most, sover-

---

38 On the importance of the development concept in framing international politics in the 20th century—both for making and diffusing claims to resources—see Frederick Cooper and Randall Packard, eds., *International Development and the Social Sciences: Essays in the History and Politics of Knowledge* (Berkeley: University of California Press, 1997).
39 The United States was particularly eager to keep social and economic rights out of discussions of human rights. Samuel Moyn sees the 1948 declaration as more of a substitute for a human rights regime than the real thing and insists that the notion of human rights as we now conceive of them took root only in the 1970s. Roland Burke presents a more supple view of rights, with a more complex relationship to the politics of decolonization. Both agree, however, that once independent, the leaders of anti-colonial mobilizations used the notion of sovereignty to immunize themselves against outside inquiries into their treatment of their citizens. Samuel Moyn, *The Last Utopia: Human Rights in History* (Cambridge: Harvard University Press, 2010); Roland Burke, *Decolonization and the Evolution of International Human Rights* (Philadelphia: University of Pennsylvania, 2010). For further thoughts on this issue, see my "Social Rights and Human Rights in the Time of Decolonization," *Humanity* 3, 3 (2012): 473–92.

eignty. Rulers act as gatekeepers—controlling the point at which national economies encounter the opportunities of the outside world. But they are challenged for control of the gate by networks that cross borders.[40]

The same logic that justified national self-determination served to justify independence movements within states. Examples include Biafra's vain and tragic attempt to secede from Nigeria, Eritrea's and South Sudan's secession from Ethiopia and Sudan respectively—successful in a legal sense but disastrous in its human dimensions. In Rwanda and ex-Yugoslavia, efforts to make the state conform to the nation resulted in genocide or ethnic cleansing.[41] In Israel-Palestine, rival nationalist movements claim the same space.

Claiming power as a state does not mean that states fulfil their promises to their citizens. States—in Europe and North America as well as Africa and Asia—have failed to deliver the services that citizens expect and need, fostering a loss of confidence in law and accountability and a turn to patron-client political relationships. Many citizens look to scapegoats—blaming outsiders and immigrants for their economic insecurity.

The state-citizen relationship is not straight-forward. Within states, some citizens are less able than others to exercise rights—because of racial, religious, or ethnic discrimination or because behavior can justify the denial of political or economic rights to the criminal or the "undeserving" poor. Rulers from China to Egypt suppress rather than reflect citizens' quests for voice. At the same time, legal migrants might have some of the rights of the citizens of host countries from education to welfare, and even voting in local elections in some cases. Many highly mobile people have both affective and political ties to multiple places. Scholars refer to "post-national citizenship," except that it isn't particularly "post," but a changing matrix of rights and obligations toward different types of states that follows from the divisible nature of citizenship.[42] People can hold

---

[40] On gatekeeping strategies in Africa states, see Frederick Cooper, *Africa since 1940: The Past of the Present* (Cambridge: Cambridge University Press, 2002).

[41] Ther, *Dark Side of the Nation-State*.

[42] There is a burgeoning literature on the "post-national." See for example Monica Heller, *Paths to Post-nationalism: A Critical Ethnography of Language and Identity* (New York: Oxford University Press, 2011); Saskia Sassen, "Toward Post-National and Denationalized Citizenship," in Engin Isin and Bryan Turner, eds., *Handbook of Citizenship Studies* (Beverly Hills: Sage 2002), 277–91. Some scholars argue that a "post-national" citizenship is now the reality in the European Union and elsewhere, as many people, especially migrant workers, derive rights to work, participate in collective bargaining, obtain welfare benefits, gain access to education, and sometimes vote in local elections, even without national citizenship. Yasemin Nuhoğlu Soysal, *Limits of Citizenship: Migrants and Postnational Membership in Europe* (Chicago: University of Chicago Press, 1994)

dual citizenship or superposed citizenship, notably in the European Union, where a European citizenship is derived automatically from citizenship in a Member State. This complex dialectic between tendencies to enforce state boundaries and patterns of migration and network building that cross them characterizes the world right today.[43]

Cross-border networks do not put everyone on an equal footing. Their most privileged users are financial institutions and multinational corporations, who can take advantage of institutional rules that facilitate capital flows, including trade agreements that provide for international tribunals dominated by business interests to take the place of state courts in regulating exchange, perhaps to the detriment of labor and environmental concerns. There are limited mechanisms—such as shaming abusers in international media—to enforce social rights.[44]

But other sorts of networks can at least raise issues publicly, and they do so across space. Organizations focus on questions of gender equality, working conditions, migration, environment, and access to health—as well as protections against state violence—articulating principles that are supposed to be universal and that are intended to stand above sovereignty.[45] Taken together, such discourses—and the organizational mechanisms to act in relation to them—seem to posit a "world citizen" whose rights should be protected. But by whom? Through what institutions? On what basis?

---

[43] For two perspectives by thoughtful political theorists on the tensions between particularistic ties and universal principles, see Seyla Benhabib, *The Rights of Others: Aliens, Residents and Citizens* Cambridge: Cambridge University Press, 2004) and Jean L. Cohen, *Globalization and Sovereignty: Rethinking Legality, Legitimacy, and Constitutionalism* (Cambridge: Cambridge University Press, 2012).

[44] Bryan Turner, "We Are All Denizens Now: On the Erosion of Citizenship," *Citizenship Studies* 20 (2016): 679–92.

[45] For examples of cross-border networks and their complex relationship to national sovereignty, see Gregory Mann, *From Empires to NGOs in the West African Sahel: The Road to Nongovernmentality* (Cambridge: Cambridge University Press, 2015) and Benedetta Rossi, *From Slavery to Aid: Politics, Labour, and Ecology in the Nigerien Sahel, 1800–2000* (Cambridge: Cambridge University Press, 2015). Gender is one question where international and national norms often conflict. As a number of studies of gender in politics in Africa have shown, women sometimes played a key role in anticolonial mobilizations but were marginalized after independence by a politics of the "big man." Susan Geiger, *TANU Women: Gender and Culture in the Making of Tanzanian Nationalism, 1955–1965* (Portsmouth, NH: Heinemann, 1997); Lynn Thomas, *Politics of the Womb: Women, Reproduction, and the State in Kenya* (Berkeley: University of California Press, 2003). On transnational issue networks—whose origins go back to the anti-slavery movements of the late eighteenth century—see Kathryn Sikkink and Margaret Keck, *Activists Beyond Borders: Advocacy Networks in International Politics* (Ithaca, NY: Cornell University Press, 1998).

Meanwhile, other sorts of connections defy the state system. Al Qaeda and Daesh are capable of recruiting fighters not only from the brittle states of the Middle East, but also from European social democracies, the UK, the US, and Russia—young men weakly integrated into the citizenship structures in which they were brought up.[46] They are capable of inflicting periodic acts of terror in established states and pose a more profound threat to states in Africa and the Middle East. But the gap between imagining an Islamic caliphate—a twenty-first century echo of a political structure created in the seventh century—and the actual shallowness of these networks leaves their future very much in question.

Taken together, all this suggests that political imaginations and institutionalized affiliations crystalize around a variety of regional, religious, or ethnic collectivities and identifications, not just on the nations that states claim to embody. Such connections are not necessarily mutually exclusive but they can lead to totalizing claims on the loyalty of individuals and groups and to intense conflict.

If the world at the end of the twentieth century was post-imperial, it was so in the sense of having passed through and been shaped by a trajectory in which empire was a fundamental factor.[47] In China, the borders established by the Qing empire defined the space political movements struggled for throughout the century—republicans, warlords, communists and the communo-capitalists of today. China faces the problem previous dynasties faced: Tibetan and Muslim peoples at the frontiers of the empire, who have remained distinct.

The breakup of the USSR at century's end was made possible—and except for the Caucuses relatively peaceful—by the supra-national structure of the Union, which came apart along the lines of its national republics. The Russian Federation remains a multinational entity, now trying to re-establish something like its previous imperial reach, relying on something like the patrimonial authority of its previous rulers. The United States continues to exercise its repertoire of power at a distance.[48] Meanwhile, the European Union represents an experi-

---

46 Islamic networks—without being Islamist—have long existed. For a study of the spatial, genealogical, and religious imaginations of an Islamic diaspora, see Engseng Ho, *The Graves of Tarim: Genealogy and Mobility across the Indian Ocean* (Berkeley: University of California Press, 2006).
47 Burbank and Cooper, *Empires in World History*, chapter 14.
48 There was a proliferation of books after 2003 attacking the US for acting like an empire—or else calling on it to do so—all of which had a short shelf life in face of the fact that the US proved unable to occupy effectively one country, let alone colonize half the world. The US subcontracts

ment in political organization: a confederation of states, ceding some of the most important sovereign prerogatives (money and control of borders) to more inclusive entities. The very name of "Union," echoing the French Union and the Union of Soviet Socialist Republics, offers a useful ambiguity, reflecting the divisible and shifting structure of power that sovereignty has always entailed.[49] Whether the European Union will capture people's political imagination, let alone solve its practical problems, is now more than ever in question. Meanwhile, Africans whose parents once entered France as citizens face a Europe trying to define them as alien and excludable; they face arguments that even Africans with "papers" are incapable of living according to Europe's supposedly universal norms.[50]

In the early twentieth century, elites in the most powerful states believed that they had forged an imperial world order based on a hierarchy of civilizations. In the late twentieth century, statesmen and scholars thought a new order based on the sovereign equivalence of all states had emerged. The idea of a self-contained sovereignty was in tension with values that to many people transcended it: rule of law, human rights, gender equality, democracy, religious tolerance. Rulers who abused their citizens could be publicly shamed, but the defenders of universal human rights often stood accused of promoting values that were in fact European. However, the radical defense of the self-contained integrity of each state misses out on the multiple interconnections that shaped every polity and the way in which norms and connections beyond the polity have been articulated with ideas and mobilizations within it.[51] Senghor had a

---

much of its occupation labor to favourite corporations, a sign that patrimonial systems of power are alive and well in a supposedly modern and bureaucratized world.

49 The Organization of African Unity also embraced this concept, changing its name to the African Union in 2001. Both international relations experts and some theorists more recently in vogue embrace a hard notion of sovereignty. Stephen Krasner, *Sovereignty: Organized Hypocrisy* (Princeton: Princeton University Press, 1999); Giorgio Agamben, *Home Sacer: Sovereign Power and Bare Life*, trans. Daniel Heller-Roazen (Stanford: Stanford University Press, 1998). But a more grounded and useful treatment of sovereignty as a "basket" of different rights, powers, and aspirations, subject to claims and counterclaims—in short as "plural and divisible"—comes from James J. Sheehan, "The Problem of Sovereignty in European History," *American Historical Review* 111 (2006): 1–15. See also Lauren Benton, *A Search for Sovereignty: Law and Geography in European Empires, 1400–1900* (Cambridge: Cambridge University Press, 2010).

50 Controversies over the head scarf and the "burkini" reveal the brittle notion in much of the French elite that one can only be French in one way—including dress while in a public space.

51 Ironically, the anti-universalist arguments echo—and sometimes even cite—arguments used to defend national and racial distinction within Europe. It is a sign of an impasse in the left in Europe and North America that some commentators are so in need of ammunition to attack the universalistic pretensions of a supposedly liberal world order that they draw on the anti-univer-

more nuanced view on the problem, pointing to a tension without trying to resolve it: between horizontal and vertical solidarities—acknowledging asymmetry in relations among people—North and South, East and West, rich and poor—and seeking the means to lessen those inequalities.

The history of empires and the history of nation-states have left their imprints on the political landscape, but they have done so in a more complex relationship to a more diverse set of alternatives than a dichotomy of colonial empires and nation-states. Can we, as scholars, think less in terms of categories and more in terms of connections? More in terms of overlapping temporalities than of linear time?[52] Can the political ideas of other people be considered without assuming that they are incommensurable with our own? Can we aspire to the universal value of protecting and enhancing human life, both recognizing and seeing beyond the particular cultural framework in which each of us is located? Can we recognize differences among people without reifying them, think realistically about inequality without perpetuating it? These are among the questions we face in living in a world shaped by empire, a world that remains unequal, differentiated, and connected.

Works cited

Afigbo, A. E. *The Warrant Chiefs: Indirect Rule in Southeastern Nigeria, 1891–1929*. London: Longman, 1972.
Agamben, Giorgio. *Home Sacer: Sovereign Power and Bare Life*, trans. Daniel Heller-Roazen. Stanford: Stanford University Press, 1998.
Allman, Jean Marie. *The Quills of the Porcupine: Asante Nationalism in an Emergent Ghana*. Madison: University of Wisconsin Press, 1993.
Ambler, Charles. *Kenyan Communities in the Age of Imperialism: the Central Region in the Late Nineteenth Century*. New Haven: Yale University Press, 1988.
Anderson, Benedict. *Imagined Communities: Reflections on the Origin and Spread of Nationalism*. London: Verso, 1983.
Baldwin, Peter. *The Politics of Social Solidarity Class Bases of the European Welfare State, 1875–1975*. Cambridge: Cambridge University Press, 1992.
Bell, Duncan. *The Idea of Greater Britain: Empire and the Future of World Order, 1860–1900*. Princeton: Princeton University Press, 2007.
Benhabib, Seyla. *The Rights of Others: Aliens, Residents and Citizens*. Cambridge: Cambridge University Press, 2004.

---

salist, anti-democratic theorist Carl Schmitt. See the thoughtful criticism of such a position in Müller, *A Dangerous Mind*, 223, 231.
52 Reinhart Koselleck, *Futures Past: On the Semantics of Historical Time*, trans. Keith Tribe (New York: Columbia University Press, 2004 [1979]).

Benton, Lauren. *A Search for Sovereignty: Law and Geography in European Empires, 1400–1900*. Cambridge: Cambridge University Press, 2010.
Berry, Sara. "Hegemony on a Shoestring: Indirect Rule and Access to Agricultural Land." *Africa* 62 (1992): 327–55;
Brocheux, Pierre, and Daniel Hémery, *Indochine: la colonisation ambiguë, 1858–1954*. Paris: Editions la Découverte, 1995.
Brubaker, Rogers. *Nationalism Reframed: Nationhood and the National Question in the New Europe*. Cambridge: Cambridge University Press, 1996.
Burbank, Jane. "Eurasian Sovereignty: The Case of Kazan." *Problems of Post-Communism* 62 (2015): 1–25.
Burbank, Jane, and Frederick Cooper, *Empires in World History: Power and the Politics of Difference*. Princeton: Princeton University Press, 2010.
Burbank, Jane, Mark von Hagen, and Anatolyi Remnev, eds. *Russian Empire: Space, People, Power, 1700–1930*. Bloomington: Indiana University Press, 2007.
Burke, Roland. *Decolonization and the Evolution of International Human Rights*. Philadelphia: University of Pennsylvania, 2010.
Campos, Michelle. *Ottoman Brothers: Muslims, Christians, and Jews in Early-Twentieth Century Palestine*. Stanford: Stanford University Press, 2011.
Cohen, Jean. "Federation," *Political Concepts: A Critical Lexicon*. www.politicalconcepts.org/2011/federation.
——. *Globalization and Sovereignty: Rethinking Legality, Legitimacy, and Constitutionalism*. Cambridge: Cambridge University Press, 2012.
Collins, Michael. "Decolonisation and the 'Federal Moment'." *Diplomacy and Statecraft* 24 (2013): 21–40.
Conklin, Alice. *A Mission to Civilize: The Republican Idea of Empire in France and West Africa, 1895–1930*. Stanford: Stanford University Press, 1997.
Conrad, Sebastian. *Globalization and the Nation in Imperial Germany*. Cambridge: Cambridge University Press, 2010.
Cooper, Frederick. *Africa since 1940: The Past of the Present*. Cambridge: Cambridge University Press, 2002.
——. *Citizenship between Empire and Nation: Remaking France and French Africa, 1945–1960*. Princeton: Princeton University Press, 2014.
——. *Decolonization and African Society: The Labor Question in French and British Africa*. Cambridge: Cambridge University Press, 1996.
——. "Social Rights and Human Rights in the Time of Decolonization." *Humanity* 3, 3 (2012): 473–92.
Cooper, Frederick, and Randall Packard, eds. *International Development and the Social Sciences: Essays in the History and Politics of Knowledge*. Berkeley: University of California Press, 1997.
Crews, Robert. *For Prophet and Tsar: Islam and Empire in Russia and Central Asia*. Cambridge, Mass.: Harvard University Press, 2006.
Davis, Muriam Haleh. "Producing Eurafrica: Development, Agriculture and Race in Algeria, 1958–1965," Ph.D. Dissertation, New York University, 2015.
Eley, Geoff, and Ronald Suny, eds. *Becoming National: A Reader*. New York: Oxford University Press, 1996.

Foray, Jennifer. *Visions of Empire in the Nazi-Occupied Netherlands.* Cambridge: Cambridge University Press, 2012.
Geiger, Susan. *TANU Women: Gender and Culture in the Making of Tanzanian Nationalism, 1955–1965.* Portsmouth, NH: Heinemann, 1997.
Gellner, Ernest. *Nations and Nationalism.* Ithaca NY: Cornell University Press, 1983.
Geraci, Robert. *Window on the East: National and Imperial Identities in Late Tsarist Russia.* Ithaca: Cornell University Press, 2001.
Gorman, Daniel. *Imperial Citizenship: Empire and the Question of Belonging.* Manchester University Press, 2007).
Grosse, Pascal. "What Does German Colonialism Have to Do with National Socialism?" pp. 115–34 in Eric Ames, Marcia Klotz, and Lora Wildenthal, eds. *Germany's Colonial Pasts.* Lincoln: University of Nebraska Press, 2005.
Guilhot, Nicolas. "The Realist Gambit: Postwar American Political Science and the Birth of IR Theory." *International Political Sociology*, 2, (2008), 281–304.
Heller, Monica. *Paths to Post-nationalism: A Critical Ethnography of Language and Identity.* New York: Oxford University Press, 2011.
Hendrickson, David. *Peace Pact: The Lost World of the American Founding.* Lawrence: University Press of Kansas, 2003.
Hirsch, Francine. *Empire of Nations: Ethnographic Knowledge and the Making of the Soviet Union.* Ithaca: Cornell University Press, 2005.
Ho, Engseng. *The Graves of Tarim: Genealogy and Mobility across the Indian Ocean.* Berkeley: University of California Press, 2006.
Hobsbawm, Eric. *Nations and Nationalism since 1780: Programme, Myth, Realit.* Cambridge: Cambridge University Press, 1990.
Hull, Isabelle. *Absolute Destruction: Military Culture and the Practices of War in Imperial Germany.* Ithaca: Cornell University Press, 2004.
Irwin, Ryan. *Gordian Knot: Apartheid and the Unmaking of the Liberal World Order.* New York: Oxford University Press, 2012.
Itagaki, Ryūta, Satoshi Mizutani, and Hideaki Tobe, "Japanese Empire." Pp. 273–99 in Philippa Levine and John Marriott, eds. *The Ashgate Companion to Modern Imperial Histories.* Farnham, England: Ashgate, 2012.
Judson, Pieter. *Guardians of the Nation: Activists on the Language Frontier of Imperial Austria.* Cambridge, Mass.: Harvard University Press, 2006.
Karl, Rebecca. *Staging the World: Chinese Nationalism at the Turn of the Twentieth Century.* Durham: Duke University Press, 2002.
Khan, Yasmin.The Great Partition: *The Making of India and Pakistan.* New Haven: Yale University Press, 2008.
Klotz, Marcia. "The Weimar Republic: A Postcolonial State in a Still-Colonial World." Pp. 135–47 in Eric Ames, Marcia Klotz, and Lora Wildenthal, eds. *Germany's Colonial Pasts.* Lincoln: University of Nebraska Press, 2005.
Koselleck, Reinhart. *Futures Past: On the Semantics of Historical Time*, trans. Keith Tribe. New York: Columbia University Press, 2004 [1979].
Kramer, Paul. *The Blood of Government: Race, Empire, the United States, and the Philippines.* Chapel Hill: University of North Carolina Press, 2006.
Krasner, Georgio. *Sovereignty: Organized Hypocrisy.* Princeton: Princeton University Press, 1999.

Kundrus, Birthe. "Colonialism, Imperialism, National Socialism: How Imperial Was the Third Reich?" Pp. 330–46 in Bradley Naranch and Geoff Eley, eds., *German Colonialism in a Global Age*. Durham: Duke University Press, 2014.
Lee, Christopher, ed. *Making a World After Empire: The Bandung Moment and Its Aftermaths*. Athens: Ohio University Press, 2010.
Leonhard, Jörn, and Ulrike von Hirschhausen, eds. *Comparing Empires*. Gottingen: Vandenhoeck anbd Ruprecht, 2011.
Lonsdale, John, and Bruce Berman, "Coping with the Contradictions: The Development of the Colonial State in Kenya." *Journal of African History* 20 (1979): 487–506.
Lower, Wendy. *Nazi Empire-Building and the Holocaust in Ukraine*. Chapel Hill: University of North Carolina Press, 2005.
Macmillan, Margaret. *Paris 1919: Six Months that Changed the World*. New York: Random House, 2003.
Maier, Charles. *Among Empires: American Ascendancy and Its Predecessors*. Cambridge MA: Harvard University Press, 2006.
Manela, Erez. *The Wilsonian Moment: Self-determination and the International Origins of Anticolonial Nationalism*. New York: Oxford University Press, 2007.
Mann, Gregory. *From Empires to NGOs in the West African Sahel: The Road to Nongovernmentality*. Cambridge: Cambridge University Press, 2015.
Martin, Terry. *The Affirmative Action Empire: Nations and Nationalism in the Soviet Union, 1923–1939*. Ithaca: Cornell University Press, 2001.
Mazower, Mark. *Hitler's Empire: Nazi Rule in Occupied Europe*. London: Allen Lane, 2008.
McClintock, Ann. *Imperial Leather: Race, Gender and Sexuality in the Colonial Contest*. London: Routledge, 1995.
McDougall, James. *History and the Culture of Nationalism in Algeria*. Cambridge: Cambridge University Press, 2006.
Migani, Guia. *La France et l'Afrique sub-saharienne, 1957–1963: Histoire d'une décolonisation entre idéaux eurafricains et politique de puissance*. Brussels: PIE Peter Lang, 2008.
Moyn, Samuel. *The Last Utopia: Human Rights in History*. Cambridge: Harvard University Press, 2010.
Müller, Jan-Werner. *A Dangerous Mind: Carl Schmitt in Post-War European Thought*. New Haven: Yale University Press, 2003.
Pedersen, Susan. *The Guardians: The League of Nations and the Crisis of Empire*.Oxford: Oxford University Press, 2015.
Pletsch, Carl. "The Three Worlds, or the Division of Social Science Labor, Circa 1950–1975." *Comparative Studies in Society and History* 23 (1981): 565–90.
Rossi, Benedetta. *From Slavery to Aid: Politics, Labour, and Ecology in the Nigerien Sahel, 1800–2000*. Cambridge: Cambridge University Press, 2015.
Sassen, Saskia. "Toward Post-National and Denationalized Citizenship." Pp. 277–91 in Engin Isin and Bryan Turner, eds., *Handbook of Citizenship Studies*. Beverly Hills: Sage 2002..
Sheehan, James J. "The Problem of Sovereignty in European History." *American Historical Review* 111 (2006): 1–15
Sikkink, Kathryn, and Margaret Keck. *Activists Beyond Borders: Advocacy Networks in International Politics*. Ithaca, NY: Cornell University Press, 1998.

Sinha, Mrinalini. *Specters of Mother India: The Global Restructuring of an Empire*. Durham NC: Duke University Press, 2006.
Sluga, Glenda. *Internationalism in the Age of Nationalism*. Philadelphia: University of Pennsylvania Press, 2013.
Soysal, Yasemin Nuhoğlu. *Limits of Citizenship: Migrants and Postnational Membership in Europe*. Chicago: University of Chicago Press, 1994.
Steinmetz, George. *The Devil's Handwriting: Precoloniality and the German Colonial State in Qingdao, Samoa and Southwest Africa*. Chicago: University of Chicago Press, 2007.
Stoler, Ann Laura. *Carnal Knowledge and Imperial Power: Race and the Intimate in Colonial Rule*. Berkeley: University of California Press, 2002.
Ther, Philipp. *The Dark Side of Nation-States: Ethnic Cleansing in Modern Europe*. London: Berghahn, 2014.
——. "Imperial Instead of National History: Positioning Modern German History on the Map of European Empires." Pp. 47–68 in Alexei Miller and Alfred Rieber, eds. *Imperial Rule*. Budapest and New York: Central European University Press, 2004.
Thomas, Lynn. *Politics of the Womb: Women, Reproduction, and the State in Kenya*. Berkeley: University of California Press, 2003.
Tooze, Adam. *The Deluge: The Great War and the Remaking of Global Order, 1916–1931*. London: Penguin, 2014.
Turner, Bryan. "We Are All Denizens Now: On the Erosion of Citizenship." *Citizenship Studies* 20 (2016): 679–92.
Vitalis, Robert. "The Midnight Ride of Kwame Nkrumah and Other Fables of Bandung (Ban-doong)." *Humanity* summer 2013: 261–88.
Westad, Odd Arne. *The Global Cold War: Third World Interventions and the Making of Our Times*. Cambridge: Cambridge University Press, 2007.
Wildenthal, Lora. *German Women for Empire, 1884–1945*. Durham: Duke University Press, 2001.
Wilder, Gary. *Freedom Time: Negritude, Decolonization, and the Future of the World*. Durham: Duke University Press, 2015.

Britta Schilling
Material Memories of Empire: Coming to Terms with German Colonialism

The memory of colonialism in Germany has been long-lived and relatively dynamic. This is because Germany's postcolonial period has been shaped by profound ruptures including the Second World War, the Holocaust and the Cold War. This article sketches out the multifaceted collective memory of German colonialism stretching from the loss of the colonies to the present day. In 1959, Theodor Adorno famously admonished Germans for not "coming to terms" with their National Socialist past in the postwar period, a statement which many intellectuals and "ordinary Germans" have taken to heart since then.[1] But has there been a comparable "coming to terms" with a colonial past?

The German case is important for scholars' understanding of wider European colonialisms and postcolonialisms because it is at once an example and an aberration.

Although some academics have revived Hannah Arendt's work on the origins of totalitarianism and sought the origins of Nazism in colonial wars at the beginning of the twentieth century, this is a problematic thesis which has come up against a number of well-founded counter-arguments.[2] Extreme violence and

---

[1] Theodor Adorno, "What does coming to terms with the past mean?," in G. Hartman, *Bitburg in Moral and Political Perspective* (Bloomington: Indiana University Press, 1986), 114–129.
[2] Jürgen Zimmerer has been the most prolific recent proponent of this argument; see for example "Krieg, KZ und Völkermord in Südwestafrika. Der erste deutsche Genozid," in Jürgen Zimmerer and Joachim Zeller, *Völkermord in Deutsch-Südwestafrika* (Berlin: Ch. Links, 2003), 45–63; see also Mark Mazower, *Dark Continent* (New York: Random House, 1998), 71–72; Marcia Klotz, "Global Visions: From the Colonial to the National Socialist World," *European Studies Journal* 16,2 (Fall 1999): 37–68; David Furber and Wendy Lower, "Colonialism and Genocide in Nazi-Occupied Poland and Ukraine," in A. Dirk Moses, *Empire, Colony, Genocide* (New York/Oxford: Berghahn, 2008): 372–400. Convincing arguments against this "continuity thesis" have been presented in Isabel Hull, *Absolute Destruction* (Ithaca/London: Cornell University Press, 2005); Birthe Kundrus, "Kontinuitäten, Parallelen, Rezeptionen," *Werkstatt Geschichte* 43 (2006): 45–62; Pascal Grosse, "What does German colonialism have to do with National Socialism? A conceptual framework," in Eric Ames, Marcia Klotz, and Lora Wildenthal, *Germany's Colonial Pasts* (Lincoln: University of Nebraska Press, 2005), 115–134; Sebastian Conrad, *Deutsche Kolonialgeschichte* (Munich: C.H. Beck, 2008), 96–106; Stephan Malinowski and Robert Gerwarth, "Hannah Arendt"s Ghosts," *Central European History* 42 (2009), 279–300. For further discussion of the debate, see Volker Langbehn and Mohammad Salama, *German Colonialism* (New York: Columbia University Press, 2011).

racism were not unique to the German colonies, and, as with other European powers, the shape of colonial rule varied across the different areas of empire. As much as it may have influenced German racialist thinking, colonial violence in itself does not explain why other colonial powers did not develop into totalitarian societies. Moreover, not all former colonialists integrated themselves into the NSDAP seamlessly. Certainly, both Nazism and colonialism made use of concepts of "race," "empire," and to some extent also "colonialism," but in very different contexts.[3] Finally, in numerous aspects, the colonial period itself was similar to and indeed entangled with other European colonial powers' patterns of governance, as Ulrike Lindner, for example, has shown with respect to British and German colonial powers in Africa.[4]

Part of what makes the German case unique is not only that the colonial period was so short, but rather that it was cut short. On the one hand, this meant that Germany never had the experience of postcolonial migration, of hundreds of thousands of ex-colonial migrants moving to live and work in the metropole, as has been the case in France and Britain. On the other hand, some scholars have argued that the colonial past still influences Germany's multicultural present to varying degrees.[5] Germany's original period of decolonization began earlier than that of many other European nations, giving it considerable time and impetus to develop a collective memory of colonialism after the fact, a memory which is

---

[3] Uta Poiger thus makes a valid plea for viewing German history as "imperial" history, but this is not contingent upon classifying the German–Herero war as "genocide." U. Poiger, "Imperialism and Empire in Twentieth-Century Germany," *History and Memory* 17,1–2 (Spring–Summer 2005): 117–143. This is echoed by Pascal Grosse in "From Colonialism to National Socialism to Postcolonialism," *Postcolonial Studies* 9,1 (2006): 48 and Shelley Baranowski in *Nazi Empire* (Cambridge: Cambridge University Press, 2011), 3.
[4] Ulrike Lindner, *Koloniale Begegnungen* (Frankfurt am Main/New York: Campus, 2011).
[5] See, e.g., Monika Albrecht, "Postcolonialism and Migration into Germany's Colonial Past," *German Life and Letters* 65,3 (July 2012): 363–377; Patrice Nganang, "Autobiographies of Blackness in Germany," in Ames, Klotz, and Wildenthal, *Germany's Colonial Pasts*, 227–240; Kien Nghi Ha, Nicola Lauré al-Samarai and Sheila Mysorekar, "Einleitung," in Ha, al-Samarai and Mysorekar, *re/visionen* (Münster: Unrast, 2007), 9–21; Hito Steyerl, Encarnación Gutiérrez Rodríguez and Kien Nghi Ha, *Spricht die Subalterne deutsch?*, 2nd edition (Münster: Unrast, 2012); María do Mar Castro Varela and Nikita Dhawan, "Mission Impossible," in Julia Reuter and Paula-Irene Villa, *Postkoloniale Soziologie* (Bielefeld: Transcript, 2010), 303–330; Cyber-Nomads/Öffentlichkeit gegen Gewalt, *The Black Book* (Frankfurt am Main/London: IKO, 2004); Maureen Maisha Eggers, Grada Kilomba, Peggy Piesche and Susan Arndt, *Mythen, Masken und Subjekte* (Münster: Unrast, 2006); Sara Lennox, "Postcolonial Writing in Germany," in Ato Quayson, *Cambridge History of Postcolonial Literature* (Cambridge: Cambridge University Press, 2012), 620–648. For a discussion of different German "postcolonialisms," see Britta Schilling, "German Postcolonialism in Four Dimensions," *Postcolonial Studies* 18,4 (2015): 427–439.

now one or even two generations ahead of that of other major European powers, but perhaps more hidden from public space. Although the scope of German colonialism discussed, for example, at international conferences has expanded, most historians still see 1945 as a stopping point, claiming that afterwards there existed only a period of colonial 'amnesia'.[6] This article proposes a different periodization, one which transcends the conventional breaks marked by the Nazi takeover and the end of the Second World War.

1. Memory in Germany: a (material) re-periodization

Looking at both historical and theoretical aspects, it addresses a problem in traditional historiography by exploring how long, following the end of formal claims to overseas territories, a 'collective memory' of German colonialism continued to exist, what forms it assumed, and how and why these forms changed over time. This paper summarizes the most important nodes in this memory narrative, which are explained more fully in the book, *Postcolonial Germany*.[7] But, unlike other *lieux-de-mémoire*-like compilations,[8] the research also opens up valuable new opportunities for considering the relationship between human memory and material culture, how *things* make us think about the past. In our own rapidly evolving digital age, which replaces material objects with ephemeral renditions (one has only to think of the evolution of the book), the relationship between the physical and the psychological may itself soon be a figment of the past, making its investigation all the more valuable. It is the latter goal on which this article focuses.

Recent attempts to define the relationship between people and artefacts have shown how memory objects are a unique means of re-experiencing the past in the present. In his work on memory and material culture, Andrew Jones, for example, argues that "we can no longer simply treat objects purely

---

[6] The term "Amnesie" has been used by Reinhart Kößler and others to describe the current state of awareness of colonialism in Germany. Kößler, "Kolonialherrschaft—auch eine deutsche Vergangenheit", in Lutz and Gawarecki, *Kolonialismus und Erinnerungskultur* (Munster: Waxmann, 2005), 33. Lora Wildenthal also refers to a "repudiation or amnesia" of imperial ambitions after 1945 in her essay, "Notes on a History of 'Imperial Turns' in Modern Germany," in Antoinette Burton, *After the Imperial Turn* (Durham/London: Duke University Press, 2003), 145–156.
[7] Britta Schilling, *Postcolonial Germany* (Oxford: Oxford University Press, 2014).
[8] For example, most recently, Jürgen Zimmerer, *Kein Platz an der Sonne* (Frankfurt am Main: Campus, 2013).

as symbolic media; rather the materiality of objects is best seen as impinging on people sensually and physically at a fundamental level."[9] This primacy of the material in social and cultural history has also been evoked in different contexts by sociologist Arjun Appadurai, historical anthropologist Nicholas Thomas, historian Carolyn Steedman, archaeologist Chris Gosden and anthropologist Chantal Knowles.[10] In German history, the function of material objects has most influenced studies on museums, exhibitions, and the history of German ethnology, including the more recent debates of the restitution of ethnographic objects and human remains housed in Berlin museums.[11] This article expands this research by refocusing the debate to consider how objects of memory function not just as symbols in public spaces such as museums, but as "physical traces"[12] of the past in private spaces such as the home.

What makes material culture a particularly useful lens through which to investigate the colonial past? Firstly, as Karen Harvey writes, "unlike 'object' or 'artefact', 'material culture' encapsulates not just the physical attributes of an object, but the myriad and shifting contexts through which it acquires meaning. Material culture is not confined to objects that people make, use and throw away; it is an integral part of—and indeed shapes—human experience."[13] Moreover, as Arjun Appadurai has argued, objects, or commodities, have "social lives."[14] They are produced, disseminated and consumed; they can be maintained, displayed and showcased, or they can be allowed to decay. The study of objects thus always includes the study of people's relationship to them and the attitudes and ideologies which inform this relationship. Furthermore, as colonial objects move in and out of "commodity phases", to borrow Igor Kopytoff's

---

9 Andrew Jones, *Memory and Material Culture* (Cambridge: Cambridge University Press, 2007), 19.
10 Arjun Appadurai, *The Social Life of Things* (Cambridge: Cambridge University Press, 1986); Carolyn Steedman, "What a Rag Rug Means," *Journal of Material Culture* 3,3 (Nov. 1998): 259–281; Nicholas Thomas, *Entangled Objects* (Cambridge, MA/London: Harvard University Press, 1991); Chris Gosden and Chantal Knowles, *Collecting Colonialism* (Oxford/New York: Berg, 2001).
11 H. Glenn Penny and Matti Bunzl, *Worldly Provincialism* (Ann Arbor: University of Michigan Press, 2003); Penny, *Objects of Culture* (Chapel Hill/London: University of North Carolina Press, 2003). Holger Stoecker, Thomas Schnalke and Andreas Winkelmann, *Sammeln, Erforschen, Zurückgeben?* (Berlin: Christoph Links, 2013); Stoecker, "Knochen im Depot," in Jürgen Zimmerer, *Kein Platz an der Sonne* (Frankfurt a.M.: Campus, 2013), 442–457. The issue has also been covered extensively in the German media.
12 Jones, *Memory and Material Culture*, 19.
13 Karen Harvey, "Introduction," in Harvey, *History and Material Culture* (Abingdon: Routledge, 2009), 3.
14 Arjun Appadurai, "Introduction: commodities and the politics of value", in Appadurai, *Social Lives*, 3–63.

phrase, we can learn how the value of colonial objects has changed over time, as well as how colonial memory itself has been commodified.[15] And finally, objects can travel; they can cross national boundaries but also the boundaries between public and private space. Essentially, it is material objects' ability to generate meaning both to larger collectives as well as to individuals which makes them such an important element in any study of colonial memory. This paper thus argues that colonial memory was intimately bound to objects of material culture in the former German metropole, but also suggests how colonial material culture remains a contested site of national heritage in many of the former colonies. I will now briefly sketch out the histories of four objects of colonial memory which were influential in determining the meaning of the colonial past in Germany from the end of the First World War to the late 1960s.

2. 1915 – 1925: Afrikabücher/Africa-books

Attempts to memorialize German colonialism start in the colonial period itself but pick up dramatically after the loss of the colonies. One of the earliest nodes of colonial memory which traversed the private and public spheres was the *Afrikabuch*, or Africa-book. *Afrikabuch* or *Kolonialbuch*, an analogous expression, are not terms that are found, for example, in literary encyclopaedias such as Hiersemann's *Lexikon des Gesamten Buchwesens* or Hiller and Füssel's *Wörterbuch des Buches*. They are, nevertheless, terms which were frequently used in everyday parlance during the 1920s and, in the specific case of *Afrikabuch*, still used today. Indeed, "Africa-books," published travel accounts and geographies of Africa for a European audience, have been in existence for hundreds of years. One of the most notable examples, said to be the first early modern European geography of the continent, was written by the Moroccan diplomat Leo Africanus in the sixteenth century.[16] *Afrikabücher* published between 1915 and 1925 were therefore certainly not the first ones to appear on the scene. They were, however, the first ones in which we clearly have a sense of the book representing the memory of a bygone era, written during a time when Germans not only were not able to travel much abroad, but were actually banned from entering some of the former colonies in Africa. These books laid the groundwork for a genre that continued to bloom all through the 1920s and well into the Nazi peri-

---

15 Igor Kopytoff, "The cultural biography of things: commoditization as process", in Appadurai, *Social Lives*, 64 – 94; also Appadurai, "Introduction", 13, 15 – 28.
16 See Natalie Zemon Davis, *Trickster Travels* (London: Faber, 2007).

od. Indeed, many of these books were reissued in the later 1930s because of their nationalist arguments and memories of a German Reich spanning the globe.

Perhaps the most successful fictionalized *Afrikabuch* of all time was Hans Grimm's novel *Volk ohne Raum*, first published in 1926, with 480,000 copies in print by 1940.[17] It was in many ways the culmination of an almost ten-year tradition of German non-fiction books about the former colonies. The story is of a young man who, frustrated with living in an overcrowded and industrialized Germany, finds fulfilment as a farmer in prewar German Southwest Africa. Known to contemporaries as "the German Kipling," Grimm inspired a generation of readers by drawing from his experiences as a journalist and businessman in South and Southwest Africa.[18] He was one of the most fervent adherents to the nineteenth-century idea of *Lebensraum*, claiming that the German race urgently needed space to expand. Indeed, Grimm's novel was more than just light entertainment. His very motto, *Volk ohne Raum*, was used by the Nazis to describe colonial living space in the East.[19] But it would hardly have been possible without the rise in the number of *Afrikabücher* making their way into German homes before and during Grimm's drafting of the story.

As a medium, the *Afrikabuch* combines both the "communicative" and "cultural" memory of the period.[20] It lies at the intersection of oral and written forms of culture, combining the traditional elements of storytelling prevalent in settler society in the colony and the more permanent elements of the written word and popular literature in the metropole. Like communicative memory as defined by Jan and Aleida Assmann, stories in the *Afrikabuch* are often tales retold, constructed in relation to others who have a common conception of the past, that is, the community of white settlers in Africa.[21] Thus, these narratives often include digressions, tales related from second-hand knowledge, or even local rumours and myths. Parts of *Afrikabücher* are told as campfire stories, with a degree of truth but also some room for embellishment, part of a local tradition

---

17 Donald Ray Richards, *The German Bestseller in the 20th Century* (Bern: Lang, 1968).
18 G. H. Danton, "Hans Grimms Volk ohne Raum," *Monatshefte für deutschen Unterricht* 27,2 (Feb. 1935): 37. See also Woodruff Smith, "The Colonial Novel as Political Propaganda," *German Studies Review* 6,2 (May 1983): 215–235.
19 Konrad Jarausch and Michael Geyer, *Shattered Past* (Princeton: Princeton University Press, 2003), 207; Jürgen Zimmerer, "Colonialism and the Holocaust," *Development Dialogue* 50 (Dec. 2008): 96.
20 Jan Assmann and Jan Czaplicka, "Collective Memory and Cultural Identity," *New German Critique* 65 (Spring–Summer 1995): 126.
21 Assmann and Czaplicka, "Collective Memory and Cultural Identity", 127.

of telling "stories."²² Such storytelling was also frequent in POW camps during and after the war, where a number of authors found their inspiration for writing.²³ At the same time, a number of *Afrikabuch* authors were attempting to fix the "shifting horizon" of this form of communicative memory, memorializing it in a more permanent way for future generations through a "cultural" formation: the medium of the written word and the physical book itself.²⁴ The *Afrikabuch* acts as a textual and physical monument to the past, a symbol for an eternal, or timeless, unalterable rendition of history, as well as an expression of a *Gemeinschaft*, or a national identity.²⁵ The need to memorialize and monumentalize German experiences in Africa stemmed from the fear that the actual era of German colonialism was over.

Afrikabücher are fascinating documents in terms of textual analysis, but we also gain additional insights when we read them not just as texts but as material objects. *Afrikabücher* can be seen as conforming to the most avant-garde trends which fashioned books as objects of mass consumption. Many of these books were advertised to "young and old alike," reflecting the new desire to provide literature for greater parts of the population, particularly children and young people.²⁶ They also made use of new advances in reprographic technology which allowed for inclusion of a far greater number of photographs, pictures, or drawings. The prolific author Hans Anton Aschenborn's *Afrikanische Buschreiter*, for example, boasts 41 drawings by the author, and his *Farm im Steppenlande* includes as many as one hundred photographs. Richard Hennig's *Sturm und Sonnenschein in Deutsch-Südwest* features 47 colored and black-and-white photos, sketches, and watercolors. The inclusion of more visual material was also a response to the growing appeal of media such as illustrated magazines and film.²⁷ Graphically intricate covers bearing exotic scenes were meant to quickly attract potential readers. Many *Afrikabuch* covers, such as August Hauer's *Kumbuke*, featured colorful renditions of the African landscape and its people. Their outward presentation thus already promised relatively inexpensive es-

---

22 Otto Inhülsen, *Wir ritten für Deutsch-Ostafrika* (Leipzig: V. Hase & Koehler, 1926), 124–125; H. R. Schneider-Waterberg, *Der Wahrheit eine Gasse* (Swakopmund: Gesellschaft für Wissenschaftliche Entwicklung, 2006), 18.
23 Karl Koch, *Im toten Busch* (Leipzig: Voigtländer, 1922), foreword.
24 Assmann and Czaplicka, "Collective Memory," 127.
25 Cf. Jan Assmann, "Stein und Zeit. Das 'monumentale' Gedächtnis der altägyptischen Kultur," in Jan Assmann and Tonio Hölscher, *Kultur und Gedächtnis* (Frankfurt am Main: Suhrkamp, 1988), 90–91.
26 *Buchhändlergilde-Blatt* 10 (1925): 175.
27 Berthold Brohm, "Das Buch in der Krise. Studien zur Buchhandelsgeschichte der Weimarer Republik," *Archiv für Geschichte des Buchwesens* 51 (1999): 272.

capism. At Christmas, Easter, and other special occasions, *Afrikabücher* were advertised as special gifts at a range of prices. General von Lettow-Vorbeck's *Meine Kriegserinnerungen aus Ostafrika*, for example, was offered by Koehler at 28.50 marks, 35 marks fully bound; his *Heia Safari!*, for a younger audience, was offered to booksellers at 13.50 marks fully bound.[28] *Kriegserinnerungen* was thus in the same price range as works by Goethe.[29]

Afrikabücher published during the first half of the 1920s were volumes which could be valued not only for their lively stories and aesthetic appeal, but also for their underlying political messages. They challenged the accusation of Germans being bad colonialists, which had been suggested by the British Blue Book[30] and was used as justification for removing the colonies from German possession. Instead of portraying German colonialists as violent perpetrators, *Afrikabücher* used tales of internment, loss and decline to cast Germans in the role of victims. A central element in all of these accounts is explaining the meaning of the *Heimat* (home) abroad, or *zweite Heimat* (second home), to those who had never experienced or felt any allegiance to it. They offered a glimpse into the community of German *Afrikaner* who felt let down by an unjust peace accepted by the Weimar government and was now struggling to survive. Whilst offering these more emotional appeals, *Afrikabücher* illustrated everyday life abroad and educated readers in the skills and knowledge needed for life in the bush. They sought to excite younger readers with their memories of a golden age, which, in the mid-1920s, some authors hoped could be reclaimed. By imbuing their audience with a sense of nostalgia for a "lost paradise,"[31] authors used their personal experiences in the former colonies as political propaganda. It is this quality which made their books attractive to the German readership not only during the early interwar period, but ensured their popularity in years to come.

In both implicit and explicit ways, the rhetoric of remembering and forgetting infuses the texts of *Afrikabücher*. Indeed, the very medium of text and words, and the more tangible objects of manuscripts and paper become highly significant to authors. When Karl Angebauer is forcibly removed from Southwest Africa, his first instinct is to swear to return. In the face of financial hardship, however, he chooses a different route: he writes about what he has lost.[32] For

---

28 *Buchhändlergilde-Blatt* 3 (1920): 68.
29 *Buchhändlergilde-Blatt* 3 (1920): back cover.
30 South-West Africa Administrator's Office, *Report on the Natives of South-West Africa and their Treatment by Germany* (London: His Majesty's Stationery Office, 1918) [British Parliamentary Papers Cd. 9146].
31 Hans Anton Aschenborn, *Die Farm im Steppenlande* (Neudamm: Neumann, 1925), 7.
32 Karl Angebauer, *Ovambo* (Berlin: Scherl, 1927), 24–26.

Otto Inhülsen, it was so important to keep a record of his time in Africa alive that he smuggled his notes and diaries out of East Africa in a suitcase with a false base.[33] Grete Kühnhold instead regrets having to cede "a few small books with scientific observations and notes on my travels in Kamerun" to British forces upon leaving.[34] On an even more elemental level, several works reference the Swahili word *Kumbuke*, or "please remember."[35] Memory was thus enmeshed with the very language of the former African homeland. As much as some books were dedicated to the memory of lives and comrades lost, then, they were also dedicated to a lost time and place.

The *Afrikabücher* discussed here were just the beginning of a genre, works which prepared the way for a revival of Africa-centered and colonial literature in years to come. Some may even have helped establish prominent publishing houses which later specialized in travel and adventure literature, such as the Safari Verlag, established in 1921.[36] In any case, every time *Afrikabücher* were read, every time children and adults leafed through the illustrated pages or gazed at the colorful covers, the memory of the German colonial past was "recharged" through the cultural framework of the present, and the memory of colonialism kept alive. This was the period during which most of the myths and legends concerning Germans in the African colonies were born. Interestingly, it was also a time in which many of these myths were not yet reified, and we see a degree of ambiguity on issues such as the loyalty of African subjects, the treatment of German POWs, and the prospects of Germans returning to the colonies in the future.

3. 1925–1935: Colonial wares/Kolonialwaren

A second node of material memories of empire in Germany is objects linked to the economic wealth (real or imagined) from the former colonies. Perhaps the best way of understanding their circulation and multiple uses is through the phenomenon of the colonial ball. The colonial ball in Germany reached its peak between the mid-1920s and mid-1930s. At this point, societies like the German Colonial Society (DKG) were in full stride campaigning for colonial revisionism in

---

[33] Inhülsen, *Wir ritten für Deutsch-Ostafrika*, 212–213.
[34] Grete Kühnhold, *In Friedens- und Kriegszeiten in Kamerun* (Berlin: Scherl, 1917), 66.
[35] August Hauer, *Kumbuke*, 4th edn (Berlin: Hobbing, 1926); Prüße, *Zwanzig Jahre Ansiedler in Deutsch-Ostafrika* (Stuttgart: Strecke & Schröder, 1929), 270.
[36] Wolfgang Schwerbrock, Hans Thiekötter, and Wilhelm Lehmann, *Safari Verlag 1921–1961* (Berlin: Safari, 1961), 8.

Germany. We can chart the rising popularity of colonial issues by looking, for example, at the membership figures for the Women's League of the German Colonial Society (FDKG). Despite the economically and politically volatile situation during the Weimar Republic, membership rose steadily. Particularly after 1925, when Tanganyika Territory was reopened for German settlement and there appeared to be renewed hope for re-appropriation of the former colonies, colonial organizations won new members. Economically, Germany at this point was also recovering from the inflation crisis of 1923 with the help of the Dawes Plan introduced the following year. In 1930 the Women's League reached the highest membership hitherto at 20,560.[37] Four years later the number had risen to 26,600.[38] In the meantime, 270 local chapters of the FDKG had been founded—over twice as many as in 1933—of which 40 were in Africa.[39] By 1936, the year of its incorporation into the Nazi Party's Reich Colonial League (RKB), FDKG membership had doubled compared with the figure for 1928 and was 7.5 times higher than in its founding year, 1906.[40] This "popularization" was attributable to a large extent to the colonial propaganda spread by the Women's League and the larger DKG. Despite the increase in membership numbers, however, the class structure of the leadership remained as middle- and upper-class as ever.

The loss of property and profits which had been, after all, the mainstay of the German overseas merchant elite and had always been at the heart of the German colonial project, left a gaping hole in the former colonialists' sense of identity. Colonial balls were the ideal means of recreating the colonial dream for middle- and upper-class Germans.[41] They can be read as an attempt to compensate for the loss of the colonies by arranging colonial and pseudo-colonial objects, or symbols, in a dream-space, and then "performing" the dream. Essential to this dream was the instrumentalization of colonial products of empire, including tropical fruit, chocolate, coffee, rubber, palm oil and sisal, as well as objectivized "blacks."

A typical theme for the evening was, for example, "Travels in the Tropics" or a "Voyage around Africa." On these occasions, the ballroom was transformed into a steamer of the Woermann Line, often with props created by local theater artists. Occasionally, even more well-known painters were enlisted to decorate

---

37 Bundesarchiv Berlin Lichterfelde (BAB), R1001/6693, FDKG Jahresbericht 1929–30, 31.
38 BAB R1001/6695, Bl. 99, Jahresbericht 1933–34.
39 BAB R8023/404, Bl. 41–2, N. von Steinmeister, "Deutsche Büchereien und Leseartikel in Afrika," 1933; BAB R1001/6695, Bl. 219, Geschäftsbericht 1935–36.
40 Else Frobenius lists membership as 30,000 on 31 May 1936 in Frobenius, *30 Jahre koloniale Frauenarbeit* (Berlin: Reichskolonialbund, 1936), 31.
41 Schilling, *Postcolonial Germany*, chapter 2.

the walls with colonial-inspired motifs. At larger events, the "Arrival in Africa" was set up in a further ballroom. After being greeted with a speech about the significance of the former colonies for Germany and the importance of their reacquisition, guests "disembarked" and wandered among vines and palm trees, past a "native *kraal*" or an interactive *pontok* or tent, into "liveliness and frolicking," accompanied by an African band. Tables were decorated with miniature elephants, monkeys, palm trees, and "small chocolate negroes." In the "native bazaar," women dressed as "colored beauties" served tropical fruits such as bananas and oranges. Often, colorful advertisements would also adorn the ballroom. Further delights could be tasted at the "oriental"-style *Mokkastübchen*, where guests were served Germany's "own" coffee, cocoa, and other colonial products. Often the entertainment included a rendition of *Zehn kleine Negerlein* ("Ten Little Negroes"), as well as jazz music and an African dance or two.

Around three to four thousand people attended these sorts of events in major cities, most of them from the colonial, political and economic elite. Corporate sponsors included AEG, Deutsche Afrika Linien, Gasag, Deutsche Lufthansa, Daimler-Benz and Maggi. They supported primarily a move towards economic imperialism, although eventually economic arguments were also used as rationale for settler colonialism. An essential part of the marketing strategy of merchants selling tropical goods was making colonial products, usually revered as a luxury, appeal to a larger group of consumers. In this regard, the display and sale of colonial products at colonial balls was not only a way of solidifying bonds within the colonial elite. It was also intended to increase awareness of the colonial cause amongst a wider band of upper- and middle-class enthusiasts, expanding the circle of potential investors in a reinvigorated imperial project overseas.

Blacks (or representations of blacks) were the means by which colonial goods were sold. Though seldom credited with the production of colonial products, Africans were highly visible as abstract advertising symbols for them. Almost always depicted in a position of servitude, black men and women were shown carrying bananas, offering chocolates, and pouring coffee, an iconography continued from the nineteenth century.[42] The trope of the African seems to have worked so well that it was extended to more ordinary household products which were also advertised at colonialist events. An exhibition stand in 1929 presented the following wares: "glistening negro caricatures, red-mouthed

---

[42] David Ciarlo, "Rasse konsumieren. Von der exotischen zur kolonialen Imagination in der Bildreklame des Wilhelminischen Kaiserreichs," in Kundrus, *Phantasiereiche*, 135–179; see also Ciarlo, *Advertising Empire* (Cambridge, MA: Harvard University Press, 2011).

and thick-lipped, tried skin cream, toothpaste or margarine, which was gobbled up by the packet."[43] Such images reinforced the stereotype of blacks as ridiculous, dirty, unhygienic, and uncivilized subjects who would benefit from a German sense of order, cleanliness, and hygiene.[44]

Examples from advertising for colonial products show a certain visual preoccupation with black and white skin in German culture in the 1920s and 1930s. A fixation on racial difference further informed the dream-world of colonial balls through another dream element: black performers. The choice of the term "black" rather than "African" is significant, because the idea of "black" took on a variety of different guises in German popular discourse at this time, including black Africans, African-Americans, and black Germans representing African-Americans. Above all, although there may have been black Africans at German colonial balls, several reports suggest that it is more likely that the physical reality of "blackness" in the context of the colonial ball was a layer of black or brown greasepaint on white bodies. Like any dream, the colonial ball thus tried to make the abstract qualities of race more plastic and concrete, solidifying a positive and economically productive memory of German colonialism.

4. 1935–1945: Educational Maps

Attempts to popularize a positive colonial memory were thus propagated during the Weimar years but had relatively little impact on a larger population. This began to change during the later National Socialist years. In response to the relative elitism of the colonial dream in the 1920s and early 1930s, the National Socialist government attempted to sell the colonial idea to "the masses" starting in the mid-1930s. Rather than organizing colonial balls, the Nazis staged events which were more accessible to a wider population. For example, a "colonial day" was held at the zoo in Berlin in 1937 under the motto "Everyone to Africa" (*Jeder einmal in Afrika*), and nation-wide colonial memorial days were established.[45] Major colonial exhibitions were held in 1937 in Frankfurt and 1939 in Dresden, while a series of African-themed films hit the cinemas between 1938 and 1943.[46]

---

43 *Mitteilungen des Frauenbunds der Deutschen Kolonialgesellschaft* 12 (1929): 147.
44 For a similar phenomenon in British advertising, see Anne McClintock, *Imperial Leather* (New York: Routledge, 1995), 207–232.
45 *Die Frau und die Kolonien* 6 (1937), 95; Willi Walter Puls, *Der koloniale Gedanke im Unterricht der Volksschule* (Leipzig: Quelle & Meyer, 1938), 147–148.
46 See Sabine Hake, "Mapping the Native Body: On Africa and the Colonial Film in the Third Reich", in Friedrichsmeyer, Lennox, and Zantop, *Imperialist Imagination*, 164.

Nowhere was colonialism more present, however, than in the classroom and, indeed, in the schoolbook and the accompanying maps. For it is through schoolbooks and didactic maps that an understanding of German history, including colonialism, was placed in every child's hands. As Simone Lässig and Karl Heinrich Pohl have noted, "textbook knowledge" is the result of contemporary discourse and therefore a reflection of zeitgeist. What is included in textbooks is "approved knowledge, accepted values, and popular memory,"[47] a consensus among the political elite, and a cultural transfer between generations.[48] It gives us insight into national stereotypes and provides points of comparison in times of social change.[49] The schoolbook and the educational map are relatively durable objects of material culture; they accompany schoolchildren in their everyday lives, making regular trips between home and school, or private and public space. Their physical longevity also means that the pages themselves may last longer than the discourse in which they were written or drawn. In fact, at times of rapid regime change, textbooks and maps can become outdated before they have even been distributed.

During the Nazi era, colonialism was written into geography and history textbooks, but there were also special editions of pamphlets on colonial heroes which could be used as supplements to the schoolbook. As in the Weimar period, the writing style under the Nazis remained emotionally charged in an attempt to enthuse young minds for the colonial idea. In order to capture their imaginations even further, a series of short, inexpensive pamphlets (*Schriften zur deutschen Erneuerung*) published by Heinrich Handel, Breslau, was distributed to classrooms to supplement standard textbooks. These included readings on Lettow-Vorbeck as part of the "Heroes of the World War" series and a separate series on "Borderland and Overseas Germans" which included "Our Colonies Past and Future" and "Our Colonies during the World War."[50] Additionally, teachers could use *Schriften der Schülerbücherei*, pamphlets which included colonial-themed titles such as Gustav Frenssen's *Peter Moors Fahrt nach Südwest*,

---

47 Simone Lässig and Karl Heinrich Pohl, "History Textbooks and Historical Scholarship in Germany," *History Workshop Journal* 67 (2009): 125–126.
48 Saskia Handro and Bernd Schönemann, *Geschichtsdidaktische Schulbuchforschung* (Münster: Lit, 2006), 4.
49 Handro and Schönemann, *Geschichtsdidaktische*, 3.
50 Georg Vogel, *Helden des Weltkrieges*, 9th edn., 3 vols. (Breslau: Handel, 1943); Paul Schmidt, *Unsere Kolonien in Vergangenheit und Zukunft*, 16th edn. (Breslau: Handel, 1941); Walter Pardex, *Unsere Kolonien im Weltkriege*, 3rd edn. (Breslau: Handel, 1938).

Bayer's *Die Helden der Naukluft*, and Lettow-Vorbeck's *Heia Safari!*[51] Other independent titles include booklets of 50 or so pages on colonial pioneers as part of the *Niedersächsische Jugendbücherei* series published by Appelhans or a similar *Erbe und Verpflichtung* series published by Teubner.[52] Some teachers also used Hans Grimm's *Volk ohne Raum* as reading material for sixteen- and seventeen-year-olds.[53]

The Nazis incorporated arguments and views of the former colonial elite and added didactic messages of their own which resonated with the National Socialist world view. These included a new legitimization of colonial violence (absent from Weimar textbooks), the portrayal of the First World War in Africa as a "race war," and additional lessons for the *Volksgemeinschaft* from the colonial experience, including military readiness, heroic leadership, and the power of the collective will. In 1937, history and geography textbooks referred to areas that had been called the "former colonies" in the mid-1920s as "our colonies." Adopting the Nazi obsession with political geography, educational maps of Africa preached a falsified history to students. A 1941 map of Africa produced by Georg Westermann, Braunschweig (Fig. 1: Westermann's Generalkarte No. 2), for example, elided the past and the future, showing both the former colonies as German possessions, as well as reaching up just far enough to Europe to also reveal the recent (re-)conquest of Poland. Both the former and future "colonies" were highlighted in red in order to make them instantly recognizable to pupils.

Like the colonialist movements which preceded them, the Nazis may not have succeeded in convincing the entire German population of the need for colonies, but the lengths they went to in order to convince the German youth were nevertheless considerable. Targeting a vulnerable age group with the most basic tools, such as the schoolbook and map, was a highly efficient way of getting the message across. Nazi propagandists built on the work done previously by colonial enthusiasts during the Weimar period, and, indeed, the colonial story stayed much the same across both eras. After 1936, when the Nazis showed a greater

---

51 W. Rödiger, "Geschichte", in Kurt Higelke, *Neubau der Volksschularbeit*, 2nd edn. (Leipzig: Julius Klinkhardt, 1941), 144.
52 E.g., Rudolf Krause, *Kaufmann im Hererolande*, Niedersächsische Jugendbücherei 2 (Brunswick: Appelhans, 1937); Carl Bradt, *Robert Koch*, Niedersächsische Jugendbücherei 5 (Brunswick: Appelhans, 1937, 1944); Rudolf Brauckmann, Karl Witt, and Walter Poppendieck, *Kolonialdienst in der Südsee*, Niedersächsische Jugendbücherei 9 (Brunswick: Appelhans, 1939); Hubert Coerver, *Carl Peters* (Leipzig/Berlin: Teubner, 1937); Heinz Nyszkiewicz and Bruno Dauch, *Deutsches Land in Afrika* (Leipzig/Berlin: Teubner, 1940).
53 H. Knust, "Grimms 'Volk ohne Raum' als Schullektüre," *Deutsches Bildungswesen* (Oct. 1933): 265.

Material Memories of Empire: Coming to Terms with German Colonialism —— 37

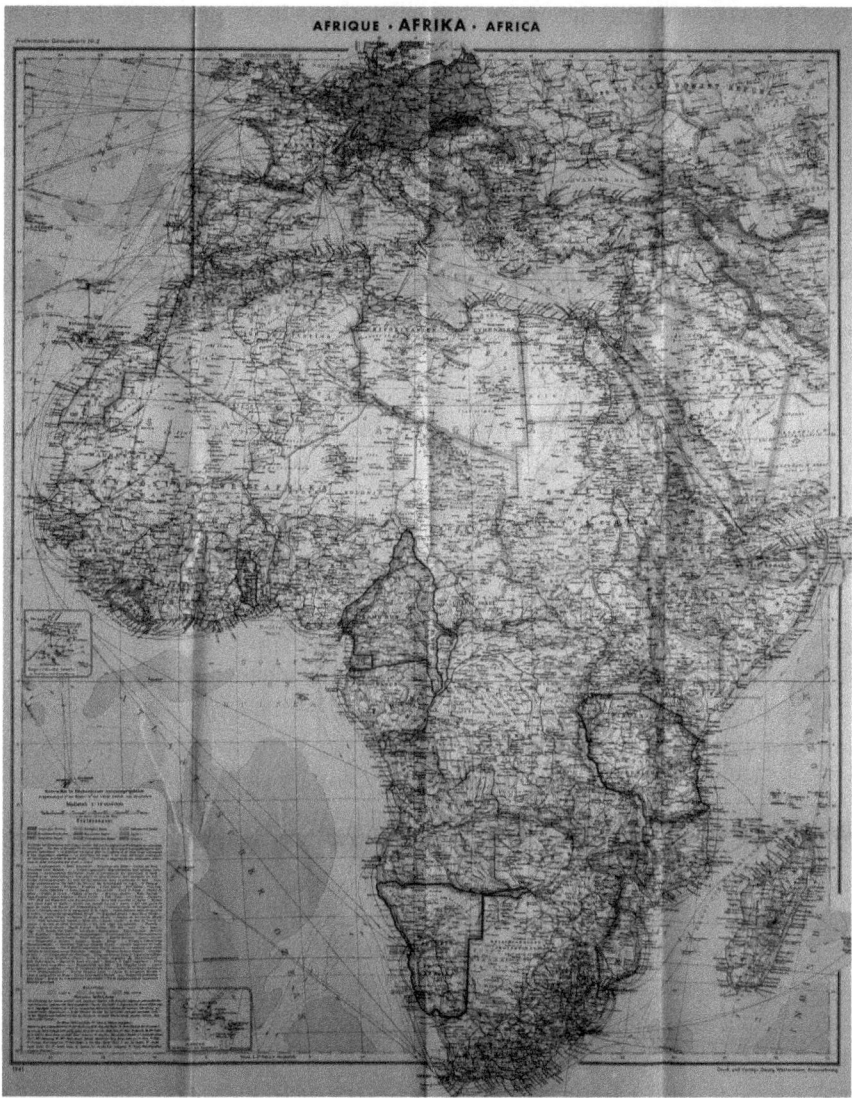

Fig. 1: A 1941 map for schoolchildren showing former colonies in Africa as German territory. *Westermanns Generalkarten (Flemings Generalkarten) Nr. 2: Afrika*, Braunschweig/Berlin/Hamburg: Georg Westermann, 1941.

commitment to the colonial cause, however, significant changes were made in the way colonialism was taught. Learning about colonialism in the Third Reich thus taught students more than just the height of the Kilimanjaro, the date of the war with the Herero, or the name of the first German settlement in Africa. It was meant to fire their imagination and encourage their willingness to defend their nation's honor both at home and abroad. In many ways, it fulfilled government aims that history should have a "connection to the immediate present."[54] The colorful, visually engaging material used to communicate these messages no doubt made an impression on young minds, and indeed many of these themes stayed with the Hitler Youth generation for years to come.

5. 1949–1968: The State Gift

For Germany, the immediate postwar period was a time of inwardness, both politically and socially. In the absence of a clearly defined German state, political interests in former overseas possessions were moot. Public memory of Germany's colonial past paled against the atrocities revealed in the more recent Nazi past, and was temporarily usurped by the lived experiences of rebuilding cities, reintegrating families, and relocating millions of people from Germany's former borderland territories in Europe. But it was not very long before Germany's colonial legacy resurfaced in public discourse. A deeper understanding of both East and West Germans' relation to the former colonies can be gleaned from analyzing objects that lie at the very heart of both the FRG and GDR's *Afrikapolitik* during the 1950s and 1960s. The official gifts from both states which were given to the former colonies at independence can provide valuable insights in this area.

In the context of Cold War competition, East and particularly West Germany's positions on the colonial past were constantly shifting, and the discourse surrounding gifts to former colonies reflect this complexity. More often than not, choosing the right gift was a cause of contention, hurried urgency and confusion. The rapid political developments in Africa kept ambassadors and consulates on their toes. West German representatives usually handed over gifts or gift certificates at the independence celebrations themselves, often presenting the item with a formal speech. Shortly thereafter, they would send over a team of delegates to secure a trade agreement with the new nation. Undeniably, for the West, development politics was, as the old colonial politics had been, a way of securing a market for exports.[55] Accusations of "neo-colonialism" by the East were thus not entirely unfounded. As African nations made up only

---

54 "Reformvorschläge" (1933), 18, in Barbara Schneider, *Die höhere Schule im Nationalsozialsimus* (Cologne/Weimar/Vienna: Böhlau, 2000), 341.
55 Bastian Hein, *Die Westdeutschen und die Dritte Welt* (Munich: Oldenbourg, 2006), 26–28.

two per cent of West German foreign trade in the mid-1960s, however, economic motivations cannot be considered the sole factor for the FRG's interest in the continent.[56] West Germans were also motivated by pressure to participate in strategic development aid from other Western powers, particularly the United States.[57]

East Germany was much slower in combining gift-giving with development aid to African countries, causing it to resent West Germans' early ties with newly emergent states. While West Germany sent ambulances and promised harbor development projects, East Germany initially sent only a congratulatory telegram. It was a slow, cautious approach, as the GDR had no pre-existing relationships with Africa. It had rejected any ties to a former colonial relationship on ideological grounds and was not able to compete with the large financial grants and credits offered by the FRG. Nevertheless, as the FRG's state gifts were often a precursor to more extensive development aid, so the GDR's telegram was often a gateway to economic or cultural agreements, or even a "solidarity program." As was the case for West German gifts, sending the congratulatory telegram was a ritual which served to promote the GDR as the one "true" Germany as much as it was meant to actually help Africans. As Marcel Mauss observed, an intense rivalry exists within and between societies to bring about exchanges of the most valuable things, for this signifies wealth and can "attract and dazzle" the other party, eventually winning them over as allies.[58] Such a rivalry eventually played itself out between East and West Germany in the selection and delivery of state gifts, for both wished to win over the newly independent nations as allies in the Cold War.

But beyond Cold War politics, a key point informing this rivalry was the dilemma of how to remember Germany's colonial past. West Germany, although aware of the negative connotations of colonialism in an age of mass decolonization, could not help but try to assume the legacy of a "good colonialist" in Africa. Its cultural memory was constructed by the convictions of government ambassadors and advisers who had been active in the former colonies before 1945, as well as alleged testimonies by former colonial subjects themselves.[59] Gifts from West Germany thus included objects which referenced the "good old days" of German colonialism, a period of "scientific colonialism" in which the Germans provided medical care, epitomized by the research of Robert Koch and Albert Schweitzer.

---

56 Rainer Tetzlaff, "Grundzüge und Hintergründe Bonner Afrika-Politik," in Helmut Bley and Rainer Tetzlaff, *Afrika und Bonn* (Reinbek bei Hamburg: Rowohlt, 1978), 30.
57 Hein, *Die Westdeutschen*, 38.
58 Marcel Mauss, *The Gift*, trans. W.D. Halls (London: Routledge, 1990), 28.
59 See Schilling, *Postcolonial Germany*, chapter 4.

Cameroon, for example received a Klinomobil, a mobile medical station, while Tanganyika received an X-ray unit, and Rwanda and Burundi received ambulances. Not to be overlooked is the fact that all of these gifts are material objects, objects which could be inscribed with personal messages of congratulations but which also physically embodied a special relationship between the two nations which dated back to the colonial period.

In contrast to the FRG, East Germany claimed to have broken with the colonial past completely. Its stance left relations to the former colonies dangling in a state of uncertainty, ostensibly with no shared memories—positive or negative— to build upon. But over time, East Germans' denial and repression of colonial memory was at times punctuated by a very limited recognition. East German congratulations started with *Glückwunschbriefe*, presented like gifts by a visiting diplomat but eschewing the crass materialism of the capitalist West. Eventually, however, the GDR also favored material signs of appreciation, notably with a gift of a printing press to Tanganyika in 1962, presented at the one-year anniversary of independence.[60] As with gifts given by West Germany, the gift given by the GDR appears to represent a paternalistic kind of relationship with the new state which implicitly references colonial times: a gift of "the word," Western education and technology. Interestingly, though, like the West German gift at independence, this state gift was selected in response to a wish expressed by the Tanganyikan government, specifically, Foreign Minister Oscar Kambona during his visit to the GDR in April 1962.[61]

The changing face of public memory of German colonialism since the end of the First World War has now been traced, noting where and how this collective memory was upheld and manipulated to fit into the dominant national paradigms. It is clear that, even after the Second World War, the public memory of colonialism was still making important appearances. And yet, it had changed: by the 1960s, there were rising uncertainties about moral implications of a colonial past, as well as an entirely novel context of Cold War alliances which framed colonial memory.

---

60 Auswärtiges Amt (AA) MfAA/A15068, Bl. 201–2, Direktive für die Delegation nach Ostafrika im Dezember 1963, 29 Nov. 1963.
61 AA MfAA/A15067, Bl. 244, MfAA an Büro des Bevollmächtigten der DDR in der VAR, betr. Tanganyika, 4 May 1963.

6. 1968–1990: The Empty Plinth

One of the most poignant moments of German postcolonial history, analyzed by several historians, is when students of the University of Hamburg tore down the statue of the colonial explorer Hermann von Wissmann in 1967–8 as part of a larger *Denkmalsturz* movement.[62] The fall of the Wissmann statue is symbolic of a broader trend concerning German colonial memory after 1968. In spite of several moments of colonial remembering after 1968, Germany's colonial past ceased to play a significant role in public space and therefore receded from the nation's (or, rather, both nations') collective memory. During this period the memory of colonialism may therefore be considered not as an artefact, but as an absence—an empty plinth where once a colonial monument stood. This is not to say that there was no interaction with the colonial past at all. In fact three potential nodes of memory did develop during this time through student activism and street protest, the work of East and West German historians, and the controversy surrounding Southwest Africa's independence. The difference from previous foci of memory, however, is that this memory no longer informed the national, collective conception of the past; it did not exist on the level of politics and government, nor did it have any real meaning in the socio-cultural space. It was a memory not internalized, but employed by small groups sharing diverse special interests, causes not necessarily directly related to German colonialism at all. These groups confronted the German colonial past in the present, but these were localized, fragmented, incomplete encounters, not tied together in a master narrative as public or national memory is. Colonial memory had thus moved from the monumental to the local, and likewise from an era of material memories to an era of traces, ghosts, and whispers increasingly related to the present rather than the past. Colonialism ceased to be a memory anchored in material relics but instead became an idea, a battle-cry, a symbol, a word. In public space at least, it moved from three to two dimensions.

In Germany, the public memory of the colonial past faded after 1968. This was because effective memory is dependent on large part on effective retrieval —the ability to call up encoded memories quickly. Not only individual memory, but also collective memory requires some outside impulse, a mnemonic device,

---

[62] Joachim Zeller, *Kolonialdenkmäler* (Frankfurt am Main: IKO, 1999); Wolfgang Speitkamp, *Denkmalsturz* (Göttingen: Vandenhoeck & Ruprecht, 1997); Ingo Cornils, "Denkmalsturz: The German Student Movement and German Colonialism," in Michael Perraudin and Jürgen Zimmerer, *German Colonialism and National Identity* (New York/London: Routledge, 2011), 197–212; Quinn Slobodian, *Foreign Front* (Durham/London: Duke University Press, 2012).

in order to be sustained. With the absence of triggers for remembering, including the physical destruction of monuments to the colonial past, the German collective memory of colonialism was rendered a taboo and subsumed in a torrent of other national memories, many of them more recent. [63] As Viktor Mayer-Schönberger points out, "Even though we may have stored it…information that cannot be retrieved easily in practical terms is no different from having been forgotten."[64] Without *things*, historical memory—like individual memory—has no longevity.

Coda 1: Family Memory

That would be the end of the story—except for two codas. The first is the remarkable resilience of family memories of the colonial past, which I have investigated in more detail elsewhere.[65] These can be divided roughly into four generations: colonial actors (born c. 1850s – 1880s), who brought back ethnographic items and hunting trophies which served as objects of memory and eventually became, over the years, decontextualized ornaments. The next generation, a "decolonized" generation (born c. 1880s – 1910s), added photographs, diaries, and more ethnographic objects, preserving them together with older items to combat a sense of loss and generate hope for a possible reclaiming of the former colonies in the future. For the next "postcolonial" generation (born c. 1920s – 1940s), the memory of colonialism was deeply enmeshed with memories of National Socialism and wrought with a mixture of pride and guilt. This generation is often now charged with managing the family archive, arranging and contextualizing photographs, particularly portraits displaying a clear iconography of colonialism, including pith helmets, hunting trophies, lush vegetation, all of which have become markers of colonial identity within the family. Other items, such as gifts from the former colonies, are kept because they represent the essential "otherness" of colonial ancestors, who are more often than not remembered as quirky, harmless characters. Finally, the "extra-colonials" (born c. 1950s – 1970s) are doubly impacted by silencing of colonial memory within the family and lack of emphasis on colonial history in education and public until very recently. By

---

[63] Joachim Zeller also suggests that the disappearance of colonial monuments from public space after 1968 may well facilitate forgetting of, and critical engagement with, the colonial era. Zeller, *Kolonialdenkmäler*, 214 – 215.
[64] Viktor Mayer-Schönberger, *Delete* (Princeton/Oxford: Princeton University Press, 2009).
[65] Schilling, *Postcolonial Germany*, chapter 6; Schilling, "Imperial Heirlooms," *Journal of Imperial and Commonwealth History* 41,4 (2013): 663 – 682.

engaging with both material and immaterial memories of the colonial past, this generation presents a clear potential for "working through" the legacies of German colonialism, perhaps even adding new layers of memory and material culture to the family archive. Together, these generations have constructed private archives of artefacts, stories, texts, and photographs which form an important part of German colonial memory, archives which at times resonates with but at other times runs counter to colonial memory in the public sphere.

Over the years, two major trends have emerged: first, the narratives produced in colonial families have become increasingly influenced by public memory; and, secondly, private, family memory's bearing on public memory has decreased. In spite of some similarities and overlaps, the memory of German colonialism is thus ultimately unlike that of Nazism, which has been increasingly infused with private recollections brought to light in published sources, talks, school projects, and similar initiatives. At the same time, because a much smaller segment of the population was involved in the colonial project, the private memories of colonialism could continue, not without impact from outside but certainly without such a full-scale intrusion as the national "working through" of the Nazi past.

In both Germanies, then, the memory of colonialism, although contested at times, frequently appeared in public life even beyond 1945. Private family memory, on the other hand, was more hidden, lying just below the surface of national narratives, in what one might call a "subterranean" space filled with odd pieces of material culture, a few anecdotes, and incomplete recollections. This eclecticism is a typical characteristic of collective memory in the family. Grandparents, as Maurice Halbwachs argues, can only communicate their family memory to their grandchildren in fragmentary ways, "within the interstices of the present family," never as a totality.[66] Moreover, as Angela Keppler has posited, the narration of what she calls "family history" is defined by occasional acts of remembering and can therefore by its very nature never be seen as unified whole.[67] Finally, the substance of family memory lies not in the profound, but, rather, in the profane. Keppler claims that family memory is above all constituted by "little" stories.[68] Colonial family memory, like other family memory, is a series of these sorts of material and immaterial fragments. In the absence of a "monumental," internationally recognized narrative of empire, and in the overwhelming absence of public monuments still actively associated with colonialism, "little" pri-

---

[66] Maurice Halbwachs, *On Collective Memory*, trans. L. A. Coser (Chicago/London: University of Chicago Press, 1992), 77–78.
[67] Angela Keppler, *Tischgespräche* (Frankfurt am Main: Suhrkamp, 1995), 207.
[68] Keppler, *Tischgespräche*, 186.

vate memories have become the primary means of engagement with Germany's colonial legacy.

Coda 2: Postcolonial Heritage in Former Colonies

Therefore, German colonialism, though begun in the nineteenth century, is a twentieth century phenomenon, not (only) because it witnessed "the first genocide of the twentieth century," but because its memory has played a decisive role in political, cultural and social—public and private—relations in Germany at key points throughout the twentieth century. The second coda to keep in mind, however, is the trajectory and continuation of colonial memory in the former colonies and its complications in terms of material heritage and postcolonial tourism. Of particular interest to me in my current research is the issue of former colonial homes in Namibia and other former European colonies in Africa. Colonial memory in the former Southwest Africa has been addressed by experts on Namibian history and anthropology such as Larissa Förster, Reinhart Kössler, Henning Melber, and other scholars. What is particularly poignant, however, is how both the German idea of *Heimat* and the physical traces of colonial-era homes complicate discussions on postcolonial heritage in the region.

Despite the recent changes to the urban landscape in places like Windhoek, German architecture is still one of the most visible traces of memory of colonial times in Namibia.[69] The National Heritage Council of Namibia lists 32 buildings from the German colonial era, ten of which were private residences, as National Monuments. All of these buildings were declared national heritage monuments by the National Monuments Council of South Africa in the 1960s through 1980s. They now have various uses, including as storage rooms, shops, hostels, museums, and guest houses.[70] Some of these are owned privately and have been preserved through private initiatives, such as the Consolidated Diamond Mines (NamDeb) which renovated the Goerke Haus (or Magistrate's House) in Lüderitz and one representative house in the nearby "ghost town," Kolmanskuppe.

---

[69] On German colonial architecture in Namibia, see for example, Itohan Osayimwese, "Colonialism at the Center," PhD dissertation (University of Michigan, 2008); Osayimwese, "Prolegomenon to an alternative genealogy of German modernism," *Journal of Architecture* 18,6 (2013): 835–874; Walter Peters, *Baukunst in Südwestafrika,1884–1914* (Windhoek: SWA Scientific Society, 1981); Peters, "Wilhelminian Historicism and Objectivity", *Restorica* 14 (Oct. 1983): 13–23; Peters, "Das Verandenhaus. Beispiel einer klimatisch wohltemperierten Bauweise," in Klaus Hess and Klaus Becker, *Vom Schutzgebiet bis Namibia* (Windhoek: Klaus Hess, 2002), 242–243.
[70] National Heritage Council of Namibia, www.nhc-nam.org, accessed 4 June 2014.

In popular tourist towns such as Swakopmund and Lüderitz public debate about the preservation of German colonial architecture and the general architectural "look" of the town has increased in recent years. Part of the reason colonial-era buildings here have not been bulldozed, I would suggest, is that this architecture is thought to "characterize" the towns' old-world "charm," something which makes them eminently attractive to tourists. In addition, any major changes to smaller townscapes would almost certainly run up against German-speaking grassroots initiatives, as has already happened in Swakopmund.[71]

Out in the veld, the owners of safari lodges are also aware of the appeal of a historic, "colonial" style. But German architecture is not just a tourist trap—it has played a significant role in the memory of the past among the German settler community both in Namibia and in Germany. And because of that, rather than being an ending point, it is perhaps an ideal starting point for thinking about a more entangled memory of colonialism in both former colony and metropole.

Works cited

Adorno, Theodor. What does coming to terms with the past mean? In *Bitburg in Moral and Political Perspective*, edited by Geoffrey Hartman, 114–129. Bloomington: Indiana University Press, 1986.

Albrecht, Monika. Postcolonialism and migration into Germany's colonial past. *German Life and Letters* 65,3 (July 2012): 363–377.

Ames, Eric, Marcia Klotz and Lora Wildenthal. *Germany's Colonial Pasts*. Lincoln: University of Nebraska Press, 2005.

Angebauer, Karl. *Ovambo. 15 Jahre unter Kaffern, Buschleuten und Bezirksamtmännern*. Berlin: Scherl, 1927.

Appadurai, Arjun, *The Social Life of Things: Commodities in Cultural Perspective*. Cambridge: Cambridge University Press, 1986.

Aschenborn, Hans Anton. *Die Farm im Steppenlande. 11 Jahre Farmerleben und Jagd in Afrika*. Neudamm: Neumann, 1925.

Assmann, Jan. Stein und Zeit. Das 'monumentale' Gedächtnis der altägyptischen Kultur. In *Kultur und Gedächtnis*, edited by Jan Assmann and Tonio Hölscher, 87–114. Frankfurt am Main: Surhkamp, 1988.

Assmann, Jan and Jan Czaplicka. Collective Memory and Cultural Identity. *New German Critique* 65 (Spring–Summer 1995): 125–133.

Auswärtiges Amt (AA), Ministerium für Auswärtige Angelegenheiten, MfAA/A15068 Tanganyika/Sansibar, MfAA/A15067 Tanganyika.

---

[71] E. g., Maggi Barnard, "Fears rife at Swakopmund that heritage being 'defaced,'" *The Namibian*, 14 July 2004: www.namibian.com.na/index.php?id=5637&page=archive-read, accessed 4 June 2014.

Baranowski, Shelley. *Nazi Empire: German Colonialism and Imperialism from Bismarck to Hitler.* Cambridge/New York: Cambridge University Press, 2011.
Barnard, Maggi. Fears rife at Swakopmund that heritage being 'defaced'. *The Namibian* 14 July 2004: www.namibian.com.na/index.php?id=5637&page=archive-read [Accessed 5 June 2014].
Bechhaus-Gerst, Marianne and Sunna Giesecke. *Koloniale und postkoloniale Konstruktionen von Afrika und Menschen afrikanischer Herkunft in der deutschen Alltagskultur.* Frankfurt am Main/New York: Lang, 2007.
Bechhaus-Gerst, Marianne and Reinhard Klein-Arendt. *AfrikanerInnen in Deutschland und schwarze Deutsche.* Münster: Lit, 2004.
Bechhaus-Gerst, Marianne and Reinhard Klein-Arendt. *Die (koloniale) Begegnung: AfrikanerInnen in Deutschland, 1880-1945, Deutsche in Afrika, 1880-1918.* Frankfurt am Main: Lang, 2003.
Bley, Helmut and Rainer Tetzlaff, *Afrika und Bonn. Versäumnisse und Zwänge deutscher Afrika-Politik.* Reinbek bei Hamburg: Rowohlt, 1978.
Bradt, Carl. *Robert Koch.* Niedersächsische Jugendbücherei 5. Brunswick: Appelhans, 1937, 1944.
Brauckmann, Rudolf, Karl Witt, and Walter Poppendieck, *Kolonialdienst in der Südsee. Brieftagebuch des Kolonialsekretärs Rudolf Brauckmann aus Uslar, gefallen im Kampf mit Aufständischen auf Ponape (Ost-Karolinen) am 18. Oktober 1910.* Niedersächsische Jugendbücherei 9. Brunswick: Appelhans, 1939.
Brohm, Berthold. Das Buch in der Krise. Studien zur Buchhandelsgeschichte der Weimarer Republik. *Archiv für Geschichte des Buchwesens* 51 (1999): 256–296.
Buchhändlergilde-Blatt 3 (1920).
Buchhändlergilde-Blatt 10 (1925).
Bundesarchiv Berlin Lichterfelde (BAB), R1001/6693, R1001/6695, R8023/404,
Campt, Tina. *Other Germans: Black Germans and the Politics of Race, Gender and Memory in the Third Reich.* Ann Arbor: University of Michigan Press, 2004.
Castro Varela, María do Mar and Nikita Dhawan. Mission Impossible: Postkoloniale Theorie im deutschsprachigen Raum? In *Postkoloniale Soziologie*, edited by Julia Reuter and Paula-Irene Villa, 303–330. Bielefeld: Transcript, 2010.
Ciarlo, David. *Advertising Empire: Race and Visual Culture in Imperial Germany.* Cambridge, MA: Harvard University Press, 2011.
Coerver, Hubert. *Carl Peters: ein Kämpfer um deutschen Raum.* Leipzig/Berlin: Teubner, 1937.
Conrad, Sebastian. *Deutsche Kolonialgeschichte.* Munich: C. H. Beck, 2008.
Conrad, Sebastian and Jürgen Osterhammel. *Das Kaiserreich transnational. Deutschland in der Welt, 1871-1914.* Göttingen: Vandenhoeck & Ruprecht, 2004.
Cyber-Nomads/Öffentlichkeit gegen Gewalt. *The Black Book.* Frankfurt am Main/London: IKO, 2004.
Danton, G. H. Hans Grimms Volk ohne Raum. *Monatshefte für deutschen Unterricht* 27,2 (Feb. 1935): 33–43.
Eggers, Maureen Maisha, Grada Kilomba, Peggy Piesche and Susan Arndt. *Mythen, Masken und Subjekte: kritische Weissseinforschung in Deutschland.* Münster: Unrast, 2006.
Eley, Geoff and Bradley Naranch. *German Colonialism in a Global Age.* Durham: Duke University Press, 2014.
Die Frau und die Kolonien 6 (1937).

Friedrichsmeyer, Sara, Sara Lennox and Susanne Zantop. *The Imperialist Imagination: German Colonialism and its Legacies*. Ann Arbor: University of Michigan Press, 1998.
Frobenius, Else. *30 Jahre koloniale Frauenarbeit*. Berlin: Reichskolonialbund, 1936.
Furber, David and Wendy Lower. Colonialism and genocide in Nazi-occupied Poland and Ukraine. In *Empire, Colony, Genocide: Conquest, Occupation, and Subaltern Resistance in World History*, edited by A. Dirk Moses, 372–400. New York/Oxford: Berghahn Books, 2008.
Gosden, Chris and Chantal Knowles. *Collecting Colonialism: Material Culture and Colonial Change*. Oxford/New York: Berg, 2001.
Grosse, Pascal. From colonialism to National Socialism to postcolonialism. *Postcolonial Studies* 9,1 (2006): 35–52.
Ha, Kien Nghi, Nicola Lauré al-Samarai and Sheila Mysorekar. *re/visionen. Postkoloniale Perspektiven von People of Color auf Rassismus, Kulturpolitik und Widerstand in Deutschland*. Münster: Unrast, 2007.
Halbwachs, Maurice. *On Collective Memory*. Translated by L. A. Coser. Chicago/London: University of Chicago Press, 1992.
Handro, Saskia and Bernd Schönemann. *Geschichtsdidaktische Schulbuchforschung* Münster: Lit, 2006.
Harvey, Karen. *History and Material Culture*. Abingdon: Routledge, 2009.
Hauer, August. *Kumbuke. Erlebnisse eines Arztes in Deutsch-Ostafrika*. 4th edition. Berlin: Hobbing, 1926.
Hein, Bastian. *Die Westdeutschen und die Dritte Welt. Entwicklungspolitik und Entwicklungsdienste zwischen Reform und Revolte 1959-1974*. Munich: Oldenbourg, 2006.
Higelke, Kurt. *Neubau der Volksschularbeit. Plan, Stoff und Gestaltung nach den neuen Richtlinien des Reichserziehungsministeriums*. 2nd edition. Leipzig: Julius Klinkhardt, 1941.
Hull, Isabel. *Absolute Destruction: Military Culture and the Practice of War in Imperial Germany*. Ithaca/London: Cornell University Press, 2005.
Inhülsen, Otto. *Wir ritten für Deutsch-Ostafrika*. Leipzig: V. Hase & Koehler 1926.
Jarausch, Konrad and Michael Geyer. *Shattered Past: Reconstructing German Histories*. Princeton: Princeton University Press, 2003.
Jones, Andrew. *Memory and Material Culture: Tracing the Past in Prehistoric Europe*. Cambridge/New York: Cambridge University Press, 2007.
Keppler, Angela. *Tischgespräche. Über Formen kommunikativer Vergemeinschaftung am Beispiel der Konversation in Familien*. Frankfurt am Main: Suhrkamp, 1995.
Klotz, Marcia. Global visions: from the colonial to the National Socialist world. *European Studies Journal*. Special Issue: German Colonialism: Another Sonderweg? 16,2 (Fall 1999): 37–68.
Knust, H. Grimms 'Volk ohne Raum' als Schullektüre. *Deutsches Bildungswesen* (Oct. 1933): 265–271.
Koch, Karl W. H. *Im toten Busch: Kameruner Erzählungen*. Leipzig: Voigtländer, 1922.
Krause, Rudolf. *Kaufmann im Hererolande. Ein niedersächsischer Bauernjunge wird Großkaufmann in Deutsch-Südwest-Afrika*. Niedersächsische Jugendbücherei 2. Brunswick: Appelhans , 1937.
Kühnhold, Grete. *In Friedens- und Kriegszeiten in Kamerun*. Berlin: Scherl, 1917.

Kundrus, Birthe. Kontinuitäten, Parallelen, Rezeptionen. Überlegungen zur 'Kolonialisierung' des Nationalsozialismus. *Werkstatt Geschichte* 43 (2006): 45–62.
Kundrus, Birthe. *Moderne Imperialisten. Das Kaiserreich im Spiegel seiner Kolonien.* Cologne: Böhlau, 2003.
Kundrus, Birthe. *Phantasiereiche: zur Kulturgeschichte des deutschen Kolonialismus.* Frankfurt am Main: Campus, 2003.
Lässig, Simone and Karl Heinrich Pohl. History Textbooks and Historical Scholarship in Germany. *History Workshop Journal* 67 (2009), 125–139.
Langbehn, Volker. *German Colonialism, Visual Culture, and Modern Memory.* New York/London: Routledge, 2010.
Langbehn, Volker and Mohammad Salama. *German Colonialism: Race, the Holocaust, and Postwar Germany.* New York: Columbia University Press, 2011.
Lennox, Sara. Postcolonial writing in Germany. In *Cambridge History of Postcolonial Literature*, edited by Ato Quayson, 620-648. Cambridge: Cambridge University Press, 2012.
Lewerenz, Susann. *Die Deutsche Afrika-Schau (1935-1940). Rassismus, kolonialrevisionismus und postkoloniale Auseinandersetzungen im nationalsozialistischen Deutschland.* Frankfurt am Main: Lang, 2006.
Lindner, Ulrike. *Koloniale Begegnungen. Deutschland und Großbritannien als Imperialmächte in Afrika 1880–1914.* Frankfurt am Main/New York: Campus, 2011.
Linne, Karsten. *Deutschland jenseits des Äquators: die NS-Kolonialplanungen für Afrika.* Berlin: Ch. Links, 2008.
Lutz, Helma and Kathrin Gawarecki, *Kolonialismus und Erinnerungskultur: die Kolonialvergangenheit im kollektiven Gedächtnis der deutschen und niederländischen Einwanderungsgesellschaft.* Münster: Waxmann, 2005.
Malinowski, Stephan and Robert Gerwarth. Hannah Arendt's ghosts: reflections on the disputable path from Windhoek to Auschwitz. *Central European History* 42 (2009): 279–300.
Maß, Sandra. *Weiße Helden, schwarze Krieger. Zur Geschichte kolonialer Männlichkeit in Deutschland 1918-1964.* Cologne: Böhlau, 2006.
Mauss, Marcel. *The Gift: the Form and Reason for Exchange in Archaic Societies.* Translated by W.D. Halls. London: Routledge, 1990.
Mayer-Schönberger, Viktor. *Delete: the Virtue of Forgetting in the Digital Age.* Princeton/Oxford: Princeton University Press, 2009.
Mazower, Mark. *Dark Continent: Europe's Twentieth Century.* New York: Random House, 1998.
McClintock, Anne. *Imperial Leather: Race, Gender and Sexuality in the Imperial Contest.* New York: Routledge, 1995.
Mitteilungen des Frauenbunds der Deutschen Kolonialgesellschaft 12 (1929).
National Heritage Council of Namibia: www.nhc-nam.org [Accessed 5 June 2014].
Nyszkiewicz, Heinz and Bruno Dauch, *Deutsches Land in Afrika. Bilder aus den deutschen Kolonien.* Leipzig/Berlin: Teubner, 1940.
Osayimwese, Itohan. Colonialism at the center: German colonial architecture and the design reform movement, 1828-1914. PhD dissertation, University of Michigan, 2008.
Osayimwese, Itohan. Prolegomenon to an alternative genealogy of German modernism: German architects' encounters with world cultures c. 1900. *Journal of Architecture* 18,6 (2013): 835–874.

Pardex, Walter. *Unsere Kolonien im Weltkriege*. 3rd edition. Breslau: Handel, 1938.
Penny, H. Glenn. *Objects of Culture: Ethnology and Ethnographic Museums in Imperial Germany*. Chapel Hill/London: University of North Carolina Press, 2003.
Penny, H. Glenn and Matti Bunzl. *Worldly Provincialism: German Anthropology in the Age of Empire*. Ann Arbor: University of Michigan Press, 2003.
Peters, Walter. *Baukunst in Südwestafrika,1884-1914*. Windhoek: SWA Scientific Society, 1981.
Peters, Walter. Das Verandenhaus. Beispiel einer klimatisch wohltemperierten Bauweise. In *Vom Schutzgebiet bis Namibia*, edited by Klaus Hess and Klaus Becker, 240–247. Windhoek: Klaus Hess Verlag, 2002.
Peters, Walter. Wilhelminian historicism and objectivity: the reception of German architecture during the period 1882 to 1914 in the former German Southwest Africa (Namibia). *Restorica* 14 (Oct. 1983): 13–23.
Poiger, Uta. Imperialism and empire in twentieth-century Germany. *History and Memory* 17,1–2 (Spring–Summer 2005): 117–143.
Poley, Jared. *Decolonization in Germany: Weimar Narratives of Colonial Loss and Foreign Occupation*. Oxford/New York: Lang, 2005.
Prüße, Albert. *Zwanzig Jahre Ansiedler in Deutsch-Ostafrika*. Stuttgart: Strecke & Schröder, 1929.
Puls, Willi Walter. *Der koloniale Gedanke im Unterricht der Volksschule*. Leipzig: Quelle & Meyer, 1938.
Richards, Donald Ray. *The German Bestseller in the 20th Century*. Bern: Lang, 1968.
Schilling, Britta. German postcolonialism in four dimensions: a historical perspective. *Postcolonial Studies* 18,4 (2015): 427–439.
Schilling, Britta. Imperial heirlooms: the private memory of colonialism in Germany. *Journal of Imperial and Commonwealth History* 41,4 (2013): 663–682.
Schilling, Britta. *Postcolonial Germany: Memories of Empire in a Decolonized Nation*. Oxford: Oxford University Press, 2014.
Schmidt, Paul. *Unsere Kolonien in Vergangenheit und Zukunft*. 16th edition. Breslau: Handel, 1941.
Schneider, Barbara. *Die höhere Schule im Nationalsozialismus. Zur Ideologisierung von Bildung und Erziehung*. Cologne/Weimar/Vienna: Böhlau, 2000.
Schneider-Waterberg, H. R. *Der Wahrheit eine Gasse*. Swakopmund: Gesellschaft für Wissenschaftliche Entwicklung, 2006.
Schwerbrock, Wolfgang, Hans Thiekötter and Wilhelm Lehmann. *Safari Verlag 1921–1961: Die Wandlung unseres Bildungsgutes in 40 Jahren*. Berlin: Safari, 1961.
Slobodian, Quinn. *Foreign Front: Third World Politics in Sixties West Germany*. Durham/London: Duke University Press, 2012.
Smith, Woodruff . The Colonial Novel as Political Propaganda: Hans Grimm's *Volk ohne Raum*'. *German Studies Review* 6,2 (May 1983): 215–35.
South-West Africa Administrator's Office. *Report on the Natives of South-West Africa and their Treatment by Germany*. London: His Majesty's Stationery Office, 1918. [British Parliamentary Papers Cd. 9146].
Speitkamp, Wolfgang. *Denkmalsturz: zur Konfliktgeschichte politischer Symbolik*. Göttingen: Vandenhoeck & Ruprecht, 1997.
Steedman, Carolyn. What a rag rug means. *Journal of Material Culture* 3,3 (Nov. 1998): 259–281.

Steyerl, Hito, Encarnación Gutiérrez Rodríguez and Kien Nghi Ha. *Spricht die Subalterne deutsch? Migration und postkoloniale Kritik*. 2nd edition. Münster: Unrast, 2012.

Stoecker, Holger, Thomas Schnalke and Andreas Winkelmann. *Sammeln, Erforschen, Zurückgeben? Menschliche Gebeine aus der Kolonialzeit in akademischen und musealen Sammlungen*. Berlin: Ch. Links, 2013.

Thomas, Nicholas. *Entangled Objects: Exchange, Material Culture and Colonialism in the Pacific*. Cambridge, MA/London: Harvard University Press, 1991.

Van Laak, Dirk. *Imperiale Infrastrukur. Deutsche Planungen für eine Erschließung Afrikas 1880 bis 1960*. Paderborn: F. Schöningh, 2004.

Verber, Jason. The conundrum of colonialism in postwar Germany. PhD dissertation, University of Iowa, 2010.

Vogel, Georg. *Helden des Weltkrieges: ein Lesebogen für die deutsche Jugend*. 9th edition. 3 vols. Breslau: Handel, 1943.

Wildenthal, Lora. Notes on a history of 'imperial turns' in modern Germany. In *After the Imperial Turn: Thinking with and through the Nation*, edited by Antoinette Burton, 145–56. Durham /London: Duke University Press, 2003.

Zeller, Joachim. *Kolonialdenkmäler und Geschichtsbewußtsein. Eine Untersuchung der Kolonialdeutschen Erinnerungskultur*. Frankfurt am Main: IKO, 1999.

Zemon Davis, Natalie. *Trickster Travels: a Sixteenth-Century Muslim between Worlds*. London: Faber, 2007.

Zimmerer, Jürgen. Colonialism and the Holocaust—Toward an Archeology of Genocide. *Development Dialogue* 50 (Dec. 2008): 95–123.

Zimmerer, Jürgen. *Deutsche Herrschaft über Afrikaner: staatlicher Machtanspruch und Wirklichkeit im kolonialen Namibia*. Münster: Lit, 2001.

Zimmerer Jürgen. *Kein Platz an der Sonne: Erinnerungsorte der deutschen Kolonialgeschichte*. Frankfurt am Main: Campus, 2013.

Zimmerer, Jürgen and Michael Perraudin. *German Colonialism and National Identity*. London: Routledge, 2010.

Zimmerer, Jürgen and Joachim Zeller. *Völkermord in Deutsch-Südwestafrika: der Kolonialkrieg (1904-1908) in Namibia und seine Folgen*. Berlin: Ch. Links, 2003.

Nina Berman[1]
Schaffe, schaffe, Häusle baue: German Entrepreneurs and Settlers on the Kenyan Coast since the 1960s

This essay explores several long-term continuities that connect our contemporary moment to the longer history of the German presence in East Africa. The activities of Germans in various economic developments on the Kenyan coast over the past fifty years provide much insight in this regard. In particular, my discussion zooms in on one of Kenya's most prominent tourism resort centers, the Diani area, which is located about thirty kilometers south of Mombasa. Tourism development in Kenya began in earnest in the 1960s, and in the Diani area it became a catalyst that led to an influx of settlers from various European countries and the emergence of an active real estate market; it has also generated diverse forms of connections between African Kenyans and (mostly) European tourists and expatriates. Together, these developments—building on processes that began during the colonial period and were continued after Kenyan independence was gained in 1963—caused shifts in landownership, social structures, and cultural and religious practices as well as, in part, an orientation of the area toward Europe. German, Swiss, and Austrian entrepreneurs played a crucial role in this process, and often pioneered the kind of enterprises that became the hallmark of coastal tourism—upscale hotels, restaurants, bars, discotheques, safari businesses, and diving schools. (For the sake of convenience and because of their significant cultural similarities, henceforth German-speaking Germans, Swiss, and Austrians will be collectively referred to as "Germans.")

Reviewing the developments in Diani provides insight into neoliberal transnational economic transactions that presently occur across the world, and that, in the case of Kenya and many other countries, perpetuate processes of land alienation that began during the colonial period. What the villagers of Diani have experienced over the past fifty years is part of a global trend: areas with attractive beachfronts are especially popular, as evidenced by developments in the Canary Islands, Thailand, Morocco, and Ghana, among other countries. The more recent trends in real estate developments are discussed in the scholarly literature as examples of "second home tourism," "residential tourism," and the effect of "time share ownership," and often are considered primarily national

---

[1] Parts of this essay originally appeared as "From Colonial to Neoliberal Times."

DOI 10.1515/9783110525625-003

phenomena; however, most examples of these types of tourism, even in Europe, have distinct global dimensions.[2] The volume and effect of expatriate and local real estate acquisitions in tourism areas has been discussed critically by Central American and European scholars, but analyses with regard to Africa and many other areas is still relatively rare.[3] Real estate activity in tourism locations across Africa and Asia, however, is apparent widely.

Germans take part in these developments not only as representatives of large corporations or agents of state-funded development aid, but also as individual entrepreneurs. Ethnographic research on the effects of tourism, lifestyle and amenity north-to-to-south migration has brought to light the impact of US citizens on communities in Central America and the Caribbean and that of northern Europeans in southern Europe and the Middle East. Little, however, is known about the actions of small-scale investors and entrepreneurs, especially in the various countries of Africa. Acknowledging the impact of individual investors, managers, and entrepreneurs through this case study of German activities in Kenya sheds light on lesser-known dimensions of globalization, dimensions that include an increasing north-to-south migration and new forms of cross-cultural hierarchies and collaborations.[4]

The story of Germans in Diani is a story of opportunities and oppression, of resilience and exploitation, of longue durée and contemporary modes of domination and accommodation. It is a story of global economic, political, and social change, one that is rooted in the deep structures of colonial history and the transformations of the global capitalist system. It also highlights the schemes that distinguish the present "Second Scramble for Africa," in which land and

---

[2] Gustav Visser and Gijsbert Hoogendoorn, "A Decade of Second Home Tourism Research in South Africa: Research Prospects for the Developing World?" *South African Geographical Journal* 97, no. 2 (2015): 122.

[3] See Richard Barkham, *Real Estate and Globalisation* (Hoboken, NJ: Wiley-Blackwell, 2012); Diego Armando Casas-Beltrán, Luis Felipe Beltrán-Morales, Aradit Castellanos, and Aurora Breceda Solís-Cámara, "Turismo residencial y migración de jubilados extranjeros en México: un estudio de caso sobre sus implicaciones ambientales y de servicios en Baja California Sur," *Estudios Fronterizos, nueva época* 14, no. 28 (2013): 51–77; Peter Keller and Thomas Bieger, *Real Estate and Destination Development in Tourism: Successful Strategies and Instruments* (Berlin: Erich Schmidt, 2008); Femke van Noorloos, "Residential Tourism Causing Land Privatization and Alienation: New Pressures on Costa Rica's Coasts," *Development* 54, no. 1 (2011): 85–90; and Julie Velásquez-Runk, Julie, "Indigenous Land and Environmental Conflicts in Panama: Neoliberal Multiculturalism, Changing Legislation, and Human Rights," *Journal of Latin American Geography* 11, no. 2 (2012): 21–47.

[4] My study, *Germans on the Kenyan Coast*, discusses these dimensions in more detail.

natural resources are leased to and left for exploitation by foreign companies, with only minimal profit to the country that owns the resources.

The essay first outlines the setting in which these interactions take place and then reviews the stages and various dimensions of German economic activities in Diani, namely developments in the area of tourism, small businesses, and real estate. The concluding section considers the effects of the German activities with regard to local culture and landownership, as examples of current global neoliberal developments.

The research results presented here are part of a larger project on the German community in Diani, *Germans on the Kenyan Coast: Land, Charity, and Romance*, that draws substantially on ethnographic fieldwork. I have been visiting the area since 1980, and pursued my first research project in Diani in 1998.[5] Fieldwork for this project was conducted from November 2009 to February 2010, in July and August of 2011 and 2012, in October and November of 2013, and during December 2014. Two brief visits in December 2015 and June of 2016 allowed me to gather a sense of recent developments. Traveling to the area over the past three decades and then conducting research over seven years have given me insight into change over time and allowed me to build crucial relationships with individuals who were willing to share their views with me. I conducted more than two hundred formal and informal interviews with close to 150 individuals from different ethnic societies and diverse age, religious, and social groups. I carried out interviews in English, German, and Kiswahili (my knowledge of Arabic also proved useful several times, for example, in conversations with the imam of the Kongo Mosque in Diani and other Muslim leaders of the area), and I followed up with a few individuals throughout the duration of the study. I observed and listened, especially to gossip, which turned out to be crucial to the process of corroborating and revising what I had learned during formal interviews. I conducted archival research at the Office of the Registrar of Marriages in Mombasa and in Kwale; gleaned statistical data from interviews and marriage licenses; visited humanitarian initiatives onsite; made use of statistical data provided by the official statistical agencies of Germany, Switzerland, Austria, and Kenya; and applied geographical information system (GIS) tools to create maps of the area. I also gathered data through *dériving*, on extensive walking and driving tours in the area. In fact, an up-close view of the building activity and the act of counting houses in Diani became indispensable in the process of

---

[5] The result was the chapter on tourism in Berman, *Impossible Missions?* I also co-organized the Nairobi Workshop on Disability in 2007. Contributions were published in Armstrong et al., *Disability in Kenya*.

archiving landownership and documenting the presence of Germans who live in the area. I was also able to get aerial views of Diani during several short flights in small passenger planes, which brought to light the extent of building activity in the area.[6] In addition, I have drawn on the insights of historians, cultural anthropologists, social scientists, filmmakers, novelists, and authors of life narratives.

I chose not to do some things, however, and also encountered some obstacles. I decided not to go to the Land Registry in Kwale, as it became obvious that the records kept there are inconsistently accurate; real estate agents and local residents suggested that about one-third of the title deeds are forged, disputed, or both. After walking through and flying over the area, I decided to register building activity rather than assess landownership. While my figures amount to estimated values, they provide insight into building activity and numbers of residents by way of a systematic assessment. With one exception, I encountered no obstacles from Kenyan authorities; the leading German real estate company in Diani and German official institutions, however, were highly resistant to sharing information. The German Embassy in Nairobi (unlike its Austrian and Swiss counterparts) refused to give out figures on the number of registered German residents in Kenya, despite several written and phone attempts on my part. The Organization for International Collaboration (Gesellschaft für Internationale Zusammenarbeit, GIZ), the key development agency of Germany, which I contacted to inquire about a scandal that occurred in the 1990s and about the murder of a development worker in Kwale in 1998, also blocked my attempts to get access to records about these issues.

1. The Setting: Diani

Diani stretches from north to south for about ten kilometers along the beach from the Kongo River to Galu Beach, and inland from the beach west to the Mombasa–Lunga Lunga Road (A14) for about two and a half to three kilometers and another four to five kilometers west of the road inland (see Map 1). The center of the area, known as the town of Ukunda, is densely populated. The indigenous people of the area are Digo, one of the nine ethnic communities known as the Mijikenda.[7] Today the area includes Kenyans of various ethnicities who have mi-

---

6 I thank Denis Moser from DM Tours for arranging these opportunities.
7 Scholarship on the Digo is scant. Some of the earliest known references to discussions in European languages date back to the mid-nineteenth century (e.g. Krapf). Several anthropological studies were conducted between the 1950s and 1970s (Gillette; Gerlach). Apart from several ar-

grated to Diani, drawn by the promise of a tourism-related economy. Since the 1960s, when Diani's original inhabitants merely numbered in the few thousands, the population has swelled to close to 75,000. Diani has become a contact zone between Kenya's various communities and also between Kenyans and a diverse group of expatriates, many of whom have settled in Diani permanently or semi-permanently.

Officially, Diani is the name of an administrative unit in Kwale County, which, according to the 2009 census, covers an area of 81 square kilometers and is subdivided into the areas of Ukunda, Gombato, and Bongwe.[8] The majority of the population lives in Ukunda (38,629) and Gombato (24,024), with a smaller population in Bongwe (10,822).[9] Most areas close to the Mombasa-Lunga Lunga Road and the road from Diani to the beach and along the beach road are very densely populated, with 2,271 (Gombato) and 1,542 (Ukunda) people per square kilometer. This relatively high population density, however, is a very recent phenomenon and is mainly a result of the expansion of the tourism industry in the area. The tourism infrastructure emerged slowly during the 1960s, 1970s, and 1980s along the beach road, but until the early 1980s the several thousand indigenous Digo villagers living there were not very affected by the changes occurring around them. Today, villagers' control over land is restricted to only about twenty percent of the land they once considered theirs, and their villages are surrounded by, among other structures, residential housing, including lavish private villas with security fences and walls; commercial buildings, such as restaurants and supermarkets; a hospital; various schools; and an airstrip. A dramatic increase in building activities and population began in the late 1980s and early 1990s, and continues to this day.

What are the main factors that have brought these substantial changes to the Diani area? How have the transformations of the past five decades affected local villagers? A review of the longer history of the Diani area reveals an astounding continuity with regard to the question of landownership. In particular, the trends that have occurred over the past fifty years, from the moment of independence in the early 1960s to the area's integration into neoliberal capitalism over the past thirty years, amount to an unremitting process of gentrification that had already

---

ticle-length analyses of various subjects, no comprehensive study exists that focuses on the Digo of the Diani area.

8 The three areas form two wards, namely Gombato/Bongwe and Ukunda, which each have one representative in the Kwale County Assembly.

9 Figures according to the 2009 census. The dataset and information about the individual villages was provided by the Chief's office in Ukunda.

Map 1. Aerial view of the Diani area, showing villages, the airstrip, the golf course, and DARAD area (Diani Agriculture and Research Development).

begun during the colonial period.[10] Germans have played a central role in building Diani's tourism infrastructure and in creating the real estate market, and thus in bringing about substantial shifts in landownership.

2. German Development of Tourism, Business, and Real Estate

German entrepreneurs appeared on the Kenyan scene during the 1960s and took on a significant role in the creation of the coastal tourism infrastructure. Until the 1960s, "the coast was the resort chiefly of upcountry expatriates who would hire beach cottages at low rates," but now hotels were being built that attracted international visitors (Jackson 62). One of the first hoteliers was Edgar Herrmann, also known as "Herrmann the German"; some have credited him with coining the slogan "Sun, Sand, and Sex," which corresponds to the dominant image of Kenya in German mainstream media. When tourism development in Diani began in the early 1960s, the German share in hotel ownership and hotel management was significant. Until the end of the late 1980s, Germans owned or managed most of the hotels on the south coast: eight of the ten major hotels of that period had a German management team. Four of them were owned or partially owned by Germans or a German company. Some of the hotels that were built during the 1990s were also owned or managed by Germans at some point (see Table 1).

Table 1. Hotel Ownership and Management, 1960s to 2013

Name of hotel (year of first opening)	Initial ownership	Change in ownership; current	General Management
1. Indian Ocean Beach Club (1992)	African Kenyan	Closed October 2013	African Kenyan; closed
2. Southern Palms Beach Resort (1992)	Ismaili Indian Kenyan	Same	First British; various European, one Indonesian-Dutch since 2006
3. Golden Beach Hotel (1980; only open for a short period)	African Kenyan	LAICO (Indian Kenyan), rebuilding into apartment complex	Swiss earlier (Hans Wittwer); no longer a hotel

---

10 For a review of developments under colonialism and a discussion of gentrification, see the discussion in Chapter 2 of *Germans on the Kenyan Coast*.

Table 1. Hotel Ownership and Management, 1960s to 2013 *(Continued)*

Name of hotel (year of first opening)	Initial ownership	Change in ownership; current	General Management
4. Diani Reef Beach Resort and Spa (1972; org. Diani Beach Reef Hotel)	Changed hands several times; Israeli (Mr. Bernin)	Indian Kenyan	Used to have German management (Siggi Jogschart); African Kenyan
5. Leisure Lodge Resort (1972)	Mostly owned by Germans (Wilhelm Meister); some African shares	Now Ismaili Kenyan (since about 1996); came out of receivership in 2001	Used to have German managers, even after 1996; now African Kenyan (John Mutua)
6. Leopard Beach Resort (1974)	Italian	Sikh Kenyan	African Kenyan manager in consulting partnership with German manager (Chris Modigell, freelance consultant)
7. Swahili Beach (2012)	Sikh Kenyan	Sikh Kenyan	South African
8. Kaskazi Beach Hotel (1991)	LTI jointly with African Kenyan	In receivership 1991 to 2012; again owned by African Kenyan	Used to have German management; now African Kenyan
9. Trade Winds (1940s)	Government, African Kenyan	Now German (Kampa / Kampa-Matthiessen); presently (2013) closed	Formerly African Tours and Hotels (Kenyan), now German; presently closed
10. Diani Sea Lodge (1981)	German owned	German owned (Kampa / Kampa-Matthiessen	German management
11. Diani Sea Resort (1991)	German owned	German owned (Kampa / Kampa-Matthiessen	German management
12. Two Fishes (1940s)	Until after WW II Mr. and Mrs. Fish; then Mr. Plumb; 1960s Karl Pollman	Various Germans until early 1990s; then African Kenyan; burnt down 1997 or 1998	Used to have German management; closed as hotel, run as beach bar and restaurant (Kim4-Love, leased)
13. Africana Sea Lodge (1978)	African Kenyan and European Kenyan (Kenneth Matiba and Steven Smith)	Sold in 2012 to Indian Kenyan (after being in receivership for 12 years)	German and African Kenyan; now closed
14. Jadini (1937; reopened 1973)	African Kenyan and European Kenyan (Kenneth	Sold in 2012 to Indian Kenyan (after being in receivership for 12 years)	German and African Kenyan; now closed

Table 1. Hotel Ownership and Management, 1960s to 2013 *(Continued)*

Name of hotel (year of first opening)	Initial ownership	Change in ownership; current	General Management
	Matiba and Steven Smith)		
15. Sands at Nomads (2005)	European Kenyan (Patricia Bonam)	Leased to Italian and European Kenyan	Austrian
16. Safari Beach Hotel (1986)	African Kenyan and European Kenyan (Kenneth Matiba and Steven Smith)	Same	German and African Kenyan; now closed
17. Ocean Village Club (1987)	Italian owned	Changed hands several times; French	Portuguese
18. Papillon Lagoon Reef (1987; used to be Lagoon Reef Hotel)	Indian Kenyan (Reef Hotel Ltd.)	Goan (Mr. Correa); REX group acquired in 1999	African Kenyan
19. Robinson Baobab (1974; then Baobab Beach Resort & Robinson Club, added Maridadi and Kolekole)	Used to be 100% German owned (Karl Pollman; Swiss; TUI)	Indian (from Tanzania, Moledina), based out of UK; TUI still owns 10–20% or more	German and Swiss management; now African Kenyan
20. Shaanti (1998; then Galu Retreat Hotel; Afrika Pearl since Dec. 2013)	Indian Kenyan	Still Indian Kenyan but since September 2013 leased to French, Africa Safari Adventure	Shaanit—Goan couple; now French management

Source: Table information is based on interviews conducted by the author from January 2010 to November 2013. Note: The hotels are listed according to their north-to-south geographic order along Diani Beach.

In 2013, only thirteen of the major twenty hotels were open, reflecting the overall decline of tourism on the south coast, and six of the seven that were closed were African Kenyan-owned or owned in partnership with African Kenyans. Four of the closed hotels were owned by Kenyan politicians, namely, James Njenga Karume (Indian Ocean Beach Club) and Kenneth Matiba (Jadini, Africana Sea Lodge, and Safari Beach Hotel). Karume, a major political figure of post-independence Kenya, died in 2012. Matiba was one of the major opposition leaders during the Moi regime. In partnership with European Kenyan Stephen G. Smith, he developed three of the hotels that were particularly popular with Germans. After Matiba's incarceration in Kamiti prison in 1990, he ran as a presidential candidate and withdrew money from his hotels and other assets, contributing to the demise of the hotels. Two of them, the Jadini and Africana Sea Lodge, were sold in July 2012; Matiba and Smith still own the Safari Beach Hotel.

While African Kenyan ownership of hotels was down, Indian (Kenyan and otherwise) ownership was up. Of the thirteen hotels open in 2013, eight (61.5 percent) were owned by Indians. The high number of Indian Kenyans who own hotels today clearly stands out and is in line with the increase in Indian business ownership generally, in Kenya and globally.[11] Only one hotel (Kaskazi Beach Hotel) that operated at the time was owned by an African Kenyan; the others were owned by Germans (two), French (one), and a European Kenyan (one). Of the thirteen hotels that were open, four still had German management (Diani Sea Resort, Diani Sea Lodge, the Sands at Nomads [Austrian], and Leopard Beach). The German manager of Leopard Beach Resort has been one of the most successful in the area for close to four decades and worked as project manager and management consultant with the hotel's African Kenyan management staff.

It can be seen that the situation with regard to major hotels along the coast has changed dramatically since the late 1990s; Table 1 shows how from the 1960s to today, German hotel management and ownership is down, and Indian and African Kenyan management is up. However, the area also features a host of cottages and boutique hotels, of which many are German owned or managed; these cottages and hotels are part of the real estate boom, a development that will be discussed below.

Hotel-based tourism also generated the development of a second area of German economic activity in Diani, especially since the late 1980s. Germans own scores of small and larger businesses in Diani, among them safari tour companies, nightclubs, restaurants, cafés, massage salons, yoga studios, diving businesses, and shopping malls. Originally these outfits targeted tourists, offering supplemental services that the hotels did not. Today, they also cater to the area's growing residential community. Many of these businesses flourish for only a short period of time, and individual owners and managers come and go, trying (and often failing) to fulfill their dream of living in a beautiful tourist destination. Many do not have the kind of expertise that might ensure success, and they leave bankrupt and disappointed, unable to adjust to Kenyan business

---

11 See, among others, Ian Taylor, "India's Rise in Africa," *International Affairs* 88, no. 4 (2012): 779–798; Jørgen Dige Pedersen, "The Second Wave of Indian Investments Abroad," *Journal of Contemporary Asia* 38, no. 4 (November 2008): 613–637. Presently, there is a lack of data regarding Indian economic activity in Kenya specifically.

practices. The successful business owners are those who pursue one of two strategies: either they adjust to the Kenyan environment and work closely with a Kenyan partner (often a spouse), or they control each and every aspect of their business themselves, ideally as a couple or family. Individuals who pursue the second approach, though economically successful, often show severe signs of burnout after a few years, primarily as a result of an overall lack of knowledge about the Kenyan business environment in combination with their attempt to retain German business practices (such as timeliness, planning, and reliability). None of the German entrepreneurs that I interviewed spoke any significant measure of Kiswahili, even after decades of living in the country, and lacked cultural and historical knowledge about Kenya, producing a significant sense of constant cultural disorientation. Despite these challenges, several of the most successful businesses in Diani are run by Germans, and some of them have been operating for more than ten years.

A third area of German business activity is in the real estate sector. The 1960s and 1970s saw new residential development in Diani. Initially it was driven mostly by British citizens who either left the Kenyan highlands to move to the coast or who came first as tourists and then bought land. But soon Diani also attracted Europeans, who left their home countries for numerous reasons; investors and heirs were joined by adventurers and criminals, and often these qualities were combined in various constellations.[12] Real estate development was still slow, but in the early 1980s Diani experienced the first major post-independence land alienation scheme, which will be discussed here in detail because it exemplifies patterns of economic and political entanglements that persist to this day.

In 1981, Dr. Wilhelm Meister (who owned the majority of shares of Leisure Lodge Hotel), Peter Ludaava (who had been employed at Two Fishes before he became Meister's right-hand man at Leisure Lodge), and Mr. Shretta (a lawyer from Nairobi who owned about 20 percent of Leisure Lodge shares) founded an organization called "Diani Agriculture and Research Development" (DARAD). This organization bought land to the north and south of the connector road, for various agricultural purposes. When DARAD bought the land, the relevant title deeds were already in the hands of a Kwale District member of parliament, Juma Boy. Part of the area at stake was known among local Digo villagers as "Chidze," which means 'outside' or 'away from the village' in Chidigo. The Chidze land, closest to the area of Mwamambi Village, served as a collective

---

[12] For a portrait of a Swedish man who led an adventurous life in Kenya and beyond, see Nina Berman, "Neils Larssen: A Life Afloat," *South Coast Resident's Association Newsletter*, 37 (August 2011): 4–5.

farming area for its inhabitants and for those living in the adjacent villages of Mwakamba, Mvumoni, and Mwaroni. Villagers would live on their various agricultural plots in the Chidze area (along with another area called Maweni) during the farming and harvesting seasons.

The loss of Chidze and adjacent areas was a significant blow to the villagers. Several recounted the events with bitterness. They said that an alliance of local leaders that included the Diani chief, the area member of parliament Juma Boy (the father of Boy Juma Boy, who continues to be an active political figure to this day, and took over from where his father left off with regard to DARAD), and the area counselor "sweet-talked village elders," who then signed a consent, thus permitting the sale.[13] The money from the sale, however, went to the alliance of local political leaders, and the villagers received nothing. So the villagers began to protest. One man recounted how he and his grandfather had been detained at the local police station after a protest against the sale of the land. Another man from Mvumoni remembered a violent fight in 1988 or 1989 outside of Club Willow on the north side of the connector road. These events, people often complained, were not properly covered in the newspapers at the time. During President Moi's dictatorship, the press was censored, and would identify incidents such as these as the actions of criminals. Villagers were not able to claim reimbursement for their land because they did not own title deeds for the land on which they had lived for centuries (and in most cases, villagers throughout the area still do not own title deeds for their land, even though allotment letters exist). The villagers were mostly illiterate and unable to represent themselves effectively, especially once their own leadership had given in to the demands of more powerful players.[14]

The officially authorized intent of DARAD (in contrast to its actual pursuits) was agricultural development. The organization conducted research on growing cloves, spices, and grasses through their *Grassversuchsfarm*, (experimental grass growing farm), for which DARAD is said to have received a loan from either the German Development Agency (Deutscher Entwicklungsdienst, DED) or the Soci-

---

[13] Juma Boy died in 1983. He represented Kwale District in parliament twice and was one of Kenya's leading trade unionists. His son, Boy Juma Boy, became a member of parliament in 1983 and served three terms until he lost his seat in the 1997 elections. He has also been implicated in the 1997 election violence (as has Kassim Mwamzandi). Boy Juma Boy was back as a political force in 2012, having being elected senator for Kwale County.

[14] Because lawsuits were pending it was difficult to find villagers who were willing to volunteer information. Information about the history of DARAD was gathered in interviews with various Diani residents, including villagers, hotel managers, and Mr. Klaus Thüsing, who was the country director for the German Development Agency (DED) in Kenya from 1988 to 1993.

ety for Technical Collaboration (Gesellschaft für technische Zusammenarbeit, GTZ).¹⁵ DARAD also featured a large carpentry training program, Diani Furniture, that was run by a German carpenter, Mr. Krüger (a "Schreinerei mit Meister, ein Herr Krüger"). The carpentry shop was evidently funded by CIM, the German Center for International Migration and Development (Centrum für Internationale Migration und Entwicklung).¹⁶ Some employees at Leisure Lodge are also said to have been paid with CIM money. While DED and GTZ were officially not supposed to work with private enterprises, CIM often collaborated with private companies and was evidently scandal-ridden at the time. DARAD also managed to secure two airplanes from the German development agencies that were meant to be used as medical transport by the Flying Doctors Society of Africa. Dr. Meister, with his training as a lawyer, is said to have been savvy in organizing these monies. His supporters included the local member of parliament (MP), the Diani Chief, other local stakeholders and government officials.

Over time, the truth about DARAD came to the surface. The *Grassversuchsfarm* turned out to be a development project for a golf course, construction on which began (with government permission) in 1991, and it opened after various delays in 1997; the planes were used for safari tourism, not doctors; and the carpentry training program was in fact a successful privately-owned furniture store, Diani Furniture, which made furniture for various hotels, among other enterprises. When the misuse of German development funds was uncovered, the scandal broke loose, though apparently with no negative consequences for the Kenya-based players.¹⁷ Dr. Meister was also involved in what became known as the "Amigo-Affair" in Germany. The Bavarian minister president, Max Streibl, who was forced to resign over a scandal involving favoritism of the kind described here had been a frequent guest at Leisure Lodge Hotel.

---

15 Under these names until 2010, now both part of the Deutsche Gesellschaft für Internationale Zusammenarbeit, GIZ (Society for International Collaboration).
16 CIM is today folded into the GIZ (Gesellschaft für Internationale Zusammenarbeit, Organization for International Collaboration) which is the result of a merger between the DED and GTZ. I contacted GIZ and CIM to corroborate data gathered during interviews, but, after an initial exchange, received no further responses once representatives realized what kind of information I was interested in. The response was that they had no access to information involving the previous organizations ("Wir führen kein Archiv zu der Arbeit der Vorgängerorganisationen der GIZ"; "Leider liegen uns keine Informationen oder Dokumente zu dem von Ihnen geschilderten Fall vor."). Email communication, February 2015.
17 Krüger's collaboration with Dr. Meister ended around that time as well, presumably because he had not been paid properly, and he left with some of his machines overnight, exacerbating the scandal.

The DARAD-scandal and the Amigo-Affair were not the only time that German development and other governmental agencies made headlines because of their activities in Kenya: in 1998, one of the German project managers who oversaw forestry development projects was murdered in the area.[18] Most likely, none of the funds provided by the German government for these instances of corporate development in Kenya were ever returned. Struggle over the Chidze and adjoining area continued, and even though DARAD was dissolved in the 1990s, the question of ownership of DARAD land remains contentious to this day.

The manipulated sale of the Chidze land during the 1980s was only the first in a series of landownership changes that led to business and real estate development in Diani. An outright building boom began in the early 1990s. Upscale housing development previously had been restricted to beachfront property, but now enclaves of luxury villas began springing up throughout the Diani area. The entire area has been surveyed and is recorded on registration maps that indicate the divisions into numbered rectangular plots, many of which are subdivided into smaller units. The various sections of the area are conceptually tied to the beach, which clearly indicates that beachfront property is valued the most: the first section is referred to as "Beachfront" property; the next section stretches to the beach road and is known as "Row 1." Afterwards, every 300 to 350 meters, another section is theoretically marked by another "road," but these roads, if they are identifiable, are not paved and often do not even cut across the entire area. As of the completion of my research in 2014, most of the development had occurred in Rows 2, 3, and 4. I have not heard anybody refer to Rows 5 or 6, even though development has taken place all the way up to the Mombasa–Lunga Lunga Road and beyond.

I divide the areas into zones based on the phase of development (see Map 2): Zone 1 combines the beachfront itself and Row 1, as this was the first area of development, through the period up until the 1970s. Development in Row 2, here Zone 2, began in the 1980s. Building activity in Row 3 and 4, which constitute Zone 3, started in the second half of the 1990s. Construction in the DARAD area also began in the 1990s. Building activity continues in all zones to this day. As a result, villagers are squeezed into a constantly decreasing area from all sides, and their villages are surrounded by modest to upscale modern housing. Most Germans and other expatriates live in Zone 1 to 3 and in the DARAD area, and make up between 90 and 50 percent of residents in these areas (about 3,400 total).

---

18 W. A. Rodgers and Neil D. Burgess, "Taking Conservation Action," in *Coastal Forests of Eastern Africa*, eds. Neil D. Burgess and G. Philip Clarke (Cambridge: IUCN, 2000), 328.

Map 2. Arial view of Diani area, showing the three zones of development.

What drove the real estate push that began in earnest during the 1990s? Particularly consequential were the Structural Adjustment Policies imposed on Kenya by the World Bank and the International Monetary Fund in the early

1990s.[19] Kenya's implementation of privatization and other neoliberal practices was promptly rewarded with an IMF loan (International Monetary Fund). The fact that these policies failed is by now widely accepted.[20] As elsewhere in the global south, and also some regions of the global north, poor people got poorer, and rich people got richer: "In Kenya, people living below the poverty line increased from 46 percent in 1992 to 49 percent in 1997, and [increased] further to 56 percent in 2000".[21] In Diani, these policies made it much easier for foreigners to invest in and to buy land, resulting in substantial changes in landownership and the development of foreign-owned businesses in the area.

German realtors were crucial in facilitating a consequential shift in landownership from villagers to settlers. One of the key agents continues to be Joe Brunlehner, who has received a lot of attention for his often contentious activities and who advertises widely: "Diani Homes—Seit 1983 Garant für Ihre Immobilien in Kenia" (Diani Homes—Since 1983 Guarantor for your real estate in Kenya; see *Diani Homes: Kenia Immobilien*," Diani Homes, "Über Uns"). Other German developers are less visible but have also acquired and resold a large number of plots. I interviewed Frank Neugebauer, an associate of Joe Brunlehner, in July 1999. He confirmed that the building boom began when the legal situation changed in 1992 and "foreigners were allowed to buy property" without the previously existing condition that a Kenyan must partner with a foreigner for a ninety-nine-year lease. As of July 1999, the company had sold about 260 houses to around two hundred families in Diani and the adjacent Galu areas; some fami-

---

19 Gurushri Swamy, "Kenya: Patchy, Intermittent Commitment," in *Adjustment in Africa: Lessons from Country Case Studies*, eds. Ishrat Husain and Rashid Faruqee (Brookfield: Ashgate, 1996), 193–237; World Bank, *Kenya: Re-Investing in Stabilization and Growth through Public Sector Adjustment* (Washington, DC: World Bank, 1992).
20 See Natalie Avery, "Stealing from the State (Mexico, Hungary & Kenya)," in *50 Years is Enough: The Case Against the World Bank and the International Monetary Fund*, ed. Kevin Danaher (Boston: South End Press, 1994), 95–101; Dambisa Moyo, *Dead Aid: Why Aid is not Working and How There Is a Better Way for Africa* (New York: Farrar, Straus and Giroux, 2009), 19–22; Sylvia Wairimu Kang'ara, "When the Pendulum Swings Too Far: Structural Adjustment Programs in Kenya," *Third World Legal Studies* 15.1 (1999): 109–51; Joseph Kipkemboi Rono, "The Impact of the Structural Adjustment Programmes on Kenyan Society," *Journal of Social Development in Africa* 17.1 (2002): 81–98; Pamela Sparr, *Mortgaging Women's Lives: Feminist Critiques of Structural Adjustment* (London: Zed Books, 1994); Howard Stein, *Beyond the World Bank Agenda: An Institutional Approach to Development* (Chicago: University of Chicago Press, 2008); Gloria Thomas-Emeagwali, ed., *Women Pay the Price: Structural Adjustment in Africa and the Caribbean* (Trenton: Africa World Press, 1995); and Roger Thurow and Scott Kilman, *Enough: Why the World's Poorest Starve in an Age of Plenty* (New York: PublicAffairs, 2009).
21 Rose Wanjiru, *IMF Policies and Their Impact on Education, Health and Women's Rights in Kenya* (Nairobi: ActionAid International Kenya, 2009), 17.

lies, Neugebauer said, had bought two and even three houses. Ninety-five percent of the buyers were Germans, with 60 percent of those coming from the former German Democratic Republic in the eastern part of the country. Neugebauer said that most of these people had been high-ranking officials ("früher hohe Tiere") or younger individuals who had made money during the first few years after German unification. Rumor in Diani has it that many of these influential figures from East Germany had worked for the Stasi, the Ministry for State Security (Ministerium für Staatssicherheit, MfS). Most of the plots were located in Rows 2 and 3, with prices for homes listed in 1999 ranging upwards from 165,000 German Marks ($100,000 and upwards at the time). Neugebauer also mentioned that the IMF and the World Bank regulations had been crucial in this regard; credits to Kenya, he said, had been tied to stipulations that made it possible for foreigners to acquire property in Kenya. Neugebauer was clearly fully aware that the company's success was intricately linked to IMF and World Bank policies.

Brunlehner (who supposedly had to leave Germany because of tax evasion charges) is known in Kenya and Germany as "Mombasa Joe," which conveys a sense of the aura he has acquired ("Prügelprozess gegen Prinz Ernst August"). Brunlehner and some of his associates are representative of a group of controversial German entrepreneurs who are operating in Kenya,[22] but the Italian community on the coast has much to show in this regard as well (Gitau; Dabbs). Beyond Germans and Italians, the Kenyan coast has been described more generally as an area "where people go to escape their pasts ... [they] have all come to Diani to avoid alimony payments, charges of tax evasion, and disgruntled clients back home" (Wadhams).

Though the German real estate boom in Diani peaked in the late 1990s, new private homes have been built continuously, and today, real estate is again on the upswing. With this recent development push, the beginning of a new phase of gentrification in Diani can be identified. Its designation as a resort town in the country's vision plan (Kenyan Vision 2030) and the prospect of a bypass that would circumvent the Likoni ferry (currently a significant obstacle to getting from the airport and Mombasa to the south coast) have brought new speculators to the area.[23] But all over the world, a rush is under way for beachfront and near-beachfront property. While many real estate transactions occur

---

[22] See the case of Andreas Költz in Steinkühler. Both Brunlehner and Pullig (his name x-ed out in this article) play a role in this story as well.

[23] The ferry at Likoni is the only means of connection between Mombasa and the south coast. Tourists traveling to and from the airport as well as commercial traffic from the north and inland have to cross via the ferries, with waiting times often reaching several hours.

through consulting firms and international real estate companies (such as Knight Frank), the only company that is registered locally in Diani as a real estate company is run by a German couple. Baobab Holidays Homes (Kenya) Ltd. has been active since 2010, evidently very successfully, and clearly competes with Diani Homes and other consulting firms (*Baobab Homes*). In an interview in November 2013, the owners, Sandra Nikolay and Frank Meininghaus, stated that the demand was high. In November 2013, Baobab Holiday Homes listed as many as 170 properties, including homes, apartments, and plots of land. The properties are located mostly in Diani and Galu Beach, but also several other locations on the south coast and in Kwale. The company was recording about two hundred visitors per day on its website. Eight-five percent of its customers came from Nairobi, among them officials of the United Nations, workers with INGOs, and businesspeople from various European countries. The owners also noted that, increasingly, African Kenyans made use of their services (a number they expected to increase in the future), which confirms the current trend toward upcountry-driven gentrification.[24] Nikolay and Meininghaus also said that they did not deal with land that indigenous villagers owned, because the legal situation was often too obscure. The law mandates that all family members have to agree to a sale, and in their view, tracking down every member of an extended family is too difficult; so they decided to stay away from these potentially conflict-laden situations. Overall, Germans continue to represent a driving force, both as realtors and buyers in the real estate market.[25]

The developments in Diani, especially as they occurred in the 1980s and 1990s when German entrepreneurs dominated the area, took place in the context of a general land-grabbing frenzy. As Paul Ndungu, the chair of the Commission of Inquiry into the Illegal/Irregular Allocation of Public Land that assessed land-grabbing practices in postindependence Kenya and published a comprehensive report in 2004, has explained: "Our conservative estimate was that some 200,000 illegal titles were created between 1962 and 2002. Close to ninety-eight percent of these were issued between 1986 and 2002".[26] Clearly, this overall lawlessness created a climate that facilitated illegal transactions of land in Diani

---

24 In late 2013, the company's online platform was voted the No. 1 realtor in Kenya by one of the largest international real estate platforms, Mondinion. Worldwide they were listed as No. 9 among 8,933 real estate companies. See Mondinion, "Kenya Realtors & Real Estate Agents."
25 For additional quantifiable data on the impact of German activities in Diani, see Berman, *Germans on the Kenyan Coast*.
26 Paul Ndungu, "Tackling Land Related Corruption in Kenya." Unpublished manuscript, last modified November 2006, 5, accessed November 11, 2016, http://siteresources.worldbank.org/RPDLPROGRAM/Resources/459596–1161903702549/S2_Ndungu.pdf.

as well. This fact does not absolve German developers from their responsibility to know whether the transactions in which they were involved were legal or not; surely many of them were aware of areas of illegality. But even when transactions occur in a legally sound manner, as indicated by recent developments, the ultimate effect on the local community remains the same: the resources of the original villagers are diminished (as stated before, Digo in Diani control only about twenty per cent of the land they once owned or used) and the local Digo community, as well as its specific history and culture, is imperiled.

3. Effects of North-to-South Transactions

For a colonized people the most essential value,
because the most concrete, is first and foremost the land:
the land which will bring them bread and, above all, dignity.
—Frantz Fanon, *The Wretched of the Earth* (44)

As Frantz Fanon and also Fred Pearce (in his study of the global extent of landgrabbing) acknowledge, landownership is central to questions of identity and dignity.[27] In Diani, Digo language, culture, and history are tied to land, and as ownership of ancestral land diminishes, so does the cultural life of the Digo in this area. The Digo who live in areas throughout Kwale County and into Tanzania do not feel their existence as a people to be threatened by what is happening in Diani; but a part of the larger Digo history that is tied to, among other sites, the kayas in the Diani area as well as the Kongo Mosque is on the verge of disappearance as lived culture.

In the absence of large-scale approaches to preserve Digo land and culture in Diani, the business activities that I have outlined here are bound to continue. Of the economic activities discussed here, the hotel industry has arguably had the most beneficial effect on the area (through job creation) and did not affect landownership immediately. However, the side effects of tourism, especially the emergence of the globalized real estate market, certainly did. Yet Digo agency will not be enhanced by way of a certain percentage of Digo privately owning land in the area. Some villages, such as those in the northern part of Diani, continue to display a significant degree of cohesion, but increasing private landownership will only divide the community further. Ultimately, all communities and cultures change, and privatization, new concepts of the family and labor, and the

---

[27] Fred Pearce, *The Land Grabbers: The New Fight Over Who Owns the Earth* (Boston: Beacon Press, 2012), 61–62.

overall scope and pace of change in the area are bound to create social energies that may also result in new communal practices. But in the meantime, the community's overall sense of loss and the multiple grievances are articulated via a discourse that emphasizes the perils associated with the loss of land. This discourse, however, addresses more than just landownership, as Digo landownership relates to an entire way of life.

Acknowledging the role of Germans in developments such as those outlined in this essay requires us to pay attention to dimensions of neoliberal capitalism that structure transnational relations in our contemporary world. Over the past fifty years, economic actions of German entrepreneurs and individual investors have affected the economic and social landscape of Diani in fundamental ways: in particular, the distribution of landownership and the business infrastructure of this Kenyan location have been shaped by the activities of Germans, Swiss, and Austrians (among others). These activities are part of a larger north-to-south trend that has yet to be studied systematically; it is a trend that builds substantially on the inequalities created during the colonial period. Future research on the ways in which German capital and social energies are shaping material realities in many locations of the world and have a tremendous impact on infrastructure and social relations in those areas will deepen our understanding of these transnational dynamics.

Works Cited

Armstrong, Philip, Nina Berman, Kimani Njogu, and Mbugua wa-Mungai, eds. *Disability in Kenya: The Nairobi Workshop on Disability, Culture, and Human Rights*. Special issue, *Disability Studies Quarterly* 29, no. 4 (2009). http://dsq-sds.org/issue/view/42. Accessed November 11, 2016.

Avery, Natalie. "Stealing from the State (Mexico, Hungary & Kenya)." In *50 Years is Enough: The Case Against the World Bank and the International Monetary Fund*, edited by Kevin Danaher, 95–101. Boston: South End Press, 1994. Print.

Baobab Homes & Holidays Kenya. http://baobab-homes-holidays.com/pages/english/home-service.php?lang=NL. Accessed November 11, 2016.

Barkham, Richard. *Real Estate and Globalisation*. Hoboken, NJ: Wiley-Blackwell, 2012. Print.

Berman, Nina. "From Colonial to Neoliberal Times: German Agents of Tourism Development and Business in Diani, Kenya," special topic, "The Future of the Past," edited by Susanne Baackmann and Nancy P. Nenno, *Transit: A Journal of Travel, Migration, and Multiculturalism in the German- Speaking World*, 10, no. 2 (2016), http://transit.berkeley.edu/2016/berman/. Accessed November 11, 2016.

—. *Germans on the Kenyan Coast: Land, Charity, and Romance*. Forthcoming. Bloomington: Indiana University Press, 2017. Print.

—. *Impossible Missions? German Economic, Military, and Humanitarian Efforts in Africa.* Lincoln: Nebraska University Press, 2004. Print.
—. "Neils Larssen: A Life Afloat." *South Coast Resident's Association Newsletter*, 37 (August 2011): 4–5. Print.
—. "Neils Larssen: A Life Afloat." *South Coast Resident's Association Newsletter* 38 (September 2011): 3–4. Print.
Casas-Beltrán, Diego Armando, Luis Felipe Beltrán-Morales, Aradit Castellanos, and Aurora Breceda Solís-Cámara. "Turismo residencial y migración de jubilados extranjeros en México: un estudio de caso sobre sus implicaciones ambientales y de servicios en Baja California Sur." *Estudios Fronterizos, nueva época* 14, no. 28 (2013): 51–77. Print.
Dabbs, Brian. "Kenyans See the Italian Mafia's Hand in Worsening Drug Trade." *The Atlantic*, July 30, 2012. http://www.theatlantic.com/international/archive/2012/07/kenyans-see-the-italian-mafias-hand-in-worsening-drug-trade/260508/. Accessed November 11, 2016.
Diani Homes: Kenia Immobilien. http://www.dianihomes.de. Accessed November 11, 2016.
Diani Homes. "Über uns." http://www.dianihomes.de/ueber_uns.htm. Accessed November 11, 2016.
Fanon, Frantz. *Wretched of the Earth*, translated by Richard Philcox. New York: Grove, 2004. Print.
Gerlach, Luther Paul. *The Social Organization of the Digo of Kenya*. Diss. University of London, 1960. Print.
Gillette, Cynthia. *A Test of the Concept of Backwardness: A Case Study of Digo Society in Kenya.* Diss. Cornell University, 1978. Print.
Gitau, Paul. "How Italian Mafia Gained Control of Malindi." *Standard Digital*, July 3, 2012. http://www.standardmedia.co.ke/article/2000061045/how-italian-mafia-gained-control-of-malindi. Accessed November 11, 2016.
International Monetary Fund. "IMF Approves Three-Year Loan for Kenya Under the ESAF." Last updated April 26, 1996. https://www.imf.org/external/np/sec/pr/1996/pr9621.htm. Accessed November 11, 2016.
Jackson, R. T. "Problems of Tourist Industry Development on the Kenyan Coast." *Geography* 58.1 (1973): 62–65. Print.
Kang'ara, Sylvia Wairimu. "When the Pendulum Swings Too Far: Structural Adjustment Programs in Kenya." *Third World Legal Studies* 15.1 (1999): 109–51. Print.
Keller, Peter, and Thomas Bieger. *Real Estate and Destination Development in Tourism: Successful Strategies and Instruments.* Berlin: Erich Schmidt, 2008. Print.
KenyaVision2030. http://www.vision2030.go.ke. Accessed November 11, 2016.
Krapf, Johann Ludwig. *Reisen in Ostafrika, ausgeführt in den Jahren 1837–1855.* 2 vols. Stuttgart: Brockhaus, 1964. Print.
Mondinion. "Kenya Realtors & Real Estate Agents." http://www.mondinion.com/Real_Estate_Agents/country/Kenya/. Accessed November 11, 2016.
Moyo, Dambisa. *Dead Aid: Why Aid is not Working and How There Is a Better Way for Africa.* New York: Farrar, Straus and Giroux, 2009. Print.
Ndungu, Paul. "Tackling Land Related Corruption in Kenya." Unpublished manuscript, last modified November 2006. http://siteresources.worldbank.org/RPDLPROGRAM/Resources/459596–1161903702549/S2_Ndungu.pdf. Accessed November 11, 2016.

Pearce, Fred. *The Land Grabbers: The New Fight Over Who Owns the Earth.* Boston: Beacon Press, 2012. Print.

Pedersen, Jørgen Dige. "The Second Wave of Indian Investments Abroad." *Journal of Contemporary Asia* 38, no. 4 (November 2008): 613–637. Print.

"Prügelprozess gegen Prinz Ernst August: 'Der Joe hat uns verarscht.'" *Spiegel Online*, July 7. 2009. http://www.spiegel.de/panorama/justiz/pruegelprozess-gegen-prinz-ernst-august-der-joe-hat-uns-verarscht-a-634878.html. Accessed November 11, 2016.

Rodgers, W. A., and Neil D. Burgess. "Taking Conservation Action." *Coastal Forests of Eastern Africa.* Eds. Neil D. Burgess and G. Philip Clarke. Cambridge: IUCN, 2000. 317–34. Print.

Rono, Joseph Kipkemboi. "The Impact of the Structural Adjustment Programmes on Kenyan Society." *Journal of Social Development in Africa* 17.1 (2002): 81–98. Print.

Sparr, Pamela. *Mortgaging Women's Lives: Feminist Critiques of Structural Adjustment.* London: Zed Books, 1994. Print.

Stein, Howard. *Beyond the World Bank Agenda: An Institutional Approach to Development.* Chicago: University of Chicago Press, 2008. Print.

Steinkühler, Karl-Heinz. "Verbrechen im Mafia-Paradies." *Focus Magazin Online*, October 8, 1995. http://www.focus.de/politik/deutschland/verbrechen-im-mafia-paradies_aid_156069.html. Accessed November 11, 2016.

Swamy, Gurushri. "Kenya: Patchy, Intermittent Commitment." *Adjustment in Africa: Lessons from Country Case Studies.* Eds. Ishrat Husain and Rashid Faruqee. Brookfield: Ashgate, 1996. 193–237. Print.

Taylor, Ian. "India's Rise in Africa." *International Affairs* 88, no. 4 (2012): 779–798. Print.

Thomas-Emeagwali, Gloria, ed. *Women Pay the Price: Structural Adjustment in Africa and the Caribbean.* Trenton: Africa World Press, 1995. Print.

Thurow, Roger, and Scott Kilman. *Enough: Why the World's Poorest Starve in an Age of Plenty.* New York: PublicAffairs, 2009. Print.

Van Noorloos, Femke. "Residential Tourism Causing Land Privatization and Alienation: New Pressures on Costa Rica's Coasts." *Development* 54, no. 1 (2011): 85–90. Print.

Velásquez-Runk, Julie. "Indigenous Land and Environmental Conflicts in Panama: Neoliberal Multiculturalism, Changing Legislation, and Human Rights." *Journal of Latin American Geography* 11, no. 2 (2012): 21–47. Print.

Visser, Gustav, and Gijsbert Hoogendoorn. "A Decade of Second Home Tourism Research in South Africa: Research Prospects for the Developing World?" *South African Geographical Journal* 97, no. 2 (2015): 111–122. Print.

Wadhams, Nick. "Fleeing Justice, All the Way to Africa." *The Globe and Mail*, March 17, 2007. M 2. Print.

Wanjiru, Rose. *IMF Policies and Their Impact on Education, Health and Women's Rights in Kenya.* Nairobi: ActionAid International Kenya, 2009. Print.

World Bank. *Kenya: Re-Investing in Stabilization and Growth through Public Sector Adjustment.* Washington, DC: World Bank, 1992. Print.

Patrice Nganang
Writing under Colonial Rule

1.

Pages from a Bamum book manuscript, 1933

German colonial rule ended in Cameroon in 1916. One book traverses that period and runs through the short British rule and a substantial part of the French rule that followed that of the Germans: it is Njoya's memoir, the *Sang'aam*.[1] It consists of 500 pages composed by Ibrahim Njoya, the Sultan of the Bamum, between 1911 and 1933, from Fumban, the capital of his kingdom, to Yaounde that had by then already become the capital of French Cameroon and where he died in exile. At the end of his book, he writes the following sentence about his own subjects:

> Listen carefully to what I am telling you here. I have observed the Bamum people. Among them there are no educated, but rather stupid people; not many courageous, but rather fearful people; only a few people who are happy of their lot, but many who are envious.

---

[1] Sultan Ibrahim Njoya, ed., *Histoire et Coutumes des Bamum*, trans. Henri Martin (Yaounde: Ifan, 1952).

DOI 10.1515/9783110525625-004

> Those who are fearful of God are not as many as those who do not fear him. Most of them do not like work, but are happy to receive many gifts. The first kings were feared, but not loved because they killed anyone who did not comply with their will. They were served because they also gave many gifts. Such service was not based on love, but on personal interest. It was not a voluntary service.
>
> I, Njoya, when I became king, I renounced this habit of having people executed. I renounced it even before the arrival of white people. Bamum people still did not love me more. What kind of a people are those, who love somebody only when they have been sufficiently fed by him? And even after being fed by you, they still don't really love you. In fact they take you for an imbecile. And if you don't give them enough gifts, for them you are a bad person. The Bamum? What kind of a people is that?[2]

Quite a startling statement, for a King who expressed gratitude towards the same people previously in the same book:

> I was made a king when I was still under age, aged nineteen. It is the Bamum who raised me. The Bamum are like my fathers; I cannot be afraid of them, and they ought not to be afraid of me. The help I can bring my fathers is infinite and will end only when God will claim me.[3]

Beyond the historical distinction between these two statements, lies a purely formal one. Even though they are written in the same book, and between them lies more than a decade, one world war, the occupation of Fumban by German (1902–1916), British (three months, in 1916) and French colonizers (from October 2, 1916), the first statement was presumably not publicly spoken, while the second is introduced in the book with the following terms: "Here are the words that King Njoya addressed to the Bamum while governing them."[4] In their different forms, the one written but not spoken, and the other both spoken and written, these contradictory statements about the Bamum people establish the Bamum sultan's distinction between the written and the spoken word in their commerce with judgment and truth. Yet, commenting on the capacity of the written word to eternally coagulate thoughts and the spoken word, he says: "it seems that after having spoken, God took their voice away, and no other king can ever find the cause of these judgments."[5] If only such a definitive account of the capacity of written words could find the agreement of his subjects! "He writes things to blind white people"[6], some said of his writing activity, an assessment that with-

---

2 *Histoire et Coutumes*, 245.
3 133.
4 Ibid.
5 136.
6 244.

out much surprise was shared by French colonial officers, as confirmed in a confidential note written in 1919 by an officer of the French colonial administration named commandant Martin, who said, "He invented a language for his people, in the hope through his vanity to halt the diffusion of European languages."[7], In 1921, this tendency of the Sultan's subsequently led to the banning of his public teaching of any form of his scriptures and to the curtailing of the language, shü-mum, which he used to write his memoir—the *Libonare*[8], the book that would be subsequently known as the *Sang'aam*.

Pose of Sultan Njoya writing. The picture, taken by the French colonial official Frederic Gadmer, shows him performing his task as a judicial accessory of the French administration, hence the stamps and European-style book notes. Fumban, 1917

Although quite unique in their kind, Sultan Njoya's struggles with writing can be read as a general trope. During colonial rule, the position and use of writing by Africans was very contested. The fate of Sultan Njoya's writing is therefore a perfect illustration of the cultural battlefield that writing opened up in the heart of the colonial enterprise. The rubble of those intellectual battles has not metamorphosed into redemptive constructions, since all Njoya's books and

---

7 Claude Tardits: *Le Royaume Bamum* (Paris: Librairie Armand Colin, 1980), 982.
8 Ibid., 81.

texts have remained sealed to most of Cameroonian literature after independence. That silence is an ironic quality he himself attributed to writing ("I will make a book that speaks without being heard", is the way he introduces his script[9]). The main issue is eloquently phrased in the question he asked, summarizing a personal frustration with his subjects and a long struggle with colonial officers, particularly the French: "The Bamum? What kind of a people is that?" This question is that of an exasperated mind as well as that of a scholar on a quest to understand who he is, and therefore who the Bamum are. It can also be used as the thread with which to read and analyze his own writing. The question will thus be understood as being a critical one. To uncover the multiple layers of the critic's answer to Njoya's own question, this article takes into consideration the rhetorical and political infrastructure from which it was voiced. Njoya's question is framed by the three poles that demarcate the contested field of writing under colonial rule. One, the colonial administration and its evolving character amongst the Bamum—German, British, French. Two, the Bamum themselves, their class struggles, and their tactical use of colonialism to create a narrative for themselves. Thirdly, Sultan Njoya whose cultural ventriloquism strategically transforms the sanction of a silent and yet vocal Cameroonian writer into a promise.

2.

Understood as a question of self-knowledge, Njoya's question, "the Bamum? What kind of a people is that?", not only installs his memoir inside a long tradition of humanism, it also defines the structure of his investigation and his method. An echo to the insignia at the door of the Heracles temple at Delphi, Γνῶθι σεαυτόν, know thyself, the book, gendered as a *Libonare* in the language invented by Njoya, stands according to its translator, Pastor Henri Martin, as a listing of the names of a mother's child. It is therefore a genealogy, but one that is inscribed in a matriarchy. And the first words are tautological as well as prospective in that respect, for they provide the beginning of an answer to who the Bamum people are:

> Here is the history book of the kings who came from Rifum.
> A long time ago, the Bamum were in Rifum. They did not know God's word. Rifum was three days away by foot. Rifum's king had three children. Nchare, Nfu Mbaam and Mufu Nsu. They went to create a plantation which each of them protected with a trench they

---

9 *Histoire et Coutumes*, op. cit., 41.

used to survive, like in a camp. Having heard that, Mfu Rifum ordered his sons to come back to him. They told their father that they would, but yet fled away. When they reached a river, Nchare told his brothers: 'Let me cross the river first.' His brother agreed, but Nchare had crossed it with his whole family, he rendered the raft unusable, to the fury of his siblings Nfu Nso and Nfu Mbaam. The latter went and settled in Nzimbaam, while Mfu Nsu, following the river Vi, settled in Nkunso.[10]

Nchare is therefore not only the founder of the Bamum people, said to be the descendants of his family, but he is also the originator of the ruling dynasty, of which Sultan Njoya was the latest heir at the time the book was written.

The construction of the *Sang'aam* thus installs the book in a specific understanding of chronology: genealogical, semi-matriarchal, collective, dynastic, narrated, but also circular. These aspects are important; after all, if it is not possible to draft a chronology without a specific concept of time, one always has to remember that time is a fiction. And yet the most unquestionable aspect of memoir writing, and of any narration, is its relation to the succession that time imposes on events. The origin of time in the *Sang'aam* has the signature of one person's ruse against his own brothers, and the shattering of his original family, that of Mfu Rifum. Through his constitutive act of erasure, Nchare did not only relegate his own father to oblivion, he also sent his two brothers into a future of nothingness:

> When a king dies, it is his son who can succeed him. Whether the king has a consanguine or uterine brother is of no relevance; that brother cannot be designated as his successor. The Bamum cannot accept such a succession.[11]

The reason for such a taboo, thus, for such bracketing of time's succession in a ruling family's life and in a community's accepted leadership ("Since the Bamum left Rifum, no one ever left the king to go and create a royalty somewhere else"[12]), lies in the original dispute that opposed Nchare to his brothers, at the banks of the river:

> Nchare recommended it because his brother refused to give him clothes, for him to be recognized as king. It angered Nchare so much that he stated that his throne shall not be given to his brother in the case of his death. Even in the case that there are thousands of candidates for the succession, his brother shall not become king. After having recommended that, Nchare buried something in Makom. He was with the elders. He then went back to Rifum to search for his clothes, boiling with anger. When he arrived, the Rifum people killed

---

10 22.
11 103.
12 103.

> him. Nji Mun Sare cut his throat and brought back his head on a banana tree. This is how it is in Makom even today. The fifteen kings of Bamum who succeeded each other kept Nchare's recommendation and added to it that if the king's brother would succeed him, the Bamum country will be destroyed that same day.[13]

Grievances die hard, one may say, particularly the ones that involve an act of regicide. That only men are considered in that succession is written in the original scene that puts three brothers against each other in a prophetic battle, this although historically some women have acted as regents in the Bamum dynasty before the maturity of their sons and although the *Sang'aam* also states: "The Bamum royalty is not yet the heritage of Nji Mamfum who can only be succeeded by her sister."[14]

The death of Nchare at his return in Rifum at the hands of Mfu Rifum's people did not reinstall the dwindling power of his father, because Nchare's act of dissent had already become constitutive of a new line, and thus of a new chronology.

> Nchare went to war, defeated the Mfubem and settled in Matam where Mfu Mben became one of his men. Thus ended that war. Nchare came from Matam to live in the palace of Mfum Mben. 'Because I have become the king of the Fumban, he said, my people will be called the Bamum. This is because I went from Rifum on the day of the futmum.' His people accepted it.[15]

The story of origins, circular in its form and content, still establishes a necessary disjunction: Nchare goes away, yet he comes back and dies in Rifum, on his father's land. While he has the time to build his own kingdom and establish his own line of succession *somewhere else,* Nchare causes the extinction of his father's line of succession and literally pays for that with his head. But he had already established his own line of succession, even if *among strangers*—the Bamum. For the sake of a continuous succession, the circle is never closed fully so as to avoid a *circulus vitiosus*. Nchare is a king to strangers whose language he adopts and with whom he is related only by a pledge of allegiance after a military defeat, and yet his most brutal act of exclusion is against his own brother. By punctuating the narration with multiple forms of repetitions and differences, the *Sang'aam* mimics the structure of passing time. Yet it is this germane concept and foundational philosophy of time that makes it become more than a chronicle rooted in a teleology—it becomes a genealogy instead.

---

13 103.
14 103.
15 22.

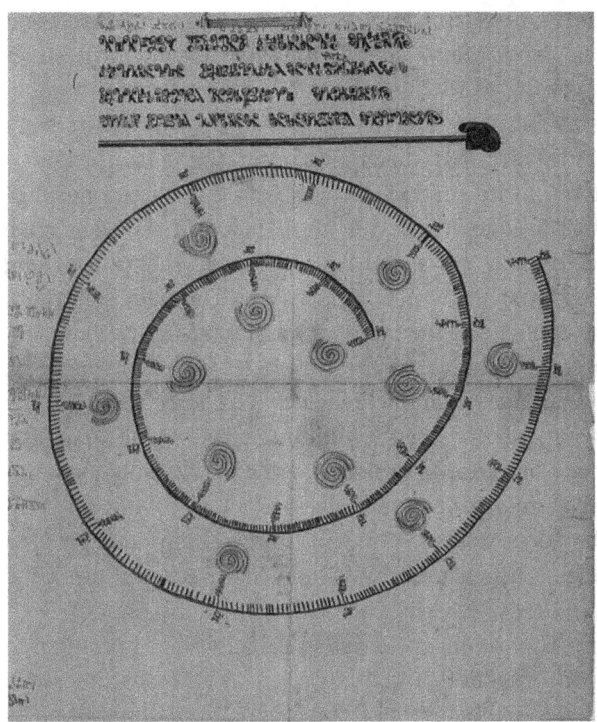

Bamum agricultural calendar, drafted by Nji Ibrahim Njoya (formerly known as Johannes Yerima), 1911

By bracketing time inside a structure of repetition and difference, Njoya's narration adopts the formal structure of a *calendar of events* of which the most vivid manifestation among the Bamum is the agricultural calendar, which follows an order of activities that is not simply chronological. The Bamum calendar is lunar and limited to a strict thirty days per month. The beginning of the year is March, with each month being marked by specific events: 1) shwop mbuu, or beginning of rains (April); 2) nzoun, or small dry season (May); 3) puure, or the time of field cleaning (June); fu nguu, green (July); 5) mfiet paam, or harvest (August); 6) mbaa ngoungaa, or yellow herbs (September); 7) sou mbaa, or harvesting of palm oil (October); 8) sou loum, or beginning of the dry season (November); 9) loum, or great bush fires (December); 10) ngu (January); 11) tonte faa, or field fires (February); 12) kukwom, or time of cultivation (March). Similarly, only a few dates puncture Njoya's book, too few for a narration that spans fifteen generations of kings, the history of the Bamum population and of many other neighboring groups. The narrative also moves between

Fumban, the capital of the Bamum kingdom, Buea, the capital of Cameroon under German colonial rule, and Yaounde, the capital of the country under the French administration. Owing to its narrative philosophy of time, the *Sang'aam* understands stories as being constitutive of chronology since events are the elemental units of narration. This distancing from the fetishisation of dates can only be understood in the context of the book's narrative concept of time. Time is a fiction, albeit an agreed-upon fiction. There are certainly some dates that appear here and there in Njoya's tale, for instance, when the writing of his book started, when the first white people arrived in Fumban, etc.; these dates still do not sufficiently punctuate the large canvass of tales that Njoya unravels on front of the reader. The change in the currencies noted in the book, from the cowries, to the German mark and the French franc, can be a way to navigate the events and the narrations that the five hundred pages of the *Sang'aam* condense. However, as a book of multiple stories, Njoya's *Sang'aam* will continue to be seen as structured by the stories themselves.

The fictive quality of time does not question its truthfulness as is underlined by the multiple cartographies of times that exist, from the Greek chronological table to today's watches, and by the different calendars that organize our human lives, from the Chinese to the Judeo-Christian calendar. The punctuation of time with events obliges one to understand its structure as kaleidoscopic, with Fumban as its center of gravity, Nchare as its originator and Njoya himself as its contemporary manifestation—as its *chronographer.* A Bamum cannot leave the Bamum kingdom, nor can he leave the tutelage of the king. Bamum history is history narrated by Njoya in his book, the *Sang'aam,* which is the primal source and definitive testament. Arrested in the framework of their definition as inhabitants of the Bamum land, as descendants of the mythical Nchare and subjects of Njoya, the Bamum people are thus invented as subjects of a dynasty, and therefore narrated as protagonists of Njoya's stories. As such, the book reads like a newspaper without dates. These stories, believable or not, are told in multiple voices and clearly involve multiple story tellers. They are placed under the sanction of laws that allow certain behaviors and forbid other ones among the Bamum, but of laws that inscribe the succession of time, both in theory and in its narrated form as praxis, inside a subjective but dynastic principle. And it is from this vantage point, from the subjective and dynastic principle, that the memoir of Njoya becomes the memoir of his people. The "I", that in the *Sang'aam,* for the first time in Cameroonian literature, defines itself as transcendental to be able to tell its story in full, does it by claiming a right to define time as a narration of the self by the self, and thus as a fiction. The words of that self-definition are in themselves historical for Cameroonian literature—and for all Cameroonians:

> I, Njoya, am the son of Nsangu Ngungure. Ngungure was the daughter of king Mbouemboue. I, Njoya, am the prince and the kingdom belongs to me, Njoya. I, Njoya, do not change things in the laws because of fear, but with courage, with the goal of helping the Bamum for them to find happiness in the land.[16]

The words of Njoya here are descriptive of his activity as a legislator. The *Sang'aam* lists indeed multiple laws he has abrogated: "King Njoya abrogated eighty five paragraphs of the law"[17], he writes. And here too succession is defined as a repetition with disjunctions. But those disjunctions are only possible from inside a principled indifference towards diverging concepts of time. It is at such a price only that succession becomes continuity. Such continuity is what Njoya defines as "happiness". For happiness is nothing else than a practical avoidance of disruptions, or its corollary, a controlled acceptance of them, of which the most repeated in his book is war. Even though the *Sang'aam* narrates multiples episodes of wars waged both in the past and the present, by Bamum kings (including Njoya himself) and by many others, happiness is always understood as self-defined. Its most brutal expression of course, is self-interest. That such definition itself can only lead to contestations is self-evident, for the fiction of one's interest and happiness necessarily collides with another one's fiction. And here, the contingent position of the Bamum people, of the ruling dynasty and of Njoya is transformed into a hegemonic principle, the principle through which happiness is defined and transformed into a politics. Tautologically, happiness is what makes the king happy, what assures the continuity of the Nchare dynasty, and the welfare of the Bamum people. Happiness is therefore both the stability of a polity, and of a policy.

It is only understandable that a concrete articulation of the self found the most difficult terrain of its experimentation during the time of Njoya's rule. And the two fictions against which the sultan's narration collided are, first colonialism and then nationalism. He writes the following about his most controversial decision not to antagonize German officials, when they entered the Bamum land in 1902:

> After that [an intestine but bloody war waged against Gbetnkum], white people arrived. 'Let us resist them, let us chase them', said the Bamum. – No, said Njoya. He has had a dream in which he saw what white people would do to the Bamum. 'If we go to war against white people, all the Bamum will be destroyed. Only a few of us will survive, and you will be unhappy.' And Njoya himself took, arms, spears and guns away from Bamum people's hands.

---

16 125–126.
17 133.

White people arrived and did not go to war against them. That is how Njoya contributed to Bamum people's happiness.[18]

As for his clash with nationalism in 1914:

The Germans were the masters of the Bamum land when Duala, the son of Manga sent Ndame to talk to king Njoya. After having allied himself with the people from the forest, Ndane came to inform king Njoya of the conflict that existed between the Germans on the one hand, and the French and British on the other. It is through him that Duala, the son of Manga, was advising Njoya to enter into war against the Germans on his land. King Njoya sent messengers to tell the following to Duala, the son of Manga: 'The Germans are my fathers and he is like my brother, how then can I enter into war against them?' He then arrested Ndane and delivered him to the German authorities who did not dislike this way of doing. Ndane was incarcerated, and after a while, Duala, the son of Manga was arrested and executed.[19]

Colonialism and nationalism were two crucial moments, two distinctive phases with their own respective chronology, their own understanding of geography, their own tumultuous drive towards hegemony, their own definition of who the subject of history is, and they collided with Njoya's narration of himself and the Bamum people. Regardless of the calendar of events that each of these phases displayed, for example conquest, sets of regulations, the World War for the first, political associations that go beyond tribal lines, solidarity of Black people and of Cameroonians against white people, independence for the second, and regardless of their *respective chronography*, they both marked the end of Njoya claim to being the sole writer of his own fiction of time, even though they all still left him with the opportunity of being the narrator of his own doom. The book he wrote through most of the period of his reign, the *Sang'aam*, can be read as a ventriloquist chronicle of his political rise and fall during a very complex time, yet this would lay claim to only one layer of his narration, to the story of his own fate in the fictions of colonialism and nationalism. Unanswered will remain the question he himself asked at the end of his book: "the Bamum? What kind of a people is that?" Born out of his frustration at the dawn of his life at not having truly made the Bamum people happy, and thus the product of the conceptual indifference of his narration during a time pregnant with new sets of definitions[20], that question does not only unravel the for-

---

18 42.
19 214.
20 It will be argued later that the king's frustration is the expression of a conflict between him and his people, a conflict rooted in a more and more unshared understanding of the concept of

mal and intellectual structure of the writing of his book; it starts the Cameroonian fiction and narration of the self by grounding it inside the philosophical question of knowledge. In it lies the possibility of all prospective Cameroonian efforts in literature, for it is Njoya who defined the fundamental task of any Cameroonian writing as being one of critique—of self-critique.

3.

It is a truism to say that contemporary African literature started with memoirs. For a formal analysis of the *Sang'aam*, defining what a memoir is, is not a philosophical predicament, in light of the fact that Njoya wrote the book using his own invented writing system and his secret language, the shümum, to ground his narration of the self inside a specific understanding of time. The question of what defines a memoir is then a historical as well as a hermeneutical question. The *Sang'aam*'s first translator, readers and interpreters were German and French colonials, and it has had no noticeable critical reception inside a Cameroonian and an African literature that has been mostly shaped by colonialism and nationalism in which Njoya's writing played no prominent part. In other words, neither negritude nor its antecedents made any reference to Njoya's extensive writing. That contemporary African literature has been produced and read mostly from inside the confrontations sparked between colonialism and nationalism has more or less condemned Njoya's narration to the critical silence of a literary bystander, for which the French colonial banning of his writing system and schools in 1921 was nothing less than an expedient pretext. The Cameroonian state has not found it necessary so far to mobilize scholars for a new translation of his books, to include them in school curricula, nor to encourage a teaching and adoption of his writing system on a larger scale such as to remove them from the restrictions that were imposed upon them by colonials. As a consequence, Njoya's texts have become hieroglyphic while at the same time the 19th century "African inventor of a script" that he is, is endlessly marveled. It is therefore from the colonial exegesis, from his translator Pastor Henri Martin in particular, that some of the most productive questions around the *Sang'aam* are voiced. Those questions address *the status of truth in fiction* in his writing, and they are formulated around the genre of that book. As such they address

---

right. For if for him right is fundamentally related to *happiness*, the Bamum people, exacerbated by colonialism and then inspired by nationalism, will view right more and more as inseparable from *freedom*.

and therefore make explicit the tension between Njoya's establishing of a fiction of time, and his book's qualification as the memoir of his life during a time of the most brutal political turmoils.

Njoya in his apartments in Fumban with German colonials, 1910

Henri Martin, who translated the *Sang'aam* as *Histoire et Coutumes des Bamum*, gives a speculatively ripe definition of 'Bamum': "According to tradition, the word 'mum' came from the verb 'yi mumme' which means: to hide. 'Pamum' therefore means: those who hide."[21]

He values this hypothesis more than other ones, for, as he writes, it "presents itself with more truthfulness, when one knows a little of the people with whom one is dealing"[22]. The two other hypotheses which he casts aside, are: first the story as told by Njoya himself in the *Sang'aam*:

---

21 Henri Martin, "Le Pays Bamum et le Sultan Njoya," *Etudes Camerounaises* Septembre-Decembre, 31–32 (1950): 8.
22 Ibid.

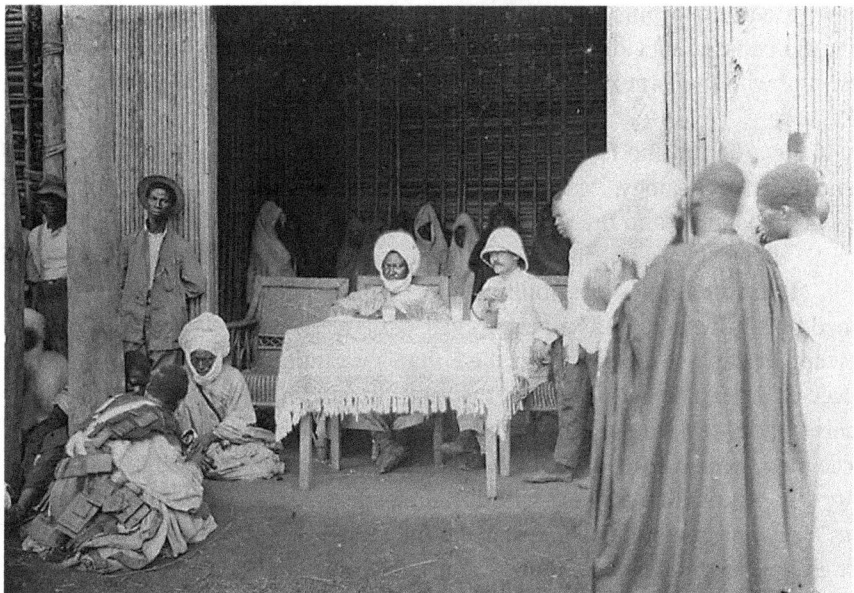

Njoya, in his apartments in Fumban with a French colonial officer, 1917

> Nchare traveled from Matam to live in the palace of Mfu Mben. I have become the king of Mfu Mben, he said, and my people will be called Bamum, because I went from Rifum on the day of futmum. His people agreed.[23]

And the second:

> Nchare proclaimed himself king of the Bamum, which means the people living in the country he had captured before Fumban. Njimmum, a village situated four hours on foot in the North-East from Fumban and where one can still see the stones on which Nchare and his principal companions sat before subduing the Pamben.[24]

In other words, immediate commerce with Bamum people convinces Martin to cast the king's narration of himself aside. His choice is both methodological and political: it is rooted in his external approach of the Bamum, as opposed to Njoya's arrival at the knowledge of who they are though an implicit route; and it is the fruit of random observations, thus of colonial ethnography, while Njoya's narration is a chronology of the self. In short what is enacted here is

---

23 Ibid.
24 8–9.

clearly a conflict of interpretations that is dramatized in the political arena as well, the consequence of which is radical: the casting aside of the sultan's definition of who the Bamum people are becomes a metaphor of his factual exile in 1921.

If Njoya found the legitimating force of his story in his dynastic right and therefore in genealogy, Martin grounds his fiction in colonial science and thus, in hypothesis and their interpretation. Martin's claim is therefore methodological, while Njoya's is epistemic. Instead of a bracketing of time as the sultan does, Martin multiplies possibilities and temporalities, all of which are sanctioned by his own choice as an interpreter—as a reader. Njoya's power is dogmatic, while Martin's is doxologic. In the sultan's narration we had the coagulating power of the writer who captures the multiple voices of the land into a single whole and the drifting and diverging possibilities of a people into a controlled succession, while with Martin it is the reader in all the colonial stigma of his activity who irrupts into the text with full force: as the sole translator so far of the *Sang'aam*, and therefore as its primeval interpreter. His tool is a proliferation of stories and his violence is that of the choice of validity. Both attributes are housed conceptually in a freedom that itself is understood as the power of judgment. The consequence is violent: Njoya's narration loses its uniqueness. The conflict between writer and reader, between the sultan and his interpreter, between Njoya and Martin, finds its more expressed manifestation around the concept of time and its application in history.

> Our Bamum tried to supplement the absence of dates. They established a chronology for their kings, and thus could make Nchare (1394–1418) become a contemporary of our king of France, Charles VII. I hold it to be pure fantasy.[25]

Because Martin's methodology is that of proliferation, his power lies in comparison and in distinction. If for the colonial officer the most visible distinction is that of a king, for the reader that he is, the most obvious distinction is that of the author.

> For the writing of his memoirs, Njoya used many notabilities of the land: those who were susceptible, either because of their age or their function, to know oral tradition very well [...]. They all wrote under the direction of the king who when necessary added his personal note or changed this or that custom.[26]

---

[25] 22.
[26] 23.

Njoya's authorship is mentioned inside the *Sang'aam* in the form of a repeated formulation: "I, Njoya".[27] It is therefore transcendental and at the same time immanent to its own narration. It is a first person and third person address, as opposed to the name of the scribes who appear inside the book in the form of an intradiegetic aside—as an *aparte* in the third person, as the doodle of *readers:* "Here are the names of those who were reading the book: Ismaila Meku, son of Njitaamen, Amadu Mfupu, son of Ngaput Njianga, Nyamnsie, Pekekue Taapit."[28]

Nji Ibrahim Njoya (formerly known as Johannes Yerima) and Nji Mama Pepekouo
Two of the scribes who contributed to writing Njoya's Sang'aam, Fumban, 1912.

The sultan's authorship is an authority that is implicit to his narration, for he is indeed the writer of his own text. However, this is not a sign of authorship that a critic would easily recognize.

Martin's multiplication of scribes sanctions the disappearance of Njoya as author, and defines him as editor. For his *Histoire et coutumes des Bamum* is writ-

---

27 125.
28 81.

ten "under the editorship of Njoya'." What is left of the author is a machine – a bureaucracy—of multiple hagiographers. Yet because Njoya's order is instead that of succession, it manifests itself in his narration as repetition and difference—in the controlled continuity of his authority and authorship. On the one hand we therefore have an explicit elaboration, and on the other, an implicit continuity. Because Martin's reading is strategic, his mode of interpretation can only be political. And this applies to the qualification of historical events as well, thus to their interpretation: it is interesting to read indeed that for Njoya, World War I is but one war amongst the many other wars the Bamum have gone through. Interesting is also to read that the belligerent forces of that war, the German, the British, the French, are but different faces of the same; that his alliance with the German and the British nurtures his expectation of a similar alliance with the French. Colonialism appears to Njoya with multiple faces, but all are united in their single manifestation as exteriority. He claims the sole right to deal with that exteriority, for the happiness of the Bamum:

> White people instilled fear in them. What was to be done? 'I will go to them, said Njoya, and will see their way of living.' He went to Buea and to Kamerun (Duala). On his return, he spoke the language of white people. He explained how they lived to the Bamum. 'If askaris come to the market and take something, or slap you, do not get angry, he told them. Leave me alone with the things of white people.' That is how he helped the Bamum people.[29]

The particularity of Martin's interpretation is that despite its general architecture of scholarship, despite its jargon of truthfulness, it cannot prove Njoya wrong, for the reason that its concept of time is a colonial manufacture. It is an invention too. It would be far too easy to subsume it into the time of a ticking clock, for that is only its most visible fetish. Colonial time is not limited to a specific calendar of events, but it too has an agenda of possibilities. In fact that agenda is the nexus to which and from which a specific understanding of history unfolds, with its ramifications whose most banal appearances in the land of the Bamum are a reorganizing polity and a quite constraining economy: bureaucracy and taxes are its most immediate figures, but yet both would not be intelligible without their organizing principle which is freedom. Freedom is the epitome of colonialism, and the new hegemonic concept.

Martin is not an innocent reader. His interest in Njoya's narration is powerful because it is scientific, and it is colonial because it is scholarly.

> Given the current state of scholarship, we have to abandon that chronology and accept the quite vague indication: a pua lare = after that, then, which marks the transition between

---

29 43.

diverse chapters of these memoirs. Furthermore, we have to have the hypothesis – knowing the power of intrigue of our Bamum – that the reign of their kings was not of the length one wants us to believe with the help of a purely fantasist chronology.[30]

His first assault goes to the heart of Njoya's text, for how can a narration whose concept of time is deemed a 'fantasy' have any claim to truth? Yet this question presents him with the most basic *aporia* of his science: how can he know anything about the Bamum when he dilutes the foundational principle of the *Sang'aam*, the time of their most hegemonic narrative and its very condition of possibility? The void that is opened between the reader and the text is marked by Martin's practical indecision: his suspension of judgment in front of the scarcity of dates in Njoya's narrations, which propels his fundamental uncertainty over the status of the book he has in front of him. He writes the following in his introduction to his translation: "This book that is not a history proper, which means a continuous narration, but a rather incoherent sample of anecdotes…"[31] And: "Some tales seems not to provide us with a reflection of truth…"[32]

To conclude:

> "Some people consider chapter 29 to be a pure product of Njoya's imagination, then in those stories there is the king's personal contribution: particularly at the end when he unloads his rancor against the French administration that was then undermining his authority it supported badly. Of course there is the king's contribution, and he gave himself a good portion in that part, and in doing so he seriously hindered truth."[33]

It is Martin who describes his translation of Njoya's narration as history. The title of his translation is *Histoire et Coutumes des Bamum*, and his title has become so authoritative that the book is routinely mentioned among the Bamum as *Sang'aam*, which means "Histoire" in their language, thus overlooking the fact that in a scholarly article he published in *Etudes camerounaises* in 1950, Martin describes the same book as 'mémoires royaux'[34]—royal memoirs.

---

30 Martin, 'Le Pays Bamum et le Sultan Njoya', op. cit., 22–23.
31 Histoire,10.
32 Ibid.
33 Ibid.
34 *Le pays Bamum et le sultan Njoya*, 8, 11, 12, etc.

4.

The principle of Njoya's time is happiness. Against that principle, colonialism and nationalism appear as two sides of the same coin. It should not be surprising, since both rather have freedom as their organizing principle, the difference between them being that freedom is mostly defined negatively by colonialism, and positively by nationalism. In any event, the sultan strategically held both at bay. Suffice it to say that in the hundreds of pages of the *Sang'aam*, there is literally no mention of the word freedom in an affirmative way. In summary, the subject of freedom is as absent from Njoya's book as the slave was non-existent in Roman law's definition of a human being[35], and the attributes of its definition are not fully evaluated just as labor was not amongst the Greeks, particularly Aristotle.[36] This does not mean that despite the lack of freedom during the sultan's reign and during the multiple regimes of corporeal restriction he mentions (serfdom, slavery, patriarchy, Christianity, sexism, colonialism, nationalism, etc.), freedom was not a necessary, legitimate and even pertinent quest for Bamum individuals. Its mention in the *Sang'aam* is in essence polemical, for it mostly addresses people whose quality as subjects having *the right to be free* was not self-evident in Njoya's jurisdiction: women and slaves in particular. These two subjects are symbolic in that they shared the singular quality of being both humans and commodities, and are therefore the bearers of a conceptual unrest. They could be given away as gifts or sold, and yet they are human beings. In an economy of happiness in which gifts were more important than exchanges, and in a system of gifts at the center of which stood the sultan, they did not possess the most fundamental attribute of the Bamum person: the capacity to give, and the satisfaction that is born from that act. They were instead the ones being given away, and as such were at the end of the chain of desire that produces happiness.

> The person who sells a pregnant woman shall bind the piece of nsinsa on her leg. It will therefore be recognized that the child who will be born will belong to the seller of the woman. After childbirth at stilling, the seller will give three thousand cowries for the care of the child. He will then take his child.[37]

---

35 G.W.F. Hegel: *Outline of the Philosophy of Right* (Oxford: Oxford University Press, 2008) p.18.
36 Karl Marx: *The Capital*, Volume 1 (London: Penguin, 1990) p. 151–152.
37 *Histoire*, 117.

Against the backdrop of the king's absolute property ("All those who are born in the land of the Bamum belong to the king"[38]), the first effective appearance of freedom takes therefore and can only take the form of escape: "Fleeing is a thing that will not disappear, and the same is valid for the drink to establish truth."[39]

Interesting is that in his presentation, Njoya contrasts exit option and narration, departure and self-expression, thus composing a historical chiasm that shows how in the end, the capacity of a Bamum subject to write its own autobiography becomes exclusive. If the Bamum people could speak, what would they say?[40] This question cannot be formulated without unsettling Njoya's status as author of his book. And as such, Martin's restriction of the sultan's prerogatives as a writer is but just an introduction to a history of unrests that is still unfolding among the Bamum. From the point of view of Njoya's concept of the self as rather having *the right to be happy* established in the *Sang'aam*, the absolute nature of freedom is therefore a clear matter of contestation, and it is not surprising that freedom is the terrain on which the king's argument with Cameroonian nationalism first, and then with French colonialism later, will unfold. The political battle around freedom will be waged with the Bamum people too. This is important to establish, for in a land in which property existed both as right to land and as right to possess slaves, the conflict of interpretation that started between the king and his subjects, between the king and other Cameroonians and between the king and the French during colonialism was rooted in the diverging nature of the principles each party echoed, and in their tactical use of them. At its core, nationalism appropriated colonialism's positing of freedom as absolute, but turned it against its principled formulator. On the other hand, Njoya defended happiness as absolute in Bamum land and used it against some early Cameroonian nationalists—amongst them the German-trained lawyer Duala Manga Bell whom he delivered to the Germans and to his death in 1914. For happiness to the sultan meant mostly happiness of the Bamum people, but also that of any one who was allied with him to the fundamental cause of Bamum happiness, Cameroonians and Germans alike: "He captured Ndane and delivered him to the German authorities, whom this way of doing did not displease."[41] To Njoya's

---

38 Ibid., p.92.
39 107.
40 Here an elaboration of a question asked by Marx in *Capital, Volume I*. For its formulation, see: op. cit., 176: 'If commodities could speak, they would say this: our use-value may interest men, but it does not belong to us as objects. What does belong to us as objects, however, is our value. Our own intercourse as commodities proves it.'
41 *Histoire*, 214.

political distinction between happiness and pleasure (including displeasure), one has to add his description of satisfaction as neutral, particularly in the moment of his shifting political allegiance against the Germans:

> The Germans were waging war with the help of the king who gave them food. They were asking the king for a thousand, nine hundred, eight hundred, seven hundred, six hundred, three hundred, two hundred carriers and the king obeyed willy-nilly.[42]

Consent, and its material form, the contract, is based on a will defined by a principled happiness whose driving impulse is self-interest. For it is self-interest that drove Njoya to accept the German tutelage over his lands, and to use them in his battle against the threatening Nso:

> When Hauptmann Graret [?] went to war in Nkunso, Ne Njapdunke [Njoya's mother] told him: 'Look after my son. Should anything bad happen to him, I will grab you by the neck and we will die together. – Nothing bad will happen to your son, I will look after him', answered Hauptmann Graret.
> When they came back from the war, Ne thanked him a lot.[43]

The principle of freedom sheds a different light over these decisions, and not surprisingly it gives them a divergent interpretation. If for nationalism this is an obvious case of collaboration, it is through the Janus face of colonialism in Fumban that one can establish a contesting reading of the same event. Indeed, the French turned the principle of happiness against Njoya's polity, and started the process of his downfall by asking if the Bamum people whom they defined as subjects of freedom, were truly happy. Colonialism's substantial redefinition of happiness transformed it into the acquisition of material riches, whose most visible incentive was wages. That the transformation of Bamum people into wage earners is their introduction into capitalism stays beyond dispute. Important is that this could not be achieved without its logical price: universal taxation. And Njoya's *Sang'aam* chronicles how, faced in his kingdom with the dual possibility of telling the truth about their growing unhappiness (which was impossible since women and slaves, the subjects in question, could not be elevated into the writers of their own narration neither by the king nor by the French) or fleeing, most people chose to go away. The exit option was formally made the more legitimate as the "drink to establish the truth", the Bamum beverage for truth-telling in judicial proceedings, was banned by the French colonial administration in 1919.

---

42 215.
43 75.

It could be argued indeed, that whereas Njoya allied himself with the Germans to realize his and the ruling class' happiness, the more wretched part of the Bamum population, women and slaves in particular, allied themselves with French colonials to undo the sultan's power over their right to freedom. Colonialism's official stance against slavery was a tactical argument of this sort. But was the transformation of all the Bamum people including the sultan into natives its fulfilled promise of liberation? That is a question only nationalism could voice. The struggle between happiness and freedom thus attained a political dimension that showed the full hypocrisy of its promise. And the majority of those who were concerned here mostly told their tale, not in writing their own book like sultan Njoya, but by walking away from the lands of Bamum. They therefore uncovered the *inner contradiction* of the *Sang'aam's* promise of happiness, for in its laws, the book transforms even a slave's earned freedom into a higher form of servitude, when it fails to pass under the scrutiny of the king's veridiction. At the same time they unsettled colonialism in its bones.

> If a slave enfranchises himself by himself by giving money to his master, and yet telling that somebody else bought him and that his master later finds out that he had bought his freedom by himself, the master should submit the case to the king. The king will have the slave drink the truth beverage. If the slave falls, it would be the proof that he bought his freedom by himself, and if he vomits it would be the proof that somebody else bought him. If he falls, he becomes the king's property.[44]

So states the *Sang'aam*. But this regulation is only one layer of the argument that voids freedom of its substance. It overlooks colonialism's practical abolition of freedom through universal taxation and its logical corollaries for the Bamum people, exploitation and impoverishment. By arguing from the principle of freedom, albeit negatively, French colonialism planted the seed of its own demise, and as a self-protecting measure it tactically allied itself at the beginning with the sultan whose power it wanted to undo. After all by simply running away, the Bamum people threatened the foundation on which its whole colonial system was built: their transformation into natives. And after the departure of German colonials, French colonial officers resorted to two methods to strengthen their presence: coercion and the sultan's authority. In other words: *mutato nomine de te fabula narratur*.

Two episodes are telling in this respect. Both present the sultan and French colonials confronted with the very unpredictable reality of unhappy Bamum people, a reality that forced even the sultan in the end to voice his frustration with

---

[44] 116–117.

them in the form of the fundamentally critical question: 'The Bamum? What kind of a people is that?' Yes, he suddenly faced the reality of a demanding Bamum people. The first episode concerns the taxation of women, and the second is an incident related to the flight of many Bamum people as a consequence of war hostilities.

> The French arrived in Bamum country in 1916, at the end of the eight month of fotimu, the twentieth day that was a futmun. The king went to meet them. When they arrived at the royal court, they found many people assembled. The Bamum greeted the French who answered back. 'Bamum country has become a French possession', the French proclaimed. The proclamation was accepted by every one. 'After the war, the newly arrived continued, we will make your country become prosperous.' The king gave them lots of food and the French were very happy with what the king gave them.
> A short while afterwards, the governor gave a medal to the king through the intermediary of lieutenant Clapot. One day the French told the king that war had ended, and informed him that his land was from now on ruled by French law. The king, the nobility and the Bamum did not object. 'Every one, they said, men, women, children, should do something. This is how the country will become prosperous. By the way, in a short while, women will start paying taxes. Don't think it is a law that has been drafted especially for your country. That law already exist everywhere, even in our own country, France.
> The king, hearing that was more or less satisfied. I called the people out, men and women, and told them the following: 'Didn't I already tell you that women should have a manual work? Didn't I already tell you that it is not good to be without work? Now lieutenant Prestat just announced that women would pay taxes by themselves, independent of their husbands. They shall work and find the means to pay it.[45]

And about those who fled:

> The white man [Prestat] told the king: 'I see that many people went away. It is not good that you, their king, shall stay at the same place. You must travel across the country and advise them to come back. The king considered those words. After the Ramadan festivities, the king went to the salty waters where he spent eighteen days. He then went to the bridge of King Mga Mfekam. Fifty servants accompanied him. When he arrived at the Bamum bridge, he found those who had fled. Hearing that it was he, King Njoya, they all came, hoping to see him. The king then sent his servant to them and told them the following: 'if you know that it is not me, the king who did you harm, but your chiefs, then come back to me.' After hearing that message, they came in large numbers.[46]

The transformation of the Bamum people into natives was therefore a joint effort of colonial officers and the sultan. But this could not be achieved without a steady dismantling of the whole economy of happiness on which his authority

---

45 216–217.
46 217.

was based, and its replacement by an economy of freedom albeit one still based on constraints and not on the fulfillment of people's rights. As a confidential note of the French colonial administration noted:

> Here we have a native potentate who had an absolute power, without any control, and whom the Germans left quite independent, with whom the British applied the same policy they do with sultans in Nigeria, and on whom the first French administrators had, it seems, a pretty weak influence, but whom Lieutenant Prestat set for the very first time in front of the hard realities.[47]

These 'hard realities' were part of the French colonial system. The destruction of Njoya's practice of gift-giving and the dismantling of the principle on which it was based was thus arrived at through a combination of the transformation of the population into wage earners, as was already started during the German rule, and of the sultan into a salaried auxiliary of the French colonial administration. That the king was not satisfied with his new position inside the colonial system can be read in his own account of one of his many public grudges with French colonials. Here is his report of a complaint he expressed to the French governor:

> Look, before, every year the Bamum would bring me provisions I used to feed the princes, my wives and the servants. Today the Bamum do not even accept to give food for my children. This is the reason why my riches are wearing out, and the reason why I would like to provide for myself. Had the governor not helped me by providing me with a salary of one thousand five hundred francs per year, what would I have done? And yet those thousand five hundred francs are not sufficient.[48]

Ironically, the multiple disruptions that followed the introduction of wages ensured the downfall of colonialism at the hands of its own brain child, nationalism, even though in the end both left the formal structure of the Bamum monarchy still standing as it does today. By establishing happiness and freedom as conceptual and historical opposites, Njoya re-writes the claim of freedom to be absolute even if he does not question the fact of its universality. More importantly, he transforms his land into an arena with philosophico-historical dimensions. The sultan narrates the unfolding of the conflict:

> One day troubles erupted in the country of the Bamum. The population was divided into two groups. Those who worked for the colonial administration were saying that people did not like the French, and the inhabitants, on the other hand, were saying that the work-

---

47 Claude Tardits, *Le Royaume Bamum*, op. cit., 986.
48 *Histoire*, 254.

ers of the administration did not like the king, that he is cruel, because when one gave them eight francs for a wedding, they asked for more money for themselves. And when they received that money, they would not show it to the white man. The people wanted that the translator be sacked. But the workers of the administration were opposed to it. It became a huge affair. M. Veauver sent a letter to M. Ripert, asking him to come and solve the issue. He had forty six people arrested and jailed for six months in Dschang.

Sooner or later, unhappy people revolt. The idea of the happy slave is an oxymoron that history has contradicted again and again. Since both freedom and happiness historically cancel each other out, they remain in a constant state of hunger and transform Fumban, the locus of their conflict into a perpetual battlefield. This surely is the most enduring lesson of Njoya's *Sang'aam*, and the key to its understanding of the Bamum people.

Works cited

Hegel, G.W.F. *Outline of the Philosophy of Right*. Oxford: Oxford University Press, 2008.
Martin, Henri. "Le Pays Bamum et le Sultan Njoya", in *Etudes Camerounaises*
    Septembre-Decembre, 31–32 (1950).
Marx, Karl. *The Capital*, Volume 1. London: Penguin, 1990.
Njoya, ed., *Histoire et Coutumes des Bamum*. Translated by Henri Martin. Yaounde: Ifan,
    1952.
Tardits, Claude. *Le Royaume Bamum*. Paris: Librairie Armand Colin, 1980.

Dotsé Yigbe
Is Togo a permanent Model Colony¹?

Togo's pronounced positive attitude towards its former colonial power, Germany, is intriguing considering that the German colonial era in Togo (1884–1914) was not rosy at all for the colonized people.² Besides this, there are a number of signs that qualify Togo to be an atypical case in the post-colonial era. These include the sudden and unexpected ending of the German colonial presence, the quick departure of the German colonial administration, suppliers and missionaries, the division of German-Togo into French and British parts, reinforced by declarations of independence by Ghana in 1957 and Togo in 1960. This series of historical and political events led to the creation of the staunch germanophile unions and to some extent, colonial and nostalgic associations that till now influence the political debate and the opinion of ordinary citizens when it comes to Togo's German colonial past as well as the relationship between the two former African colonies and the neighboring country, Ghana.

This article shows that the roots of Togo's attachment to Germany can be found in the post-German period of the country.

1. Warning voices from the scientific world

Four years after the centenary celebrations of the Germany-Togo friendship, the for historians fundamenta tudy *Togo 1884–1914 Eine Geschichte der deuschen "Musterkolonie" auf der Grundlage amtlicher Quellen (1988)* of the historian Peter Sebald was published by Berlin's Akademie-Verlag.

In his study, Sebald highlights four aspects of German colonial rule in Togo. Firstly, he shows that colonial rule is based on military power and the conquest of the regions, especially the hinterland, was achieved by way of military force.

---

1 This article is the actualised and illustrated English version of a text published in German some months ago in the Journal of CAMES.
2 See amongst others Peter Sebald, *Togo 1884–1914. Eine Geschichte der Musterkolonie auf der Grundlage amtlicher Quellen* (Berlin: Akademie-Verlag, 1988); Adjaï Paulin Oloukpona-Yinnon, "<<Devoir d'indignation>> – <<devoir de mémoire.>>: Prolégomènes à l'étude de la résistance des Togolais sous l'administration colonial allemande (1884–1914)," in *Le refus de l'ordre colonial en Afrique et au Togo (1884–1960)*, eds. Essoham Assima-Kpatcha and Koffi Nutefé Tsigbé (Lomé : Presses de l'UL, 2013), 161–183; Kuassi Ametowoyona Akakpo, *Discours et contre-discours sur le Togo sous l'empire allemand* (Paris: Le Manuscrit, 2014).

DOI 10.1515/9783110525625-005

So not only was the recognition of the political rule of the German empire was forced and made it possible to begin a campaign of colonial economic exploitation. Colonial rule came with its forms of justice, in which punishment methods used included beating, chained detention and hard labour. Secondly, all the factions of the German colonial rulers were involved in the economic plundering of Togo. The German administration and businesses were living at the expense of Togolese people, and therefore, the established German colony ensured not only huge profits to the German trade capitalists, but also covered administration costs through customs tax. This is how the economic foundations came to belaid for the legend of the Model Colony.

Third, the German colonization generated socio-economic changes and new social classes in Togo. It also changed the way the former social structures functioned through the machinery of power, such that traditional social orders were in complete disarray.

Fourth, the Togolese fiercely resisted the German colonial conquest, and after the establishment of the colonial system, the social African forces or a leading African middle class was created. This group opposed the German colonial masters because they were treated as second-class citizens without rights or individual civil freedoms and discriminated on the basis of race. In the beginning, the Togolese protest was not directed against the colonial system as much as against the arbitrary use of power by individual colonial civil officers. In the last few years prior to the First World War, anti- colonial writings by prominent Togolese figures appeared in African newspapers of the neighbouring colony of Gold Coast. These writings found an audience beyond the German colonies at an international level.

With Sebald's study, a turning point began in the scientific perception of the German "Model colony" and in Togo's historiography. Since the 1990s, various conferences were organized by historians and German scholars, during which German colonization in Togo was debated, and, subsequently, a few volumes have been published.

In addition, historical monographs referred to Sebald and this discussion moved into the broader public and into politics, and viewed Togo's German past critically.

At the end of 1990s, a colloquium on the conquering of the hinterland and the establishment of German colonial power over Togo was organized. In this colloquium, the different stages of the conquering, the so-called stages of pacification, the submission of the northern Togo kingdoms and the brutal suppression of rebellions became matters of discussion[3]. The last two conferences addressed the anticolonial uprising in Togo during the German colonial era[4] and the end of German colonial power in the First World War.[5] Among the many monographs, that of Kuassi A. Akakpo (2014) not only denounces the misuse of power by the colonial administration, but also shows how the historical facts of the German colonization have been covered up officially by political or ideological opinion. The resulting scientific opinion distorted the hard realities of German colonial power in favour of a romantic legend of the model-colony.

2. The African assistants of the North German mission as forerunners

For some years now, a debate has raged on why the majority of Togolese have a positive attitude toward German colonization and are not critical (1884–1914).[6] This debate does not take into account German evangelical missionaries who worked for decades in the West African Gold Coast before colonization officially began. Despite their sudden departure during the First World War and the division of their working areas, these missionaries have still maintained contact with the evangelical Presbyterian Church in Togo and Ghana of today.

At the former so-called Slave Coast, the German protestant Missionaries in the Lutheran tradition endeavored to master the native Ewe-tongue as much as possible. They then collected, transcribed and translated proverbs, folktales, songs as well as other forms of expressions from the Ewe-tradition into German. Ethnographic studies on different aspects of social life were conducted and a book on Ewe-grammar and Ewe dictionary written. The Bible was translated into Ewe, which became a major part of Togo's intellectual heritage.

The Protestant missionary society, especially the Norddeutsche Mission, that opened the first missionary station in the southern part of the current Togo and Ghana, in the middle of the 19th century in order to bring Christianity to Africa were of the view that the Lutheran translation turned the Bible into a folk book

---

[3] See Badjow Tcham and K. Thiou Tchamie, eds., *L'intégration de l'hinterland à la colonie du Togo* (Lomé: Presses de l'UB, 2000).
[4] See Assima-Kpatcha and Tsigbé, *Le refus de l'ordre colonial en Afrique et au Togo (1884–1960)*, op. cit.
[5] Koffi Nutefé Tsigbé and Dotsé Yigbe, *Août 1914 – août 2014: Bilan de l'oeuvre coloniale allemande en Afrique et au Togo, cent ans après* (Lomé: Presses de l'UL, 2015).
[6] See Oloukpona-Yinnon, "<<Devoir d'indignation>>," *art. cit.*

and laid the basis for public education. The Lutheran translation is considered a success story in Europe by the missionaries that other groups want to replicate in Africa. Since many African people in the region of the Norddeutsche Mission were speaking the Ewe-language, the Bible had to be translated into it. But, this translation of the Bible into the unwritten Ewe-language turned out to be much more challenging than the reformation translation. The German missionaries in Togo had to translate the Bible into the Ewe-language; a language in which Christian ideas had not yet been thought about or written. Furthermore, being a foreign language to the missionaries, they had to master it within a few years to accurately translate the message of the Bible. In order to do so, they had to depend on the support of Togolese assistants who became exceptionally important in the translation of the Bible into the Ewe-language.[7]

In Togo, right from the beginning, missionaries had established schools in which Togolese children and youth were educated. Some of these youth had been even sent to Germany, where they were educated between 1884 and 1900, first in Ochsenbach and then in Westheim in the Deutsche-Ewe-Schule.[8] These Togolese youth became teachers, evangelists, catechists and pastors after completing their education. They not only worked as employees for missionaries in established secondary stations, but they also served as reliable evangelists, who were integral to spreading Christianity and western culture even after the departure of the missionaries.

During their education in Germany and their participation in the missionary activities on behalf of their own people and in the transcription of their native language, they served as transmitters between the German and the African indigenous culture and as well as between the German metropolis and its colony Togo. Since the educated youth were the representatives of the Togolese, when the missionary message came through them, it was mostly well received, which was crucial for the development of German-Togolese relationships.

---

[7] Dotsé Yigbe, "Von Gewährsleuten zu Gehilfen und Gelehrigen. Der Beitrag afrikanischer Mitarbeiter zur Entstehung einer verschrifteten Kultur in Deutsch-Togo," in *Mission global. Eine Verflechtungsgeschichte seit dem 19. Jahrhundert*, eds. Rebekka Habermas and Richard Hölzl (Köln, Weimar, Wien: Böhlau Verlag, 2014), 159–175.

[8] Kokou Azamede, *Transkulturationen? Ewe-Christen zwischen Deutschland und Westafrika 1884–1939* (Stuttgart: Franz Steiner Verlag, 2010), 39–224.

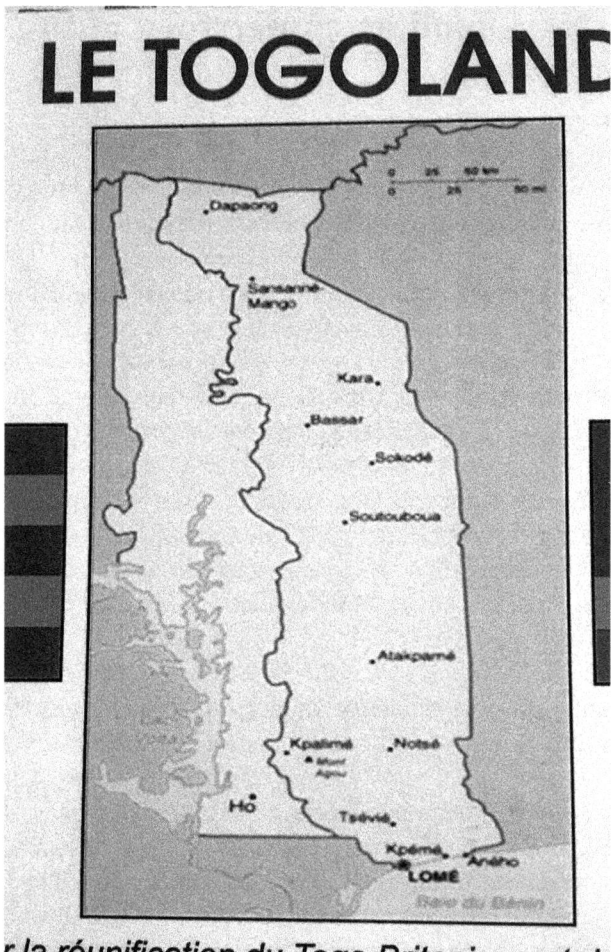

Map of Togo during the German colonization (1884–1914)

3. The Deutsch-Togo-Bund as cornerstone of the germanophilia in Togo

In 1984, the centenary celebrations marking "100 years of German-Togolese Friendship" was a big affair. The Togolese government seized the opportunity to shed light on the close relationship between the late president Eyadema and Franz J. Strauss, the prime minister of Bavaria and the speaker of the German Senate. Strauss was seen by the Togolese authority as the representative of the German government and consequently as the legacy of German Empire. Thus, Togo belongs to acquisitions of the northern German tradespeople and missionaries that were established after the 1884 Congo-conference under the protection of the German Empire. It was after this conference that the current borders to the south, east and north of Togo were established. The border in the west, that underwent changes during the First World War after the departure of the German colonial managers, was clearly demarcated under the Versailles treaty and after the division of German-Togo between France and England. Present-day Togo is the eastern French zone and the so-called British Togo is now part of the Republic of Ghana.

The 100th commemoration (in 1984) of the first arrival of the Germans in Togo (1884) was not meant only to celebrate the signing of the agreement between Togo and Germany; but also that of all events after the sudden departure of the Germans.

The former employees of the German missionaries[9] and colonial managers reacted in 1924 against the partition of Togo and what was seen as anti-German decisions[10] through the foundation of an association, the *Deutsch-Togo-Bund*. The objectives of this group have changed over time except for solidarity with Germany which remains a constant. This association has contributed greatly to the phenomenon of germanophilia in Togo.[11]

In the early 1920s, the association requested the reunification of East-Togo (56, 000 km^2) and West-Togo (33, 000 km^2) and the return of German tradespeo-

---

[9] Paul Wiegräbe, "Zwischen den Zeiten," in *150 Jahre Norddeutsche Mission 1836–1986* (Bremen: Norddeutsche Mission, 1986), 104–112.
[10] Komlan Kouzan, "La germanophobie française au Togo de 1920 A 1939," *Annales de l'Université de Lomé, Série Lettres, Tome XXXI–1*, Juin 2011, 211–231.
[11] Komlan Kouzan, "Quelle contribution du Deutsch-Togo-Bund à la fête du 27 avril 1960 au Togo?" in *Les indépendances en Afrique. L'événement et ses mémoires 1957/1960–2010*, eds. Odile Goerg, Jean-Luc Martineau and Didier Nativel (Rennes: Presses Universitaires de Rennes, 2013), 112.

ple, missionaries and colonial managers to Togo. In a sense, the association functions as a cultural protest movement that exists regardless of the divisions that split the former German colony. In the 1930s, the Deutsch-Togo-Bund claimed to have its roots in National Socialism.[12]

The partition and occupation of Germany at the end of Second World War by the Allies strengthened the dependence of Deutsch-Togo-Bund on the Federal Republic of Germany. However, in the 1940s the Deutsch-Togo-Bund rejected all nationalist offers for autonomy and instead worked with the national Union party Committee of Togolese Unity (CUT), whose leader Sylvanus Olympio later became the first president of independent Togo. Olympio was also a very committed member of the Deutsch-Togo-Bund.[13]

At the end of the 1950s, one of the co-founders of the association, Johannes Kofi A. Agboka (1893–1972) founded the so-called Togobundschule in order to offer German education to Togolese youth.[14] This was after the declaration of the independence of Ghana and in reaction to the imminent declaration of independence of Togo.

Togo declared independence on the April 27, 1960 and soon after because of the strained local political situation and the declarations of annexation by Nkrumah and the strong French influence, the Deutsch-Togo-Bund was better structured. In addition to the German school, that in the honor of the last German Governor was called 'Herzog-Adolf-Friedrich-Schule', the Deutsch-Togo-Bund had secured a logo with the meaningful inscription "Deutsch-Togo-Bund", as an advocate of German- loyal Togolese people. A branch of this association was founded in Germany with Stuttgart-based Günter Hermann as its director in the 1960s. Regular correspondence and communication with the German branch as well as with the German and Togolese authorities existed at this time. The mission as set by the German section of the association led by Günter Hermann, Vice-President of Deutsch-Togo-Bund included:

---

12 Helmut Stoecker, "Germanophilie und Hoffnung auf Hitler in Togo und Kamerun zwischen den Weltkriegen," in *Studien zur Geschichte des deutschen Kolonialismus in Afrika. Festschrift zum 60. Geburtstag von Peter Sebald,* eds. Peter Heine and Ulrich v. d. Heyden (Pfaffenweiler: Centaurus, 1995), 496.
13 Film DVD Ablodé (Freedom), 2010.
14 Dapou Ph. Napo-Issa and Adjaï Paulin Oloukpona-Yinnon, "Wir Togoleute wollen gern 'rassisch' Neger, aber technisch deutsch bleiben": Profession de foi de Johann Kofi A. Agboka (1893–1972), Fondateur du "Deutsch-Togo-Bund"," in *Plumes allemandes. Biographies et autobiographies africaines („Afrikaner erzählen ihr Leben"),* eds. A. P. Oloukpona-Yinnon and J. Riesz (Lomé: Presses de l'UL, 2003), 281–282.

- becoming member of Deutsch-Togo-Bund in the 11 states of the Federal Republic of Germany;
- looking for sponsorships in the Federal Republic of Germany for Togolese students from Herzog-Adolf-Friedrich-Schule;
- publishing the German- loyal Togolese people's newspaper in Stuttgart (see letter from Hermann to Agboka in Agboka family archiv dated 14–5–1962)

The claims of Deutsch-Togo-Bund in the early 1960s were closely related to the political events in Germany and Togo. They proved to be an illusory reaction to the partition of the country through the building of the Berlin wall and the declarations of independence of both parts of former German-Togo.

A letter from Vice-president Günter Hermann of Deutsch-Togo-Bund to the President Johannes A. Agboka says, "The Togoland should again become a member of the German family of the peoples! We were a people and we want to become again a people!" Most likely, Hermann was indirectly linking the status of East-Togo to that of East Germany since in both cases they were divided and the hope is to come together as a reunited country.

In fact, no one in Germany has taken these claims seriously except for a few who are nostalgic about colonial power. But this declaration is part of the so-called 'Sofortprogramm des Deutsch-Togo-Bund', of April 27, 1962 that was summed up in six points:

i) The Deutsch-Togo-Bund decided that the Republic of Togo/West Africa becomes a free-state of the Republic of Germany;
ii) The fusion of the Republic of Togo and the Republic of Germany should not be viewed as a way back to colonialism, but a further evidence that the German people and Togolese people suffer no difference of race;
iii) The free-state Togo becomes the twelfth state in the Republic of Germany and will be administered by the Togolese. Only on the matters of foreign and defense policy, Togo will remain under the supervision of the Republic of Germany;
iv) The free-state Togo controls the export and import activities within the country. French suppliers and whole salers would be stripped of business ties, compensated and sent out of the country. The French suppliers are parasites, scroungers of the Togolese people;
v) the Republic of Germany takes on responsibility for the economic development of Togoland. The structuring of Lomé's harbour, the extension of the railway line up to Mango, the reconstruction of the railway line into the 1-metre-gauge European standard; and

vi) the Prime Minister, ministers, teachers, wholesalers, suppliers, craftspeople will all be Togolese. Togo does not need French capitalists and pro-French ministers. German language will be introduced again.

Viewed from the German perspective, this program appears to be colonial revenge. This is contrary to the Treaty of Versailles, signed at the end of the First World War, but with the difference that Togo is no longer unlawfully conquered, but would decide through a vote whether Togo should become the twelfth federal German state or not. But in fact, the Germans were indirectly pulling the strings to maintain a strong relationship with Togo.

Viewed from the Togolese perspective, this immediate program is a matter of concern for a country that has just become independent. But, this was just a reaction from a powerless association that could not bring East and West Togo together. This is due mainly to the misunderstanding between the former political parties and the perceptible influence of the French colonial power.

4. Political exploitation of germanophilia in the 1970s and 1980s in Togo

In the deteriorating situation brought about by the murder of the pro-German President Sylvanus Olympio, the idea of Deutsch-Togo-Bund was partly illusory and an expression of the Togolese people's need for order and discipline. Sylvanus Olympio was the hope of the germanophile Togolese people, because he had a good relationship with Germany during the process of the country's independence.[15] His assassination on January 13, 1963 under suspicious circumstances shocked the Togolese people. The former sergeant Etienne Eyadema, who belonged to the section carried out the murder and claimed responsibility for the putsch. As a result, he based his power on the military mainly from his ethnic group who were trained by the French army officers.

In addition to the geopolitical situation in the 1970s and 1980s in the West African region and his ideologically pro-Western attitude, Eyadema's German-friendly policy along with his close relationship with the former Bavarian Prime Minister Franz Josef Strauss were inspired by tactical reflections. This pro-German policy enabled him to maintain a link to the Togolese people.

---

15 Atsutsè Kokouvi Agbobli and Sylvanus Olympio, *Le Père de l'indépendance togolaise* (Lomé: Graines de Pensées, 2007), 232–239.

DEUTSCH-TOGO-BUND
Organ der deutschtreuen Togoleute
Sektion Deutschland

Schirmherr: Seine Hoheit Herzog Adolf Friedrich zu Mecklenburg
Ehrenpräsident: Seine Durchlaucht Fürst Franz Joseph von Thurn und Taxis

**VIZEPRÄSIDENT
GÜNTER HERRMANN**
Träger des Deutsch-Togo-Bund-Ordens
Leiter der Sektion Deutschland
Direktor der Deutsch-Togolesischen-
Ausbildungsstätte (DTA)

STUTTGART, 29. Juli 1968
Postscheckkonto:
Stuttgart Nr. 191 31
Telefon:
Briefanschrift:
7 Stuttgart-Weilimdorf
Postfach 82

ZAHL 893/68
Bei Beantwortung bitten wir um Angabe obiger Zahl

Einschreiben

Herrn
Präsidenten des "Deutsch-Togo-Bundes"
Schulleiter Johannes A. A g b o k a

L o m é , Republik Togo, Westafrika

P. O. B o x 106

Sehr geehrter Herr Präsident !

Am Samstag, den 23. September 1967, traten alle Herren der Bundesleitung des "Deutsch-Togo-Bundes", Sektion Deutschland, in Stuttgart zusammen und gründeten die DEUTSCH-TOGOLESISCHE-AUSBILDUNGSSTÄTTE (DTA). Zum Direktor der DEUTSCH-TOGOLESISCHEN-AUSBILDUNGSSTÄTTE (DTA) wurde ich berufen.

In der DEUTSCH-TOGOLESISCHEN-AUSBILDUNGSSTÄTTE (DTA) soll jungen deutschen und togolesischen Jugendlichen im Alter von 16 bis 18 Jahren eine Fachausbildung ermöglicht werden.

Schüler der deutsch-togolesischen "Herzog Adolf Friedrich - Schule" aus Lomé werden bevorzugt in die DEUTSCH-TOGOLESISCHE-AUSBILDUNGSSTÄTTE (DTA) aufgenommen.

Verhandlungen mit der "Fürstlich Thurn und Taxisschen Domänenkammer" über eine Übereignung des fürstlichen Schlosses Sulzheim an die DEUTSCH-TOGOLESISCHE-AUSBILDUNGSSTÄTTE (DTA) sind vorerst gescheitert. Die Bundesleitung des "Deutsch-Togo-Bundes", Sektion Deutschland, hofft aber zuversichtlich, daß die DEUTSCH-TOGOLESISCHE-AUSBILDUNGSSTÄTTE (DTA) noch in diesem Jahr eine Heimstätte im süddeutschen Raum finden wird.

bitte wenden

Letter from the Vice-president Günter Hermann of Deutsch-Togo-Bund to the President Johannes A. Agboka (July 1968)

The above-mentioned commemoration of the hundred-year jubilee of the German-Togolese relationship reached its climax on July 6, 1984 in the presence

Is Togo a permanent Model Colony? — 107

Monument of German-Togolese Friendship in Togoville (1984)

of the Bavarian Prime Minister Strauss during which Eyadema delivered a speech and reminded him of the agreement of July 5, 1884. This agreement had marked the beginning of a successful cooperation between Togo and Germany as well as a friendship that was maintained despite the two World Wars and the subsequent political and economic crises that followed it. Before he acknowledged the achievement of his German friends in many areas during the colonial and post-colonial period in Togo, Eyadema praised German colonization in Togo and again revived colonial myths connected to Togo.

> Nous sommes heureux de constater que l'action courageuse et méthodique que les Allemands de bonne volonté ont menée au Togo pendant cette période [1884–1914] qui hélas fut de courte durée, a profondément marqué notre pays et laissé dans la mémoire du Peuple, des souvenirs qui suscitent encore de nos jours une vive nostalgie aussi bien chez les jeunes qu'auprès des témoins de cette époque. En effet, les trente années pendant lesquelles l'Allemagne a administré le Togo ont permis aux Togolais d'apprécier à l'œuvre, le génie, le savoir-faire, le courage et la volonté des Allemands qui ont su hisser notre pays au rang d'une colonie modèle et d'un Etat pilote en Afrique. Mais le grand mérite de l'administration allemande est d'avoir su développer chez nos populations, l'esprit d'initiative, le goût du travail bien fait, l'ordre et la discipline sans lesquels aucune nation ne pourrait mobiliser ses forces vives et conduire ses propres destinées.[16]

Besides this revival of the German colonial past, the occasion was marked by the obvious silence of Togolese exiled politicians who had not only tried to overthrow the Eyadema-regime, but also were known for taking a stand when it came to important events in Togo. These exiled Togolese constantly denounced the constant interference of the French government in African internal affairs and especially in the local affairs of the Togolese. They also made it a point to denounce military support of the French army to dictatorial and corrupt African regimes. The close relationship between Eyadema and French politicians was criticized as a neocolonial relationship of the hated Françafrique.

---

16 Nouvelle Marche N° 176 du 7.7.1984, 4. English translation: We are happy to notice the courageous action and method that the Germans of goodwill have undertaken in Togo during the short period (1884–1914) which has profoundly affected our country and has left good memories in the Togolese, the memoire that still arouse nostalgia in both the young of today and the old who experienced German colonization. Indeed, the thirty years during which Germany colonized Togo enabled the Togolese to appreciate at work, the genius, the expertise, the courage and the will of Germans who have lifted up our country to the rank of model colony and a pilot state in Africa. But, the great merit of the German administration is to have developed among our population, the spirit of initiative, the taste of good work, order and discipline without which no nation can mobilize its vigorous forces and secure its destiny. (My own translation D.Y.)

Friendship with Germany was a fundamental consensus in Togo's politics.[17] President Eyadema's speech reflected the prevailing trend of Germanophilia in a tactical and populist manner. In fact, the unexpected departure of German colonial rulers on August 27, 1914, three weeks after the beginning of the First World War, and the occupation of the German-Togo colony by the French and British troops prevented both the German and the Togolese from going through an appropriate process of decolonization. This could be seen as a contributing factor in activism such as that of the Deutsch-Togo-Bund that came later.

With Deutsch-Togo-Bund's campaign against the continuous presence of the French who were seen as the enemy of the people, germanophilia took on a consensus in Togo. This prompted the pro-German speech delivered by the late president Eyadema on the occasion of the hundred-year jubilee of the so-called German-Togolese Friendship and also explains the silence of the otherwise voluble exiled Togolese politicians.

Conclusion

Today, the Deutsch-Togo-Bund no longer exists in the original form, even though from time to time some association groups define themselves as the successors of the German- loyal Togolese people.

There are associations with names that reflect decades of German friendship including Verein Deutsche Freunde, Association of German speaking people, DESKTO (Community of German speaking people in Togo), ASTRA (Association of Togolese Trainees from Germany), and so on. As cultural associations, they are completely apolitical.

However, in French-Togo as well as in former British-Togo, movements or associations which campaign for the reunification of the two parts of former German-Togo do exist. Each group knows about the existence of its counterpart beyond the border between Ghana and Togo. But their activities are not coordinated. In Togo, the association called *Mouvement National pour l'Unification du Togo Britannique & Togo Français* (MNUT) pushes for the reunification of East-Togo and West-Togo. A press conference scheduled for April 16, 2016 in Hotel Sarakawa was officially postponed sine die on the grounds of security. In Ghana, the movement is based on the 1956 agreement under the auspices of the former UN General Secretary, according to which British-Togo should

---

[17] Kouzan, "Quelle contribution du Deutsch-Togo-Bund à la fête du 27 avril 1960 au Togo?" *art. cit.*, 112.

take part in the so-called Union Government after 50 years. Today, the movement fights for the separation of the Volta region from Ghana and its restitution to Togo. Unlike the Togolese movement MNUT, the ethnic Ghanaian movement demands a connection to the Ewe-people. The two movements' common demand is that the current border between the two countries be reconsidered. A reasonable management of this colonial legacy goes beyond a West African regional integration.

Works cited

Agbobli, Atsutsè Kokouvi 2007, *Sylvanus Olympio. Le Père de l'indépendance togolaise*, Lomé: Graines de Pensées.
Akakpo, Kuassi Ametowoyona 2014, *Discours et contre-discours sur le Togo sous l'empire allemand*, Paris: Le Manuscrit.
Assima-Kpatcha, Essoham & Tsigbé, Koffi Nutefé (ed.) 2013, *Le refus de l'ordre colonial en Afrique et au Togo (1884–1960)*, Lomé : Presses de l'UL.
Azamede, Kokou 2010, *Transkulturationen? Ewe-Christen zwischen Deutschland und Westafrika 1884–1939*, Stuttgart: Franz Steiner Verlag.
Film DVD Ablodé (Freedom), 2010
Kouzan, Komlan 2011, "La germanophobie française au Togo de 1920 A 1939" in *Annales de l'Université de Lomé, Série Lettres, Tome XXXI-1*, Juin 2011, pp.211–231.
Kouzan, Komlan 2013, "Quelle contribution du Deutsch-Togo-Bund à la fête du 27 avril 1960 au Togo?" in Odile Goerg, Jean-Luc Martineau et Didier Nativel (dir.), *Les indépendances en Afrique. L'événement et ses mémoires 1957/1960–2010*, Rennes: Presses Universitaires de Rennes, p. 97–115.
Napo-Issa, Dapou Ph. & Oloukpona-Yinnon, Adjaï Paulin 2003, "Wir Togoleute wollen gern 'rassisch' Neger, aber technisch deutsch bleiben": Profession de foi de Johann Kofi A. Agboka (1893–1972), Fondateur du "Deutsch-Togo-Bund"" in A. P. Oloukpona-Yinnon & J. Riesz (dir.), *Plumes allemandes. Biographies et autobiographies africaines („Afrikaner erzählen ihr Leben")*, Lomé: Presses de l'UL, S. 271–284.
Oloukpona-Yinnon, Adjaï Paulin 2013, "<<Devoir d'indignation>> – <<devoir de mémoire.>>: Prolégomènes à l'étude de la résistance des Togolais sous l'administration colonial allemande (1884–1914)" in Assima-Kpatcha, Essoham & Tsigbé, Koffi Nutefé (ed.) 2013, *Le refus de l'ordre colonial en Afrique et au Togo (1884–1960)*, Lomé : Presses de l'UL, p. 161–183.
Sebald, Peter 1988, *Togo 1884–1914. Eine Geschichte der Musterkolonie auf der Grundlage amtlicher Quellen*. Berlin: Akademie-Verlag.
Stoecker, Helmut 1995, "Germanophilie und Hoffnung auf Hitler in Togo und Kamerun zwischen den Weltkriegen" in Peter Heine/Ulrich v. d. Heyden (Hg.), *Studien zur Geschichte des deutschen Kolonialismus in Afrika. Festschrift zum 60. Geburtstag von Peter Sebald*, Pfaffenweiler: Centaurus, S. 495–500.
Tcham, Badjow & Tchamie, K. Thiou (dir.) 2000, *L'intégration de l'hinterland à la colonie du Togo*, Lomé: Presses de l'UB.

Tsigbé, Koffi Nutefé & Yigbe, Dotsé 2015, *Août 1914 – août 2014: Bilan de l'oeuvre coloniale allemande en Afrique et au Togo, cent ans après*, Lomé: Presses de l'UL.

Wiegräbe, Paul 1986, "Zwischen den Zeiten" in Eva Schöck-Quinteros u. Dieter Lenz (Hg.), *150 Jahre Norddeutsche Mission 1836 – 1986*, Bremen: Norddeutsche Mission, S. 104–112.

Yigbe, Dotsé 2014, "Von Gewährsleuten zu Gehilfen und Gelehrigen. Der Beitrag afrikanischer Mitarbeiter zur Entstehung einer verschrifteten Kultur in Deutsch-Togo" in Rebekka Habermas, Richard Hölzl (Hg.), *Mission global. Eine Verflechtungsgeschichte seit dem 19. Jahrhundert*, Köln, Weimar, Wien: Böhlau Verlag, S. 159–175.

Werner Hillebrecht[1]
Monuments – and what else? The Controversial Legacy of German Colonialism in Namibia

> "German monuments are everywhere.
> We are trying to create our own monuments."
>
> President Hage Geingob on 5 April 2016[2]

In discussing the 'cultural legacy' of German colonialism in Namibia, the seemingly obvious starting points are the rather symbolic presences, and absences: the presence of colonial monuments remaining in Namibia, and the absence of human remains removed to Germany. Both are highly symbolic and emotionally charged markers representing the impact of German colonialism on the country and its inhabitants. Without touching on the issue of human remains and their repatriation, which is also a wider issue of ethical approach to science, pseudoscience and museology,[3] this contribution will proceed from the discussion of monuments to other German "remnants" and their historical context, which is not always as straightforward as it appears on first sight. It will explore their touristic marketing as well as the seemingly paradoxical manifestations in indigenous cultures. The discussion closes with the socio-economic impact of colonialism which is, as shall be seen, the bedrock of the far-reaching cultural impact of the German colonial intervention in Namibia.

1. The Rider: "…and shall forever be?"

The two-phased removal of the Rider Monument from its prominent position above the Windhoek Central Business District has been a much-debated issue

---

[1] werner.hillebrecht@gmail.com. The author was involved in solidarity activities for Namibian independence in Germany, and compiling a comprehensive Namibian bibliography, since 1978. From 1992 until his retirement in 2015, he worked alternatingly at the National Library and the National Archives of Namibia. He lives in Windhoek as a free-lance consultant on history and heritage.

[2] As reported in "The Namibian Sun" of 6 April 2006, p.1.

[3] About this topic, see Stoecker, Holger, Thomas Schnalke, Andreas Winkelmann (ed.). *Sammeln, Erforschen, Zurückgeben? Menschliche Gebeine aus der Kolonialzeit in akademischen und musealen Sammlungen*. Berlin: C.H. Links, 2013.

DOI 10.1515/9783110525625-006

in Namibia. Despite objections from the tourism industry (arguing that it was the most-visited and most-photographed landmark for German tourists), and objections coming from some of the descendants of the Namibian genocide survivors (arguing that it was a highly visible reminder of the genocide), the consensus was that it should be moved from its prominent position. The triumphalist monument was inaugurated in 1912 by the German Governor who said "The brazen rider of the Schutztruppe shall look from this place in the future across this country and tell the world that we are the masters here and shall forever be".[4] The statue had occupied the central place between four other German monuments—the *Alte Feste*, Windhoek's oldest surviving building, erected as a military fort in 1891, and now a museum under renovation; the *Kaiserliche Realschule*, now the headquarters of the National Museum; the *Christuskirche* German Lutheran Church, inaugurated in 1908; and the *Tintenpalast*, the administrative building from 1913 which today serves as the Namibian Parliament.[5] Now the centre-piece of this ensemble is the towering Independence Memorial Museum, which embodies the contradictions of much of Namibia's (and Africa's) memorial culture: while the idea is approved, the execution of it is faces criticism as non-African, and imposing a foreign (to be specific: North Korean) style language upon what should be an expression of Namibian creativity.[6]

Namibia's colonial history provides the context to understand these events. The country, once called German South West Africa was colonized by the German Empire in a series of military campaigns between 1884–1914, culminating in the genocidal war of 1904–1907, and lost again after only thirty years in the First World War against invading South African troops. By then, it had become a settler colony, and that is what distinguishes it from other former German colonies where German relics might be viewed with a certain sense of nostalgia. The Versailles Peace Conference handed the colony as a League of Nations C-Mandate to the British Crown, to be administered by South Africa, with almost no restrictions, replacing one colonial master with another. South Africa ruled Nami-

---

[4] As reported in "Der Südwestbote" of 31 January 1912.
[5] A quite comprehensive—although nostalgic and apologetic—overview of the monument's history is provided by: Kuiseb Verlag. *The Equestrian Monument (Reiterdenkmal) 1912–2014. A chronological documentation of reports, newspaper clippings and photos/illustrations*. Windhoek: Kuiseb Verlag, 2014.
[6] Not only the architectural design and construction work, but also details of ornamentation and interior design were done by the Korean firm Mansudae Overseas, which specialises in monumental objects in Africa (and elsewhere).

bia for 75 further years and relinquished control only in 1990 after a sustained and escalating liberation war that lasted almost 25 years.[7]

2. Integration into Apartheid Policies

Nevertheless, the relatively short German colonial period is perceived as having shaped the face of present-day Namibia in many ways as President Hage Geingob pointed out in the quote at the beginning of this article. There is a widespread sense of weariness about the perceived preponderance of German relics in Namibia—from street names, war graves, and architectural remains, to the much-publicised Rider monument, which has now been relegated from its previous location to the courtyard of a museum.

As it often happens with such popular perceptions, different issues and phenomena are conflated into one. Many of the monuments and street names and other details that serve as reminders of German rule in Namibia do not actually originate from the German colonial period, although they might be inspired by the wish to glorify that period. For instance, Windhoek's suburb Pioneerspark, which was established only in the 1950s, had all streets named after white so-called "pioneers"—mostly Germans who are so obscure that it requires serious historical research to establish any details about them.

Furthermore, the stiff and awkward statue of Curt von François, a Prussian officer of Huguenot origin and the alleged founder of the capital city, Windhoek was only erected in 1965 in front of the town hall. In fact, Windhoek was not founded by von François when he arrived in 1890, but had been established as an urban settlement about 50 years earlier by the Orlam leader Jonker Afrikaner, who also gave the town its Cape Dutch name.[8] Nevertheless, right until Namibian independence the City of Windhoek maintained the fiction that it had been founded by a white man.

The origins of the François monument and the "pioneer" street names have the same rationale. During the height of apartheid, from the 1950s to the 1960s, the history of Namibia was being actively sanitized to become solely the white man's history. The Historical Monuments Commission, later renamed the National Monuments Council, placed a disproportionate number of German period sites

---

[7] The most comprehensive and authoritative overview of Namibian history is provided by Wallace, Marion. *A history of Namibia from the beginning to 1990*. London: Hurst, 2011.
[8] Lau, Brigitte. *Namibia in Jonker Afrikaner's time*. Windhoek: National Archives, 1987, p.33. – The Orlam were Nama-speaking communities of mixed origin from South Africa who moved northwards into central and southern Namibia in the 19th century.

and buildings, along with pre-colonial settler and missionary relics, under protection, while almost completely neglecting indigenous historical sites and relics.[9]

This attitude was epitomized in the National Museum's (known as the State Museum before independence) dichotomy of exhibitions: the old German Fort built for Curt von Francois' soldiers housed a "historical" exhibition celebrating the White Man's coming and a "cultural" exhibition of the furniture and household implements of settlers. Visitors were also greeted at the entrance by a portrait bust of Emperor Wilhelm II. In contrast, the black people of Namibia were relegated to a different museum location further down the road and were depicted in diorama exhibits of "tribal life" set in a timeless ethnographic present, alongside wildlife dioramas portraying the different ecological zones of Namibia. History did not have a place in these exhibits.

These pre-independence perceptions, which to a large extent were preserved and perpetuated well into Namibian independence, highlight a legacy of German cultural influence that remains divisive—one that is selective as well as ahistorical. It reflects an insistence on the German character of a former colony, alluding to the "good old times" of Emperor Wilhelm and the alleged economic development and peace brought about by German colonization. It is this image, this façade that is reinforced by the monuments, buildings, and names which invariably turn up in travel guides and popular magazine articles about Namibia. It is further reinforced by a burgeoning literature dealing in colonial nostalgia, mostly in German language and therefore not noticed and consumed by the wider Namibian public, copiously illustrated from the rich pictorial archives of colonialism.

This façade serves various functions. Firstly, it boosts the tourism industry, one of Namibia's biggest foreign exchange earners. While these colonial remnants might not be the main reason that tourists visit Namibia, they are an added bonus because they function as a reassuring factor to visitors that this is a safe country. "Africa for beginners" is a term that is often used to refer to Namibia. Even in instances when the tourist narrative is not framed by colonial nostalgia, these relics serve to add an exotic touch, in the same manner that a sundowner picnic on a Kalahari sand dune with cold champagne and fresh oysters might. It is a reminder that one can order an *Eisbein* in a restaurant without needing a dictionary.

Secondly, the colonial relics also reassure the German-speaking locals of their privileged place in society to the present day. Statistically speaking, they

---

9 See Vogt, Andreas. *National Monuments in Namibia*. Windhoek: Gamsberg Macmillan, 2004.

represent the wealthiest section of the population and despite being a minority of less than 20,000 people, economically they hold an important position and are very visible.

As detailed before, apart from a few public sculptures and an interesting architectural heritage in some places, much of the perceived German characteristics, are not a direct relic of the short period of German colonialism but rather a result of several immigration waves from Germany *after* the German colonial period. These include in particular economic refugees that migrated after the First and Second World Wars. These refugees were welcomed by the South African colonial power to boost white hegemony in the region. Highly visible gestures, including using German street names assisted in the effort to integrate the German-speaking settlers into the fold of apartheid policies, and creating a sense of continuity of colonial rule in the spirit of white brotherhood against a black majority. This continuity was briefly halted for a few years during the Second World War, when a sizeable majority of German speakers were interned as enemy aliens suspected of being a Fifth Column of Nazi Germany's war effort, and threatened with deportation after the war. Eventually, they were allowed to stay in the country due to the efforts of the National Party of South Africa—an effort which greatly helped the National Party secure a parliamentary majority in 1948 so that it could raise the existing racist policies to a significantly higher level under the policies of *apartheid*.

3. The Cradle of Apartheid?

The ideological underpinnings of this continuity of colonialism from German to South African rule were embodied in the patriarchal figure of missionary Heinrich Vedder. When he arrived in Namibia and worked at Swakopmund in 1905, he was still horrified by the conditions in the town's concentration camp, about which he reported back to the mission society in graphic detail.[10] But he soon assimilated into the white settler society and became the most influential local ideologue of colonialism. In the 1920s, he was asked by the South African administration to write a history of the country, which he wrote with a preconceived idea of the civilising mission of the white man. It depicted the settlers as peacemakers who were in Namibia to bring about peace between genocidal warring tribes, who needed the firm hand of the Europeans to restore harmony.

---

10 Archiv- und Missionsstiftung Wuppertal. Archiv der Rheinischen Mission. RMG 1660a Vedder, Heinrich, Dr.Dr.h.c. 1876–1972

The book's original German version has been continually reprinted ever since, and a new reprint of the English translation was published in 2016. It earned him not only two honorary doctorates from the Universities of Tübingen and Stellenbosch, but also the everlasting gratitude of both German and South African settlers and the South African government.

Vedder was also influential in training black teachers with his version of history, and writing school textbooks in local languages, with the result that later efforts to collect oral history from Namibians sometimes resulted in memorised verbatim citations from his books. In 1951, he was appointed to the Senate, the second chamber of the South African Parliament, to represent "the Natives of South West Africa". There Vedder's most notable contribution was a speech where he praised apartheid and proudly proclaimed that it had been invented by the Germans, and that "in South West Africa we have the only country in the world where apartheid has been exercised in an increasing degree since 50 years" and, can you believe it, the "Europeans and non-Europeans are pleased about those apartheid laws". [11]

It would be unfair towards the missionaries to contend that this callous attitude was generally shared by his brothers in Christ. But there is no doubt that missionaries accommodated the apartheid ideology up until the 1970s when the African clergy had begun to speak out against oppression and South African rule. A few missionaries supported them and were promptly deported by the South African authorities.

However, when speaking of German cultural influences, it cannot be denied that the Christian missionaries from Germany, who arrived long before colonialism took the form of territorial claims, shared the attitude that the culture of the indigenous Africans needed to be destroyed and replaced with European ideas and ideals. The extent of this delusion that they harboured about their idea of salvation is summed up in the following citation by the Director of the Mission Trade Society, F.A. Spiecker,

"What the trade did not achieve, and what also had by and large been denied to the mission—namely to sever the Herero from these ignoble ties of servitude to their cattle—has in a certain sense been achieved by the rinderpest, which occurred around the turn of the century in those countries and for the large part annihilated the large and rich herds of the Herero [...] But still even this ordeal of God seems not yet have had the intended effect; for I have been assured that the unrest starting in January last year have largely been caused

---

11 United Nations, Report of the Committee on South West Africa, General Assembly, Official records. Twelfth Session, Supplement no.12 (A/3626), 1957, p.10

by the fact that neither the traders nor the German government bodies showed a proper understanding for the intimate ties binding the Herero to his holy cattle."[12]

This shocking attempt to ascribe the rinderpest epizootic, which devastated the entire African continent following its introduction by Italian troops in Somalia in 1897, to God's will to convert the Ovaherero, adequately characterizes the missionary fervour to destroy the cultural foundations of a people. Furthermore, in this case the German government furthered what they called God's ordeal to help the Ovaherero get rid of their cattle, not only by expropriating the survivors of the genocide by the stroke of a pen of all their land and cattle, but also by forbidding them to acquire own cattle again after this.[13] The intention of the German government was clearly to destroy the economic basis of the Ovaherero and Nama, and to force them to become a cheap labour force. At the same time, this measure also served to destroy their cultural practice, as was becoming evident in the mass conversions to Christianity in the aftermath of the war.

4. Creative adaptations

A very visible and enduring legacy of German colonialism are the uniforms that are now considered traditional Ovaherero men's clothing and worn on formal occasions and sometimes in rural areas, in everyday life. It is noteworthy to see how these uniforms came to be adopted by the Ovaherero, and eventually creative modifications made.

---

12 "Was dem Handel nicht gelungen war, und was auch der Mission im Großen und Ganzen versagt geblieben war – die Loslösung der Herero von diesen unwürdigen Banden der Knechtschaft unter ihre Rinder – das hat freilich in gewissem Sinne die Rinderpest zuwege gebracht, die um die Jahrhundertwende in jenen Ländern auftrat und die großen und reichen Herden der Herero trotz der von der deutschen Kolonialverwaltung angewandten Schutzimpfung zum größten Teile dahinraffte. Und doch scheint auch dieses Gottesgericht noch nicht die gewollte Wirkung gehabt zu haben; denn es wird mir versichert, daß die im Januar vergangenen Jahres ausgebrochenen Unruhen zum großen Teil auch darauf zurückzuführen sind, daß weder die Händler, noch die deutschen Regierungsorgane das rechte Verständnis gezeigt haben für die innigen Bande, die den Herero mit seinen heiligen Rindern verknüpfen." Spiecker, F.A. Handel und Mission unter den Nama und Herero in Südwest-Afrika. Berlin: Buchhandlung der Berliner evangelischen Missionsgesellschaft, 1905, p.25.

13 Bekanntmachung des Gouverneurs von Deutsch-Südwestafrika, betreffend Einziehung des Stammesvermögens der Herero, Zwartbooi- und Topnar-Hottentotten, vom 23. März 1906; Verordnung des Gouverneurs von Deutsch-Südwestafrika, betreffend Maßregeln zur Kontrolle der Eingeborenen vom 18. August 1907

There have been various socio-psychological attempts to explain this striking phenomenon. However, terms such as "mimicry" or "identification with the aggressor" are rather inadequate. It is worthwhile to recall how the uniforms were adopted: after the genocide of 1904 and following years, Ovaherero society was destroyed. Most of the traditional leadership been driven into exile, killed in battle, or been court-martialled and executed. The post-war imperial ordinances had also confiscated their land and cattle and even prohibited the ownership of cattle, the cornerstone of Ovaherero culture, religion, economy and social organisation. Imprisonment and the native labour ordinance had scattered the Ovaherero as farm labourers throughout the country, away from their original homes, and made it difficult for them to travel and to re-connect to old ties. The war had also destroyed families and created an enormous number of orphans and displaced children, who were socialised in German military camps. They were known as "Bambusen", serving as casual workers and personal servants of the soldiers. Clothed in discarded uniforms, they began copying the drill, the commands, and the swearwords of their masters. To this day, expletives such as *Schweinehund* are part of the vocabulary of their descendants.

But the Ovaherero recovered from this fragmentation, in a long and sometimes contradictory process, which had already begun under German rule but accelerated under South African rule between the two world wars. While on the one hand, traditional family ties and the traditional chieftainships or royal houses were resurrected, this period also saw a parallel development of a new social movement with multiple functions. Mutual cooperation, social and ceremonial gatherings and a country-wide structure according to military organisation principles and ranks derived from the German commando structure came into being. *Oturupa* (the word is derived from the German *Truppe*) is the common expression for these structures and their activities, such as gatherings and ceremonial marches. The *Otjizerandu*, or "Red Flag Movement" was and is the largest and most influential of these structures, though by no means the only one. It seems the generation that had been socialized as children in the German Army had a decisive influence in the development of the movement and introduced the uniforms as part of their identity. In the beginning, these movements ran counter to the re-establishment of traditional leadership structures and with another rallying point for the reconstruction of Ovaherero community, namely the Christian churches. A long process of numerous political and social developments eventually brought them together, leading to the general adoption of the uniform as a "national dress code".[14]

---

14 Gewald, Jan-Bart. Herero heroes: a socio-political history of the Herero of Namibia, 1890 –

The uniforms, the German ranks and drill commands as well as the black-white-red colours used by the *Otjizerandu* were interpreted by some Germans between the two world wars as a demand to revert to German colonial rule. That was of course wishful thinking of the colonial revisionist movement which dreamt of rolling back the results of the Versailles Peace Conference, but it is an idea that still survives in the form of a widespread myth among German-speaking Namibians that German rule is fondly remembered as 'strict but just'.

The distinctive dress code of many Ovaherero women is said to have German roots with the long cotton dresses that were promoted by the missionaries to replace the traditional leather clothing designed to satisfy their idea of modesty. A comparison of photographs from history reveals that there is a very long evolutionary line between the nineteenth century missionary dress and today's exuberant fashion statements with the only resemblance being the ankle length and high waistline of the dresses. However, a tradition that has carried on is that of baptising women with German male names with a female *ine* suffix—Theopoldine, Gustafine, Ernestine, Engelhardine, and so on. These names were common during the rule of Emperor Wilhelm but have since gone out of fashion in Germany. They seem to have survived in Namibia because the multi-syllable vowel-rich names fit well with Otjiherero phonology.

There are without doubt many traces of German culture that have taken root in Namibia, especially when it relates to food where items such as bread and bread rolls and sausages are popular to the extent that the word *Brötchen* is part of the standard vocabulary in other Namibian languages, although it is pronounced "brettchen". Locally brewed German-style beer is very popular and has almost become a national symbol and it is defended vigorously against strong competition from South African Breweries. Additionally, the German language is officially recognized as one of the thirteen national languages and it is taught in the Namibian education system. Children are expected to learn to read and write in their mother-tongue before they switch to the official language which is English.

1923. Oxford: James Currey, 1999, passim; Hendrickson, Anne Alfhild Bell. Historical idioms of identity representation among the Ovaherero in Southern Africa. PhD dissertation, New York University, 1992, passim.

5. Living in a Cocoon

But all this cannot hide the fact that the remaining ethnic German presence in Namibia is widely perceived as not being integrated into the new nation, and German speakers are viewed as living in a cocoon of their own language, clubs, educational and other institutions. This includes reading the only German language daily newspaper in the southern hemisphere.[15] In the absence of representative opinion polls, it is difficult to assess how far this perception corresponds with the situation on the ground. The letters and emails to the editor of the German newspaper *Allgemeine Zeitung* seem to confirm the impression that German-speaking Namibians are out of touch with modern times and an emancipated black majority, feeding their opinions with the abovementioned Vedder mythology. A frequent trope in the letters to the newspaper seems to be "we developed this land, we built the railways", forgetting that the main reason to build the railways was to secure supply lines for the war, and secondly, that they were built with slave labour using prisoners of war.

These letter-writers might be a very vocal minority within a minority because many of the most outrageously racist and colonial letters are sent by readers from the right-wing fringe in Germany where the online version of this newspaper seems to be read eagerly. There are definitely many Namibians of German ancestry, including artists and filmmakers, musicians, architects and engineers, who do not follow this line of thinking and are dealing actively and creatively with their difficult heritage. However, there have been a few local incidents that point to a shocking insensitivity to the feelings of black people. Recently, some children in the local carnival event in the coastal town of Swakopmund dressed up in Ku-Klux-Klan gowns and the German newspaper published a photo of the event and described the masquerade as being "creative".[16]

The carnival deserves to be mentioned as a cultural import from Germany, an invented tradition that was introduced on a small scale in the 1930s and which developed to its present form during the 1950s. It is based on the Rhineland style of carnival with a public procession of floats satirising current events and includes evening celebrations with alcohol, the crowning of a prince and princess and humorous speeches. It is striking that despite its very public performance, and despite a few attempts to broaden participation beyond the tradi-

---

15 For a detailed analysis, see Schmidt-Lauber, Brigitta. *Die abhängigen Herren: Deutsche Identität in Namibia*. Münster & Hamburg: LIT Verlag, 1993; Schmidt-Lauber, Brigitta. *"Die verkehrte Hautfarbe": Ethnizität deutscher Namibier als Alltagspraxis*. Berlin & Hamburg: Reimer, 1998.
16 "People outraged at KKK images in newspaper", *New Era* (Windhoek), July 1, 2015

tional ethnic boundaries, carnival essentially remains a German event that is observed with detached amusement by the others. On the other hand, the popularity that stand-up comedy has gained in Namibia during recent years is quite a different phenomenon and has certainly not been fertilised by the carnival tradition of *Büttenreden*.

6. The Legacy of Expropriation

The most important cultural impact of German colonialism in Namibia is its enduring socio-economic impact. In particular, the wholesale expropriation of land from the original owners, which up to this day determines the map of Namibia.

Without going into the details of the genocidal war that started in Namibia in January 1904, it has to be noted that this genocide has finally come to the attention of a wider German public and is now the subject of bilateral negotiations between the governments of Namibia and Germany. The fact to be highlighted is that the outcome of the war amounted to a cultural genocide for the surviving members of the Ovaherero, Nama, Damara and San communities, because the culture of a people cannot be separated from their economic subsistence and mode of production. Right after the war, the German government brought into effect a series of laws which confiscated all land and property of the Ovaherero and Nama, a measure which also disowned the Damara and San communities who had been living on the same land, an often overlooked fact. These laws further prohibited them from owning cattle and horses, enforced a strict control on their movements with the issuing of passes, included an obligation to seek wage labour, and included measures to prevent larger settlements outside strictly controlled urban locations. It was a clearly formulated policy to reduce the former owners of the country to a class of landless disposable labourers for the colonial economy and to minimise their ability to organise themselves. The Nama, deemed "worthless" as labourers by influential colonial ideologues,[17] fared even worse than the Ovaherero as they had a prisoner of war status until

---

17 "Über die Hottentotten [Nama] geht das Urteil meist dahin, dass sie wirtschaftlich im weiteren Sinne unbrauchbar sind und insofern kein Interesse an der Erhaltung der Rasse besteht." Rohrbach, Paul. *Deutsche Kolonialwirtschaft. 1. Band. Südwest-Afrika*. Berlin: Buchverlag der "Hilfe", 1907, p.349.

World War I. They were displaced from the regions they considered home or deported to another colony, Cameroon, as late as 1910.[18]

The cultural devastation such measures wrought on a people whose entire economy was based on raising cattle, whose daily rituals and oral traditions revolved around cattle, and about speaking to their ancestors at their graves was immense. Furthermore, the pastoral economy in a dry country like Namibia depended on moving herds over vast distances according to pastural conditions, and knowledge of water sources. There exists a rich oral literature of praise poems that interweaves the history of persons, individual cattle, and places, but it loses all meaning if there are no means to travel to those places anymore. Over the past hundred years, the resilience of the Ovaherero has enabled them to recover and maintain some elements of this cultural heritage, besides adding new elements, such as the uniforms.

Independent Namibia has at last removed the legal impediments to free movement of people that were introduced under German rule, and maintained and intensified under apartheid. But the land ownership pattern remains largely unchanged. When German rule ended in Namibia, large tracts of land were formally the property of the German government, but had not yet been taken up by settlers, leaving some land for the Africans to live on—even if was deemed illegal and therefore dangerous. It was the foremost goal of the South African government to fill all this available land with white settlers to gain total control, and it proceeded to do so. The current land reforms are a slow process, and do not aim to restore communal ownership. Instead, they change the private owners of the land and therefore still restrict free movement. This result of colonialism has become irreversible.

The land ownership issue remains the most fraught legacy of colonialism in Namibia today and it is in this context that the controversy regarding monuments comes up. An illustrative example is the battle-field of Hamakari, better known as the Battle of Waterberg. It is a vast area, owned by a white German-speaking farmer, and his permission is needed to enter the area. The only visual reminders of this battle are the well-maintained graves of German soldiers. There is no indication that even a single Omuherero died on this land. These are the types of cultural legacies that sustain bitterness.

Namibia is a peaceful country. On an individual level, one rarely encounters animosity or ill-feelings on the grounds of German ancestry. The recent upgrad-

---

[18] Hillebrecht, Werner & Henning Melber. Von den Deutschen verschleppt: Spurensicherung. In *Ein Land, eine Zukunft, Namibia auf dem Weg in die Unabhängigkeit*, N. Mbumba, H. Patemann, U. Katjivena (eds.), 132–150. Wuppertal: Peter Hammer, 1988.

ing of the Goethe Centre in Windhoek to a full Goethe Institute is seen as welcome and long overdue. The substantial German contribution to direct investment, and assistance in the development of transport infrastructure, amongst other sectors, is gratefully recognized. But that does not mean that the destructive historical legacy of the Germans can or should be forgotten. It is time that there is closure with a full recognition of the German responsibility.

Cited works

Gewald, Jan-Bart. *Herero heroes: a socio-political history of the Herero of Namibia, 1890–1923*. Oxford: James Currey, 1999.

Hendrickson, Anne Alfhild Bell. Historical idioms of identity representation among the Ovaherero in Southern Africa. PhD dissertation, New York University, 1992.

Hillebrecht, Werner & Henning Melber. Von den Deutschen verschleppt: Spurensicherung. In *Ein Land, eine Zukunft, Namibia auf dem Weg in die Unabhängigkeit*, N. Mbumba, H. Patemann, U. Katjivena (eds.), 132–150. Wuppertal: Peter Hammer, 1988.

Kuiseb Verlag. *The Equestrian Monument (Reiterdenkmal) 1912–2014. A chronological documentation of reports, newspaper clippings and photos/illustrations*. Windhoek: Kuiseb Verlag, 2014.

Lau, Brigitte. *Namibia in Jonker Afrikaner's time*. Windhoek: National Archives, 1987.

Rohrbach, Paul. *Deutsche Kolonialwirtschaft. 1. Band. Südwest-Afrika*. Berlin: Buchverlag der "Hilfe", 1907.

Schmidt-Lauber, Brigitta. *Die abhängigen Herren: Deutsche Identität in Namibia*. Münster & Hamburg: LIT Verlag, 1993.

Schmidt-Lauber, Brigitta. *"Die verkehrte Hautfarbe": Ethnizität deutscher Namibier als Alltagspraxis*. Berlin & Hamburg: Reimer, 1998.

Spiecker, F.A. *Handel und Mission unter den Nama und Herero in Südwest-Afrika*. Berlin: Buchhandlung der Berliner evangelischen Missionsgesellschaft, 1905.

Stoecker, Holger, Thomas Schnalke, Andreas Winkelmann (ed.). *Sammeln, Erforschen, Zurückgeben? Menschliche Gebeine aus der Kolonialzeit in akademischen und musealen Sammlungen*. Berlin: C.H. Links, 2013.

Vogt, Andreas. *National Monuments in Namibia*. Windhoek: Gamsberg Macmillan, 2004.

Wallace, Marion with John Kinahan. *A history of Namibia from the beginning to 1990*. London: Hurst, 2011.

Yixu Lü
Colonial Qingdao through Chinese eyes

The story of colonial Qingdao can be told from many contrasting perspectives with widely divergent factors which determine the differences between such narratives. These factors may be the political persuasions of the writers, cultural traditions and influences, the targeted recipients of the writing or, indeed, the editorial policies of the medium in which the writing appears. The most important determining factor is, without doubt, whether the author is German or Chinese.

This essay discusses the representations of the German colony Qingdao in Chinese writing. It analyses the perception of Qingdao in texts from various genres including fictional and academic texts, online blogs and discussion forums and juxtaposes it with German imaginings. While there have been extensive discussions about how Germans viewed Qingdao as their "model colony"[1] and a few on Chinese views on the German colony,[2] it is necessary to contrast and compare the views on both sides in order to bring fresh insight into the complex history of German imperialism in China as well as the manner in which it was received in China.

The texts chosen for this analysis are from various genres, both academic and non-academic. This combination of scholarly and popular writing is necessary if we want to gain a complete picture of the sentiments about the city's colonial past held by the Chinese people in general and the contemporary dwellers of Qingdao in particular. As Hayden White demonstrated convincingly in his analysis of the narrative techniques used by nineteenth century historians, the objectivity that historical writing may claim is contingent on the selection of events and narrative forms.[3] By looking at Chinese historiography alongside literary texts and online postings in social media, the aim is to present a perspec-

---

[1] Mechthild Leutner and Klaus Mühlhahn have provided an excellent summary of the German views on Qingdao: "Die 'Musterkolonie'": Die Perzeption des Schutzgebietes Jiaozhou in Deutschland," in *Deutschland und China. Beiträge des 2. Internationalen Symposium zur Geschichte der deutsch-chinesischen Beiziehungen*, ed. Heng-yü Kuo and Mechthild Leutner (Munich: Minvera, 1993), p. 399–423.

[2] Jianjun Zhu, *Zimindi jingli yu Zhongguo minzu zhuyi. Dezhan Qingdao 1897–1914* [The colonial experience and modern Chinese nationalism. Qingdao under German occupation 1897–1914] (Beijing: Renmin chubanshe, 2010).

[3] Hayden White, *Metahistory: The Historical Imagination in Nineteenth Century Europe* (Baltimore: Johns Hopkins University Press, 1973).

tive that is more representative of Chinese views on colonial Qingdao than if the analysis were confined to only one genre.

The main question that this essay seeks to answer is the manner in which Chinese intellectuals and present-day inhabitants of Qingdao describe the colonial past of the city and what significance they assign to it. In the first part, the views that Germans held of Qingdao are outlined. It will be followed by the analysis of similarities and differences between the German image of Qingdao and that of the Chinese, especially contemporary Qingdao dwellers. Furthermore, the divide between the views of the colonisers and the colonised shall be studied to determine whether the divide between them remains as stark as it once was or whether it has undergone any change with the passing of time.

1. The trope of the "model colony"

Descriptions of Qingdao in German writing prominently include the phrase "model colony" (*Musterkolonie*). Journalists from the colonial period as well as present day ones use this phrase as frequently as tourists and scholars do. Although there have been numerous scholarly investigations regarding Qingdao's colonial past, there is still no clarity about when this term was first coined and used. Moreover, since there is no precise definition of the term, a literary scholar would classify it as a *trope*. This indicates a type of collective memory of images that are passed from hand to hand in the sphere of representations that may be regarded more as a rhetorical device than a representation of reality.

The most famous evocation of Qingdao as heralding a new "world politics" (*Weltpolitik*) under Kaiser Wilhelm II comes from Bernhard von Bülow, Secretary of State in the Foreign Office. Informing the *Reichstag* that the navy had occupied Jiaozhou Bay, he proclaimed,

> Germany now stands at the inception of its development into an international world power. Taking possession of Kiautschou Bay represents the first initiative in securing a firm basis for our trade and industry to exploit China, and I hope this will bring us rich rewards from those lands where our goods are sold. [...] Those times are past when Germans left to one neighbour the earth, another the sea and kept the heavens, where pure doctrine reigns, for themselves. [...] In short, we wish to put no other nation in the shade, but we also demand our place in the sun.[4]

---

4 Rüdiger vom Bruch and Björn Hofmeister, eds., *Kaiserreich und Erster Weltkrieg 1871–1918. Deutsche Geschichte in Quellen und Darstellung* (Stuttgart: P. Reclam, 2000), pp. 268–270. All translations in this essay are done by the author.

From this moment on, Qingdao became inextricably linked with the emperor's "world politics". It was their first success and at the same time it serves as an emblem of the legitimation of Germany's claim to a "place in the sun".[5] Although Qingdao became the most expensive project of German colonialism and was a financial disaster, within the symbolic world of German writing the city remained a shining example of German progressiveness and efficiency. Critical remarks alluded to the fact that with the 110 million marks in subsidies that had been expended up to 1908 on Qingdao, even the Mark Brandenburg could have been turned into the most beautiful garden on earth.[6] However, they did nothing to weaken the myth of the exemplary colony. This obituary for Qingdao after it had fallen in November 1914 clearly indicates the prevailing sentiment:

> Tsingtau was the defiant and impressive exemplary achievement of the genuine German spirit, particularly imposing in the drab environs of Chinese backwardness and causing especial offence to foreign powers. [...] Tsingtau became an exemplary exhibition of Germanness in the far east, a place of pilgrimage for admiring Chinese, Japanese, English and Americans. A spotlessly clean city with that order for which Germany is renowned [...], for Tsingtau remains a crowning achievement of the German naval administration [...] and it was the entry port for the German spirit, for German education, for German thought in the world.[7]

From today's perspective, the consciously crafted and widely disseminated image of Qingdao can be termed as the triumph of the domestic over the exotic. Under the political and financial protection of the Imperial Naval Office, there arose a miniature Germany on the coast of Shandong. The favourable climatic conditions, especially for Asia, and the opportunity of creating both the city and the landscape anew favoured the creation of a "paradise" that was intended to reflect "genuine Germanness". This was carried out to the extent that the Chi-

---

[5] For a more detailed analysis of Qingdao's significance in the propagation of Wilhelm II's "world politics" see Yixu Lu, "Tsingtau," in *Kein Platz an der Sonne: Erinnerungsorte der deutschen Kolonialgeschichte*, ed. Jürgen Zimmerer (Frankfurt/New York: Campus Verlang, 2013), p. 204–226.
[6] Petra Kolonko, "Wie die Hunnen es den Chinesen zeigten. Tsingau, eine Episode deutscher Kolonialherrschaft," *Die Zeit* (Hamburg), March 8, 1997.
[7] Fritz Wertheimer, *Deutschland und Ostasien* (Stuttgart and Berlin: Deutsche Verlagsanstalt, 1914), p. 22–23: "Tsingtau war die trotzige und eindrucksvolle Musterleistung echt deutschen Geistes, besonders imponierend in einer trostlosen Umgebung chinesischer Zurückgebliebenheit und besonderen Anstoß bei den fremden Mächten erregend [...]. Tsingtau wurde eine Muster-Ausstellung des Deutschtums im fernen Osten, zu der Chinesen, Japaner, Engländer und Amerikaner bewundernd pilgerten. Eine blitzsaubere Stadt mit deutschester Ordnung [...], denn Tsingtau bleibt eine Ruhmesleistung der deutschen Marine-Verwaltung [...], und war das Einfallstor für deutschen Geist, deutsche Bildung, für den deutschen Gedanken in der Welt."

nese surroundings were largely lost from view. For here, German "mother earth" was being cultivated. Exoticism was simply not desired. The capacity of the Chinese workforce to adapt to German orderliness guaranteed that there were hardly any concessions that were required to be made for the Asian context. This theatrical production of Qingdao in the service of German nationalist expansion is unmistakable here:

> Tsingtau had now become the centre of German culture in East Asia for our lifetimes, the harbour for exports in the trade between China and Germany [...]. The German entrepreneur in East Asia finds here native German soil, protected by the prestige of concentrated military power on sea and land. Here he can soak up new national strength and by this means preserve his Germanness and become bound more closely to it.[8]

This trope of the transformation of Qingdao from a "desolate" fishing village into a modern and—above all—German city is characteristic of descriptions of the city and has survived not only the fall of the colony in 1914 but also all the social and political changes of the twentieth century. After almost a hundred years have passed, one can still find similar descriptions of Qingdao in German journalism today:

> Anyone who strolls through the cobbled streets of the Old City discovers, among the neon advertising panels, architecture of *Jugendstil* and Neo-Romanticism, preserved through a whole century. In Qingdao there is more intact Wilhelminian architecture than in Hanover, Düsseldorf, Cologne and Hamburg together.[9]

2. Colonial Qingdao in Chinese writings

If German characterisations of Qingdao are marked by the trope of the transformation of a "desolate" fishing village into an exemplary German city, how do the Chinese represent it? How do Chinese writings process the fact that the German

---

8 Wertheimer Fritz, *Deutschland und Ostasien* (Stuttgart and Berlin: Deutsche Verlagsanstalt, 1914), p. 24f.: "Tsingtau war jetzt eben in unseren Jahren das Zentrum des Deutschtums in Ostasien geworden, das Ausfallstor für den chinesisch-deutschen Handel [...] In diesem Milieu, gestützt durch das Prestige der dort konzentrierten militärischen Macht zu Wasser und zu Lande, findet der in Ostasien tätige Deutsche Muttererde, aus der er neue nationale Kraft zieht und so sein Deutschtum erhalten und ihm fester verknüpft bleiben kann".
9 *Welt am Sonntag*, April 8, 2001: "Wer durch die Kopfsteinpflastergassen der Altstadt geht, entdeckt zwischen Neonreklamen Jugendstil und Neuromantik, hinübergerettet durch die Zeitläufte eines kompletten Jahrhunderts. In Qingdao gibt es noch mehr intakte wilhelminische Architektur als in Hannover, Düsseldorf, Köln und Hamburg zusammen."

government forcibly annexed the "leased territory" of Jiaozhou? Does Chinese writing have a corresponding, dominant trope to the one in the German texts discussed above?

The educated elite of China reacted with great indignation to the occupation of the Jiaozhou Bay. "Germany has the reputation of being an old civilisation. Yet the occupation of Jiaozhou is the act of bandits and barbarians," – this was how the event was presented to the readers of a Shanghai newspaper.[10] For Yan Fu, one of the leading scholars of the age, the behaviour of the German government infringes on every moral and legal code: "Whilst our officials were searching for the murderers [of the German missionaries] and the Court had only just been informed of the incident, the Germans already occupied our fortress, destroyed our telegraph lines and drove away our soldiers. This conduct is surely like that of a robber who robs a bank in broad daylight."[11]

This feeling of rage at the blatant wrongdoings committed by Germany is typical of many later Chinese narratives on the history of Qingdao. It fits in perfectly with nationalist and Marxist discourses on colonialism in China for most of the twentieth century. For the growing Chinese nationalism, the German occupation of Jiaozhou was a catastrophe and a disgrace for all of China. For the Marxists, it was a typical example of imperialist aggression against people in other parts of the world. In research on the colonial past of Qingdao, moral condemnations of imperialism and narratives of the suffering of the Chinese populace under German rule were the dominant themes.

However, a paradigm shift in Chinese historiography has taken place since the 1980s, as has been observed by Mechthild Leutner and Klaus Mühlhahn.[12] Current Chinese historical writing has taken cognisance of and internalised the paradigm of modernisation that had been prominent in German historical writing on Qingdao. In his article on the Shandong railway, the Chinese historian Xu Lu writes:

> Although the railway was constructed in the service of German colonial rule, the railway, as a progressive means of transport, did contribute to the development of capitalism in China, which led the transformation of China from a feudal society to a semi-feudal, semi-colonial

---

10 *Shengbao*, Dezember 12, 1897: "讶德人久称开化之国，而行事类盗 贼野蛮也。"
11 "今官吏方在缉捕，朝廷甫及闻知 ... 夺我要塞，毁我电线，逼我守土之官，逐我驻防之兵。...其与海盗行劫，清昼攫金之子，又何以异哉。" Fu Yan, "Protest against the commentary on German occupation of Jiao'ao in the *Times*," in *Collected works of Yan Fu*, ed. Wang Shi. (Beijing: Zhonghua Shuju, 1986), Vol. 1, p. 55–57.
12 Mechthild Leutner, "Dekolonisierung einer Kolonie: Jiazhou im deutschen Diskurs," in *Alltagsleben und Kulturaustausch, Deutsche und Chinesen in Tsingtau 1897–1914*, ed. Hermann J. Hiery and Hans-Martin Hinz (Wolfratshausen: Edition Minerva, 1999), p. 294–305.

society. It promoted the modernisation of Chinese railway systems and led to China's modernisation in other areas as well.[13]

This statement is remarkably similar to most of the German historical writings on Qingdao which tend to see equal benefit for both sides in this colonial undertaking. As Hermann J. Hiery writes, "it was precisely European imperialism that offered pathways to modernisation." [14]

How may we explain this growing similarity between the two schools of historical writing? Is it merely that the period of a hundred years has softened the traumatic experience of what was termed as a "national disgrace"? Or have the Chinese, having sought an independent path of development for decades, now joined the chorus of Western globalisation? Would it be too provocative to assert that German historiography has now brought to a conclusion the German Empire's colonial project in China, since Chinese writing on Qingdao now shares a similar paradigm of modernisation? In other words, has the colonial undertaking reached its end in the Chinese assimilation of a German perspective?

Looking back at Chinese reactions to German colonial rule at the time, Yan Fu's sharp condemnation stated, "The Germans use the murder of the missionaries as a pretext to occupy Jiaozhou. That is not only a barbaric act against China but against Germany itself."[15] This statement also speaks of the disappointment that Chinese intellectuals felt about this country that had enjoyed the reputation of a civilised land.[16] This ambivalent attitude to Germany, which emerges amid the general indignation over the invasion, was perhaps not consciously intended, but becomes more pronounced during the course of German rule over Qingdao. This ambivalence is illustrated through the memoirs of two Chinese writers.

---

13 "德国在华修筑铁路，固然是为其殖民统治服务的，但铁路作为先进的运输工具，促进了中国资本主义因素逐步增长，从而使中国从封建社会转化为半封建半殖民地社会，也一定程度上刺激了中国铁路的近代化，进而刺激其他方面近代化的发展。" Xu Lu, "Deguo qinzhan jindai zhongguo tieluquan de fangshi tanxi [On the methods used by the Germans to seize the railway rights in China]," *Liuzhou shizhuan xuebao* [Journal of Liuzhou Teachers Colleage], Vol 29 (1) (2014): p. 50.
14 Hermann J. Hiery, introduction to *Alltagsleben und Kulturaustausch: Deutsche und Chinesen in Tsingtau 1897–1914*, ed. Hermann J. Hiery und Hans-Martin Hinz (Wolfratshausen: Edition Minerva, 1999), p. 20.
15 *Collected works of Yan Fu*, ed. Wang Shi (Beijing: Zhonghua Shuju, 1986), Bd. 1, p.57: "夫德人借端教案。此不特以野蛮生番之道待吾中国，直以野蛮生番之举动自待而已欤。"
16 Kai Hu, *Zhongde Fengyun Jihui. Shiyu 1840 Nian de Deguo zai Hua Xingxiang* [Stormy encounters between China and Germany. The image of Germany in China from 1840] (Shanghai: People's Press, 2013), esp. p. 59–111.

> I saw how a German tried to arrest a Chinese. The Chinese could run very fast. He vanished around a corner and seemed to be out of danger. The German now set his Alsatian loose on the Chinese. The dog held the man fast and waited for his master, who was able to arrest him after all. As this Chinese had been hunted like an animal, I thought he was a thief. But a passer-by told me this was not so: 'He was on the railway lines as a train was coming. The German called to him. He got a fright and tried to run away. The faster he ran, the faster the pursuit, as the German was now determined to catch him. If you live here, you have to keep to the rules to avoid disasters. A trivial piece of carelessness can result in severe punishment. The world belongs to the Germans, and we must be careful and wait until we get the leased territory back again.' Ah, these are the words of a coolie.[17]

While the German Shepard in this description symbolises a special type of humiliation for the Chinese, a similar dog appears in another memoir to represent German order in a positive light:

> I saw scarcely any police in the streets. But everything in them proceeded in an orderly manner. It was not necessary to lock the doors at night. Qingdao cannot be compared with Hong Kong and Port Arthur, where there are so many thieves and burglars. There are two reasons for this: diligent police and ... German shepherd dogs. The police in Qingdao have over a hundred of them. After dusk they patrol the streets. If they discover burglars they can quickly warn the police and help in the arrests, as these dogs have a very fine sense of smell and can quickly sniff out burglars.[18]

These examples are meant to show how the Chinese perception of the German colonial rule oscillated from the beginning between moral indignation and practical adaptation to a situation that from their perspective could not be changed, but could potentially bring some advantage to their own situation. While hardly any historian makes this explicit, this form of "inverted exotism" was a contributing factor to young male peasants from surrounding areas migrating to Qingdao during the German rule. These young people were far more interested in stories

---

17 "又一日,亦见洋人狂奔,捉前之人,前一人步行捷,转一墙角,可避捉矣。洋人大碳其随行之犬。。。。竟噬得若人衣角,而待洋人来获,是以猎兽之法待华人。吾意此必为窃,询之他人,曰:"不然,火车将至,轨道例不许行人。渠犯其章,洋人喝之,渠茫无措手足,于是奔。洋人必得而甘心,亦奔。彼奔亦厉,追亦厉"且曰:"居此间者,必谨守法度,乃可免祸,稍不慎,罚即随之。洋人当运,吾辈日惴惴。此等租界,必收赎后,吾人乃得有生命。" 此之说似出于一苦工者,呜呼!" Se Fu, *Qingdao Huigu Ji* [Memoires of Qingdao] (Shanghai: Zhonghua Shuju, 1921), p. 21.

18 "街上不见有多数巡警植立,然其秩序之佳,乃有夜不闭户,路不拾遗之况。较之香港旅顺,盗贼辈出者,不可同日而语。细论起得力之故,盖有二端,一侦探能尽职 ... 二利用猎犬,青岛警厅畜犬百余头,黄昏以后,纵之四出,遇有穿潜之事,报告迅速。其踩缉窃案,赖猎犬嗅觉之力,四出觅贼,得之亦甚。有此二端,治安不足虑也。" Shen Hong, "Qingdao wenjian lu [Stories from Qingdao]," *Xiaoshuo Yuebao*, vol. 6, (1–2), (1915): p. 6.

about the exotic way of life the Germans led than in tales of German cruelty to Chinese coolies. Stories about how the Germans baked their bread and threw away the crusts as well as how they transported their food in horse-drawn carts were fascinating to them.[19] The appeal of the exotic and the expectation of better wages were the main reasons for peasants from neighbouring villages to come and live in Qingdao. The size of the Chinese population in the territory increased almost fivefold in the last ten years of German rule. Many contemporaries also perceived that the Chinese population of Qingdao was becoming European:

> Many inhabitants of Qingdao have assumed a Western way of life. Let us take their dwellings as an example. The furniture in the living room and the bedroom is quite European. Only the meals remain Chinese. Also as far as their daily activities are concerned—entertainment, sport, going for walks, swimming—in all of this they imitate the Germans. The result is that the educated and wealthy Chinese in Qingdao have all become Europeans.[20]

The acceptance of German rule goes hand in hand with an improved image of Germany. From the mid-1920s one could detect an almost nostalgic sentimentality, especially when it came to comparing the two foreign rulers that the citizens of Qingdao have had. In this comparison, the Germans come off better than the Japanese for the Chinese observed that the Germans had invested a great deal in infrastructure and had at least tried to impress the Chinese with their zeal for modernisation. In contrast, the Japanese were concerned solely with looting the city. Anything that they could dismantle was carried off to Japan, including the monument to Admiral Diedrichs and German books from the library. Thus we read in a description from the year 1926:

> The Germans are like an eagle. It carries off fat hares and chickens, but leaves the worms as a reward for its slaves. The Japanese are different. With them the junk merchants, drug dealers, thieves and prostitutes arrived. They sent crowds of men and women from Osaka and Kobe to their new colony, so that the Chinese inhabitants, who were previously able to make a little profit, are now afraid. Because the Japanese are so hated, the positive qualities of the Germans are now recognised. If one has a conversation with the citizens of Qingdao

---

19 Martin C. Yang, *A Chinese Village: Taitou, Shantung Province* (Columbia University Press, 1945).

20 Yonglong Gan, "The achievments of German administration in Qingdao," *Eastern Review*, vol. 5 (7) (1908): p. 24: "青岛市大部分的居民，大都是出入这些高矮重叠的洋房里，因此他们的生活，便也随着洋化起来了。先从住屋说起，卧房和会客室的陈设，都欧化了... 只有吃，还保持着本国的滋味，而日常生活如娱乐，运动，散步，游泳，也都一个劲儿跟了外国人学。结果，生活在青岛市内的一般职业较高或较为有钱的人，都成了欧化型的中国人了。"

about their two overlords, one inevitably hears: 'The Germans were much better; the Japanese are the worst'.²¹

While in the People's Republic, recollections of the violent annexation and other brutal humiliations that the Chinese populace had to suffer from the Germans were official dogma for historians until the 1980s, the Marxist interpretation of imperialism does permit a change of perspective that would allow the interpretation of colonialism as promoting modernisation, given a favourable political climate. Karl Marx wrote on the British subjugation of India in an article of 1853 for the *New York Daily Tribune:* "It is a twofold mission that England will carry out in India: one destructive and one conducive to renewal—the destruction of the old Asiatic social order and the creation of the basis for a Western social order."²²

With the opening of China to the world intensifying, the very word "renewal" in Marx's commentary becomes the dominant paradigm in Chinese historical writing from the 1990s. There is a clearly observable transvaluation of the colonial project from exploitation of the subjugated into something positive. The Qingdao historian Lü Mingzhou, for example, has appealed for a return to the origin of Marxist doctrine on colonialism in 1999. He stresses that one should not only take into account the destructive effects of colonialism, but also the aspect of "renewal". According to Lü Mingzhou, German colonialism was indeed a national catastrophe for China, but it also awakened the national awareness of the Chinese. The traditional economic and social structures in Shandong were destroyed, but this also gave rise to the initial impulses towards modernisation. The missionaries indeed brought the spiritual opium of Western religion, but their schools also spread modern sciences throughout China, trained specialists and promoted cultural exchange between China and the West. In this sense, Lü Mingzhou has pleaded the case for a differentiation between moral judgements and historical research. To quote from his writings:

---

21 Tongzha Wang, *Portrait of Qingdao. Anthology of modern and contemporary Qingdao-themed poetry and prose,* edited Qingdao Archiv (Qingdao, 1997), p. 32–33: "德国人像一只掠空的鹫鹰，他单拣地面上随时可以取得的肥鸡，跑兔；至于小小虫子则不足饱他的口腹。他是情愿把小小的恩惠赏给奴隶们的。可是　　xx人却不然了。挟与俱来的：街头的小贩，毒品的制造者，浪人，红裙队，什么都来了。一批一批的男女由大坂，神户向这个新殖民地分送。于是以前尚有微利可图的中国居民也渐渐感到恐慌。因为对xx人的诅恨，更感到德国人的优容。直到现在，与久居青岛市的人们谈起话来，说到两位临时主人，总说："德国人好得多，xx最下三烂。"
22 Karl Marx, "The British Rule in India", *New-York Herald Tribune* (New York, NY), June 10, 1853. Quoted from https://www.marxists.org/archive/marx/works/1853/06/25.htm, accessed May 5, 2016.

> In researching the history of the aggression of the imperialist powers against China, we should distinguish moral verdicts from historical facts. Our strong condemnation of their barbaric aggression and criminal exploitation of the colonies belongs to the sphere of morals and ethics. Historical research, however, must consider the twofold mission of imperialism. Our moral judgements relate to the injustice of aggression; but research is concerned with its historical consequences, and, in assessing these, one should not confuse emotion with research. [23]

Is it a historical coincidence or an intellectual affinity when, in the same year, the German historian Hermann Hiery writes the following introduction to the symposium "Everyday Life and Cultural Exchange: Germans and Chinese in Tsingtau 1897–1914":

> I think it is completely inadequate to anchor one's historical evaluation of the late Empire, the Ching/Manchu Dynasty, solely or primarily in the traumatic experiences, which cannot be denied, with the imperialist desires of foreign nations [...] I am not a sinologist but a historian, but for me there are many other possible interpretations [...] China is so vast and so manifold [...] and what characterises the Chinese experience with previous foreign conquerors and cultures is that these become integrated like those before them, indeed could have become assimilated without doing damage to the real character of China. [24]

A century after the occupation of Qingdao, the Chinese and German historians appear to view each other in a similar manner. This outlook is that of Karl Marx who was convinced that capitalist means of production were a force to carry forward history, precisely in his thesis of the twofold mission of colonial-

---

[23] Mingzhou Lü, "The twofold impact of the German occupation of Jiaozhou on modern China," *Literature, History and Philosophy*, 1/1999, p. 50: 德占胶澳对近代中国的双重影响。文史哲，1/1999, p. 50: "我們在评定帝国主义侵华史时，应该把道德评价与历史研究区别开来。我們严厉谴责帝国主义对殖民地的野蛮侵略与罪恶掠夺，这是一个道德范畴的问题，而具体评价帝国主义侵略殖民地的"双重使命"，则是一个历史研究问题。前者所关系的是侵略的不应该，非正义性问题，后者所关系的是这一侵略结果的历史作用问题，评价时不应以感情代替研究。"

[24] Hermann J. Hiery, introduction to *Alltagsleben und Kulturaustausch: Deutsche und Chinesen in Tsingtau 1897–1914*, ed. Hiery, Hermann J. and Hans-Martin Hinz (Wolfratshausen: Edition Minerva, 1999), p. 20: "Ich denke, es ist völlig unzureichend, die historische Bewertung des späten Kaiserreiches, der Ch'ing/Mandschudynastie, allein oder auch nur vordinglich an der – zugegebenermaßen – traumatischen Erfahrungen mit den imperialen Gelüsten fremder Nationen festmachen zu wollen. ... Ich bin kein Sinologe, sondern Historiker, aber für mich sind viele andere historische Interpretationen denkbar, ... Dieses Land ist so groß und vielgestaltig, ... seine historischen Erfahrungen mit fremden vorhergehenden Eroberern und Kulturen derart ausgeprägt, daß auch diese neuen Eroberer und Kulturen ähnlich wie vorhergehende integriert, vielleicht sogar assimiliert hätten werden können, ohne Schaden für den eigentlichen Charakter Chinas."

ism. For him, the victory of capitalism over the Asian village system was an "organic" necessity, thus ineluctable.

3. Colonial Qingdao in the Chinese everyday

Since the Germans were forced to leave Qingdao, a whole century has passed. The twofold Japanese occupation of the city in both world wars, the civil war between the Communists and the Nationalists, the Cultural Revolution and China's economic rise have all transformed most of Qingdao. Yet many German buildings, such as the Governmental Administrative Building and the Imperial Law Courts, have survived. What do today's inhabitants think of the colonial past of their city? To gain an understanding of this, a survey was conducted using a questionnaire in March 2016. Respondents who were selected included those had lived in Qingdao for at least five years and had a university degree. The university qualification ensured that they would have heard the official interpretation of imperialism at least once. The answers revealed that the respondents were surprisingly well-acquainted with the German past of their city. They could all correctly name at least two German buildings and describe their function in the colonial period. The most popular German building was the Governor's residence, followed by the Christ Church. A few also named the Bismarck Barracks, now part of the Ocean University campus. All of them answered the question about whether the German architecture of Qingdao should be preserved, in the affirmative. The main reasons given were that these buildings represent the history of the city and that together with the mountains, the forests and the sea, they accounted for the uniqueness of their city, of which they were very proud. All respondents rejected the idea that Germany should take some responsibility for the preservation of the buildings from the colonial time. For today's inhabitants of Qingdao, these buildings are not German at all. Rather, they are considered to be Chinese buildings in a German style. This is the most informative result of the questionnaire since it indicates that the educated inhabitants of Qingdao have undertaken their own form of decolonisation. The representative public buildings that constitute proof of the 'exemplary colony' in German writings are in the eyes of these present-day dwellers of Qingdao, entirely Chinese. They consider them to be authentic Chinese buildings with a German appearance.

How can this reinterpretation of the German "exemplary achievement" that turns the symbol of colonial power into a decorative style that Chinese can unreservedly esteem and enjoy be understood? For, instead of calling forth painful memories of humiliations suffered in the past, these buildings are seen to symbolise the uniqueness and identity of their city. Historians may see this transvaluation as the expression of the increasing confidence of the Chinese nation. Sociologists could use this example to test the validity of the concept of "communicative memory". Optimistic adherents of globalisation might perceive the dawning of a world-wide cultural federalism, characterised by the universal conviction in urbanisation. But exponents of cultural studies would point to a well-known explanation that the evocation of the Other has always been in the service of self-representation or self-criticism. The following example clearly illustrates this.

The system of sewers that the Germans left in Qingdao has a legendary reputation in today's China. Searching with the keywords "sewers in Qingdao" in Chinese online forums produced almost half a million hits. All pointed to the German origin of the sewerage system with mainly positive remarks, such as "Rolls Royce of drainage", "visionary", "symbol of Germany's engineering genius". In such contributions we find no trace of indignation over German colonial masters:

> The Germans ruled for seventeen years in Qingdao and built twelve sewerage canals [...] A century later these still serve hundreds of thousands of inhabitants. Separate systems for storm water and waste water are still not being built in many cities. What decides on a nation's spirit and system of values? The sewerage system in Qingdao makes us wonder. [25]

In the numerous, clichéd expressions of praise used to describe the sewerage system in Qingdao, no serious attempt is made to come to terms with any historical facts. In other words, the authors of these comments have little interest in giving an accurate picture of the Germans or of their sewage system, but rather use their German origins as a rhetorical device for criticising the incompetence of contemporary Chinese bureaucracies. We could almost term this an inversion of "Orientalism". By transforming the German "cultural achievements" in China into a simplified image of efficiency, the authors lay claim to the power to reinterpret the past and the Other.

However, this is not to claim that there are no longer any voices in contemporary China that criticise German colonialism. In 2001, the Nobel Prize winner Mo Yan published the novel *The Sandalwood Torture* (檀香刑). Written during the

---

[25] www.kannewyork.com/culture/2014/12/16/1581.html: "德国人在这17年间，他们总共修了12个相互独立又彼此连接的排水系统，包括若干条地上明渠和地下管道、暗渠，至今覆盖着整个青岛西部老城区…这些极具前瞻眼光的下水道，百多年后仍在运转，令数十万人青岛人受益。其中雨、污水分流的模式即使到今天也还有很多城市没能做到。一个民族的精神、行为准则和行为规范是由什么决定的? 这真的值得人们深思!" Accessed April 10, 2016.

era of Jiang Zemin and echoing the xenophobic attitudes current at the time, the novel takes an unremittingly hostile stance to the German presence in Shandong.[26] The novel is set, not in Qingdao but in Gaomi, a short distance along the railway under construction at the time of the Boxer Rebellion. The perspective from which the novel is narrated is nostalgic, and the railway is portrayed as a purely destructive force. The Germans are simply "foreign devils" who serve to magnify the conscienceless power already incarnate in the tyrant Yuan Shi Kai, and the author has no further use for them or interest in them. The only wholly positive characters are the anonymous masses of the oppressed peasantry who express themselves both in the Boxer Rebellion and in the "cat opera", a popular art-form, and it is ultimately this that dominates the whole work. Western impulses towards modernisation have no redeeming features in the world of this novel. There is great complexity in the novel's plot and characterisation, but the negative view of the Germans and their technology is simple and straightforward. Clearly, works of fiction are not obliged to differentiate moral judgements from historical fact.

4. Conclusion

In summary, one may say that Chinese perceptions of Qingdao's colonial past display some parallels to those of the Germans. Both sides have adapted their "Master Narrative" to the changing tides of history. For the Germans, Qingdao transforms itself from a "glorious achievement" on the part of the Imperial Navy into a project of civil modernisation from which both Germans and Chinese could profit. Yet the trope of the "ideal colony" remains dominant despite all the political and social changes affecting Qingdao. Perceptions on the Chinese side are more differentiated. Moral indignation over the German occupation and the feeling of national disgrace have been tenacious and even find expression in the most recent literature, but the discourse of modernisation gradually comes to determine the tenor of the discussion. In the everyday life of present-day Qingdao, the colonial period is seen as a brief episode in the city's long history which may occasion both exotic fantasies and disguised social criticism. The German colonisers belong to the past. The visible traces of the colonial period are enjoyed

---

[26] For an detailed analysis of this aspect of the novel, see Yixu Lu, "Germans and the Death-Throes of the Qing: Mo Yan's *The Sandalwood Torture*," in *German Colonialism revisited: African, Asian and Oceanic Experiences*, ed. Nina Berman, Klaus Mühlhahn and Patrice Nganang (Ann Arbor: University of Michigan Press, 2014), pp. 271–283.

and admired by the present-day inhabitants with full self-awareness. They are part of their own identity.

Works cited

Fu, Se. *Qingdao Huigu Ji* [Memoires of Qingdao]. Shanghai: Zhonghua Shuju, 1921.
Gan, Yonglong. "The achievments of German administration in Qingdao." *Eastern Review*, vol.5 (7) (1908).
Hiery, Hermann J.. Introduction to *Alltagsleben und Kulturaustausch: Deutsche und Chinesen in Tsingtau 1897–1914*, edited by Hiery, Hermann J. and Hans-Martin Hinz. Wolfratshausen: Edition Minerva, 1999.
Hong, Shen. "Qingdao wenjian lu [Stories from Qingdao]." *Xiaoshuo Yuebao*, vol 6, (1–2), (1915).
Hu, Kai. *Zhongde Fengyun Jihui. Shiyu 1840 Nian de Deguo zai Hua Xingxiang* [Stormy encouters between China and Germany. The image of Germany in China from 1840]. Shanghai: People's Press, 2013.
Kolonko, Petra. Wie die Hunnen es den Chinesen zeigten. Tsingau, eine Episode deutscher Kolonialherrschaft. "*Die Zeit* (Hamburg), March 8, 1997.
Leutner, Mechthild. "Dekolonisierung einer Kolonie: Jiazhou im deutschen Diskurs." In *Alltagsleben und Kulturaustausch, Deutsche und Chinesen in Tsingtau 1897–1914*, edited by Hermann J. Hiery and Hans-Martin Hinz. Wolfratshausen: Edition Minerva 1999.
Lu, Xu. "Deguo qinzhan jindai zhongguo tieluquan de fangshi tanxi [On the methods used by the Germans to seize the railway rights in China]." *Liuzhou shizhuan xuebao* [Journal of Liuzhou Teachers Colleage], Vol 29 (1), 2014.
Lü, Mingzhou. "The twofold impact of the German occupation of Jiaozhou on modern China." *Wen Shi Zhe* [Literature, History and Philosophy], 1/1999.
Lü, Yixu. "Tsingtau." In *Kein Platz an der Sonne: Erinnerungsorte der deutschen Kolonialgeschichte*, edited by Jürgen Zimmerer, 204–226. Frankfurt/New York: Campus Verlang, 2013.
Lü, Yixu. "Germans and the Death-Throes of the Qing: Mo Yan's *The Sandalwood Torture*." In *German Colonialism revisited: African, Asian and Oceanic Experiences*, edited by Nina Berman, Klaus Mühlhahn and Patrice Nganang, 271–283. Ann Arbor: University of Michigan Press, 2014.
Marx, Karl. "The British Rule in India." *New-York Herald Tribune* (New York, NY), June 10, 1853. Accessed May 5, 2016. https://www.marxists.org/archive/marx/works/1853/06/25.htm.
Vom Bruch, Rüdiger and Björn Hofmeister, eds., *Kaiserreich und Erster Weltkrieg 1871–1918. Deutsche Geschichte in Quellen und Darstellung*. Stuttgart: P. Reclam, 2000.
Wang, Tongzhao. *Portrait of Qingdao. Anthology of modern and contemporary Qingdao-themed poetry and prose*, edited by Qingdao Archiv. Qingdao, 1997.
Wertheimer, Fritz, *Deutschland und Ostasien*. Stuttgart and Berlin: Deutsche Verlagsanstalt, 1914.
www.kannewyork.com/culture/2014/12/16/1581.html. Accessed 5 May 2016.
Yan, Fu. "Protest against the commentary on German occupation of Jiao'ao in the *Times*." In *Collected works of Yan Fu*, edited by Wang Shi. Beijing: Zhonghua Shuju, 1986. Vol. 1.

Yang, Martin C.. *A Chinese Village: Taitou, Shantung Province*. Columbia University Press, 1945.

Zhu, Jianjun. *Zimindi jingli yu Zhongguo minzu zhuyi. Dezhan Qingdao 1897–1914* [The colonial experience and modern Chinese nationalism. Qingdao under German occupation 1897–1914]. Beijing: Renmin chubanshe, 2010.

Malama Meleisea and Penelope Schoeffel
Germany in Samoa: Before and After Colonisation

1. Introduction

The association between Germany and Samoa is usually thought of in relation to the period in which Germany ruled Samoa in the years 1900–1914. However German influence in Samoa began in the mid-nineteenth century and there were many German interests involved in what has been referred to as the Samoan "imbroglio"[1] or the "Samoan Tangle".[2] By the 1850s, a German company was on its way to become the largest land holder in Samoa and by the 1890s, German interests had become dominant in the international rivalry of the period, despite strenuous efforts by missionaries and settlers in Samoa to engage Britain and the US in a contest to colonise the islands. In 1892, the famous British novelist Robert Louis Stevenson, who had settled in Samoa, wrote bitterly about the former German consul and Godeffroy & Sohn plantation manager, Theodor Weber: "His name still lives in the songs of Samoa ... how all things, land and food and property pass progressively as by a law of nature into the hands of *Misi Ueba*, and soon nothing will be left for Samoans."[3] This paper outlines German involvement in Samoa's history and reflects on modern resonances from the German period.

2. Samoan conflicts in the 19th century

The nineteenth century was a period of revolutionary change and upheavals in Samoa and by the middle of the nineteenth century, Samoans had all converted to Christianity. Conversion had political consequences because of the transformation of Samoan theology and eschatology under Christian teaching. The Samoans had previously believed that their highest chiefs were descendants of the god Tagaloa, who created the world. Genealogical descent from god was

---

[1] See Henry C. Ide, "The Imbroglio in Samoa," *The North American Review*, Volume 168 (1899).
[2] See Paul M. Kennedy, *The Samoan Tangle: A Study in Anglo German Relations 1878–1900* (New York: Barnes and Noble, 1974).
[3] Stevenson, Robert Louis, *A Footnote to History: Eight Years of Trouble in Samoa* (London: Dawsons of Pall Mall, 1967 [1892]), 35.

the principle underlying the rank order of Samoa. But the new faith taught that all were equal in the eyes of the new triune God. Nevertheless the Samoans did not let go of the focus of their political contests of the eighteenth and early nineteenth century. These concerned the bestowal of four honorific "royal" titles Tui Aana, Tui Atua, Tamasoalii and Gatoaitele which, when held together by one high chief, made the holder the paramount in Samoa. The titles were bestowed by a number of orator groups in Samoa, the most prominent being the Pule from the island of Savai'i, and Tumua from the island of Upolu. When the first missionaries arrived in Samoa in 1830, the four titles were held by Malietoa Vainu'upo, the titular head of one of two of Samoa's great overarching chiefly lineages, who converted to Christianity believing the missionaries to have arrived in response to an ancient prophesy. In 1841, when Malietoa Vainu'upo died, he willed that the four titles be divided among other chiefs in his lineage. Perhaps he did so because having become Christian; he wanted no more wars over the titles. Nevertheless, the wars over succession to these and other high titles continued.

3. Foreign settlement

During the 1850s, a foreign settlement sprung up around Apia harbour and Apia had become one of the main ports in the South Pacific, along with Papeete in Tahiti and Levuka in Fiji. The settlers in Apia built stores, hotels and liquor saloons to cater to the increasing number of ships arriving at the harbour. Aside from seamen and traders Samoa began to attract growing numbers of Germans, as well as Europeans and Americans seeking land on which to plant tropical crops in the hope of making their fortunes.

From 1830s onwards, naval vessels from Europe and America intervened on behalf of their citizens in Samoa. For example during a war between rival Samoan districts in the late 1840s – 1850s a number of Europeans claimed damages from the Samoans who were accused of destroying European-owned property. This war had enabled European settlers to lay claim to areas of land which had been deserted by Samoans during the war. Although the settlers paid for the land thus acquired, there was doubt and confusion about whether the chief receiving payment had rights to sell village-owned land. However, any time that settlers' rights were challenged by the Samoans, the setllers were likely to call in support from naval vessels of their own nationality.

Since the ideas that Europeans had about property rights were very different in comparison to those that the Samoans had, European claims were usually upheld. An initial code of laws had been drawn up in 1838 which had no effect on the Samoans but which were obeyed by at least some of the visiting ships for the first few years. British and American consuls were appointed in this period, both of whom had connections with the mission of the London Missionary Society. One problem that arose for the Samoans was when the chiefs of Apia lost control over the Apia municipal area. As a result the Samoan leaders faced a situation of lawlessness and trouble-making amongst Samoans as well as between Samoans and Europeans.

4. First attempts to establish a monarchical government in Samoa

The consuls, mission leaders and a few of the European settlers felt that it was essential to establish a central government which could make laws and set up courts. While many of the chiefs of Samoa thought this was a good idea and a few even had passed laws in their districts, there was no central authority in this period representing all of Samoa. The long history of two rival aristocratic lineages in Samoa meant that many Samoans either feared that their enemies might gain control through such an arrangement, or found it hard to understand how all parties in Samoa could be equally represented in the central government in a way that would avoid jealousy. It was also very hard for foreigners to understand Samoan ideas about political authority. For the Samoans, paramount chiefs were like flags representing the dignity of the two great lineages, while political decisions were made by groups of orator chiefs groups who represented the villages and districts of Samoa. This division of political authority was different from European ideas about monarchy.

The British Consul thought that Malietoa Laupepa (grandson of Malietoa Vainu'upo) should be made king since he had the support of Tuamasaga district, which had the biggest foreign population. Centralised monarchies had been established with European encouragement in several parts of Polynesia and it was an arrangement of this kind which Williams had in mind. In the 1830s, in Tonga, Taufa'ahau Tupou had made himself "King George I", with missionary assistance. He had succeeded in establishing a centralised monarchy because he had become king immediately after winning a war which gave him unchallenged power. In addition he made genealogical claims to all the highest ranking titles in Tonga. The situation with Malietoa Laupepa in Samoa was quite different. The Savai'i branch of his family did not recognise him and he held none of the four royal titles which in the old days would have given him sacred authority throughout Samoa. Nevertheless, Malietoa Laupepa's supporters made plans for a confederation based at Matautu (Apia), in which all the districts of Samoa would be represented as a kind of parliament, with Malietoa Laupepa as the king. When this news reached Tonumaipe'a Talavou, the rival claimant to the Malietoa title, he and his supporters, among whom there were also many Europeans, established a rival headquarters at Mulinu'u near Apia. So, in 1869, a new war began between the supporters of the two titles. The war was fought in and around the Apia area because of the location of the two rival headquarters. It continued later in 1869 with settler involvement, the trading of guns and other supplies in exchange for land. Following peace talks between the rival Malietoa factions, it was agreed that Malietoa Laupepa would be joint king with a representative of Samoa's other great lineage the Sa Tupua, Tupua Pulepule. The new government was made up of the two kings, and councils of village and district leaders. For the remaining 24 years of the 19th century, conflict between the Samoan factions was to become increasingly complicated by the land claims and quarrels of the foreign settlers and the international rivalry of the nations whose citizens they were.

5. The second Samoan government

In 1872 Captain Meade of the US Navy conducted a survey of Pagopago harbour on Tutuila and negotiated an agreement with the Mauga, the high chief of the area for recognition of American shipping rights at the harbour in exchange for US protection. Due to these American interests in Samoa, the US President, Ulysses S. Grant authorised Colonel Albert B. Steinberger to visit Samoa as his emissary. Steinberger spent three months investigating the situation in Samoa and made promises to German plantation interests which will be discussed later in the article. Steinberger had no definite undertaking from the US Government that they would establish a protectorate, but he carried a letter of greeting from President Grant and gifts for the chiefs. Steinberger gave the Samoans the impression that the US Government wanted to establish a protectorate over Samoa. This was understood by the Samoans to mean that the US would protect their land from foreign intrusion and allow them internal self-government. In fact the US Congress was opposed to the idea of American colonies and resisted President Grant's territorial interest in the South Pacific and the Caribbean. It is not clear whether Steinberger knew this and was deliberately deceiving the Samoans, or whether he genuinely believed that he could make Samoa an American Protectorate in time. He arrived on the US Naval ship Tuscarora which made a great impression upon the Samoans. He arranged a great assembly which was attended by 8,000 Samoans, who presented the Captain and crew of the Tuscarora with a huge feast. Steinberger presented the gifts and read the letter from the

President, which was translated into Samoan by George Turner of the London Missionary Society (LMS). As a result, in 1875 Steinberger was appointed the first Prime Minister of Samoa in the newly reorganised government under King Malietoa Laupepa.

The new government passed many laws which were clearly applicable to everyone. A few of the laws placed moral restrictions on both Europeans and Samoans, such as the one regarding the sale of liquor. Many of the Apia traders disliked these laws and European feelings against Steinberger began to grow. Steinberger stated he wanted to protect the Samoans from bad influences and he also declared a possible intention to hold an enquiry into land matters. The new American Consul, S.S. Foster, had originally come to Samoa to work for a group of American land speculators, disliked Steinberger and suspected that he was using the Samoan government to further his own personal interests and those of Germany in Samoa. An influential leader of British LMS in Samoa, George Turner also turned against Steinberger. Although the LMS had originally approved of him, and certainly the code of laws he promoted, rumours of his German involvement worried them. The LMS were of the hope that Samoa would become a British Protectorate, since Britain had just established a crown colony in Fiji. Steinberger, despite his probable earlier involvement with the American land speculators, opposed the land claims of this company, with which the American Consul S.S. Foster was still involved. Although the company had gone bankrupt, Foster was selling its land interests. This provided further reasons for Consul Foster's hostility and in 1876 he used his official position to denounce Steinberger's actions as "unauthorized" by the American Government. When a British warship arrived at Apia, the Captain found all the American and British residents opposing Steinberger. However as European opposition grew, Samoan support for Steinberger became stronger. The Captain and the Consuls informed the Samoan government that they had no jurisdiction over Europeans, which made the Samoans even angrier. Finally, Consul Foster obtained evidence from the American Government that Steinberger had no official backing. This was the news he was waiting for, and with the help of Turner, Foster persuaded King Malietoa Laupepa to sign a deportation order. Steinberger was arrested and taken aboard the British warship. Although Steinberger never returned to Samoa, the British Captain and the British and American Consuls were eventually dismissed from their posts for the actions they had taken.

The Samoan government retaliated by deposing Malietoa as the king and ignoring attempted interventions by the Consuls. However, finding a substitute king became a new source of conflict because of disagreements in the Sa Tupua, who were divided into factions supporting Tupua Pulepule, Tamasese Titimea and Tui Atua Mata'afa Iosefo. Meanwhile, Malietoa Laupepa established a rival government outside Apia with the support of a number of chiefdoms. The foreign cliques of Americans, Germans and British became entangled in the Samoan factions, adding a foreign-backed power rivalry to the already existing complicated divisions among the Samoans. Malietoa's rival government was supported by the Germans and eventually by a number of Americans. Samoans support was once again divided between the Sa Tupua and the Sa Malietoa

In 1871, a company of land speculators was registered in California; the Central Polynesian Land and Commercial Company (CPLCC). They took advantage of the wars of the late 1860s to buy land from the Samoans who wanted money for guns, and the company intended to sell the land thus acquired to European settlers for plantations. In 1872, the company claimed to have acquired 300,000 acres of Samoan land—half the land area of the islands. If this was added to German and other foreign land claims, there would have been no land left for the Samoans. Samoan leaders had been selling the same pieces of land to different buyers. One such leader sold the entire lands of the village of Vaitele, including the land where the village settlement was built. Some of the land claims included 12 square miles at Sale'imoa, 38,400 acres at Falealili and 6 square miles of land at Malie. The American land speculators tried to influence their government to colonise the islands or to declare a "protectorate" which would allow their land claims to be, legally recognised, surveyed and registered. Fortunately for the Samoans, the CPLCC went bankrupt before it could press its land claims with force. Trading posts were being operated by foreigners throughout the islands and if the claims of European settlers are to be believed, Samoans were selling their land recklessly and indiscriminately. It is unlikely that in this period the Samoans understood the difference between use-rights and outright alienation of land.

In 1876, the faction led by Tupua Tamasese Titimaea was victorious but unable to govern effectively due to conflicting demands, influences and rivalry of the foreign consuls and their settler nationals. Fighting broke out again and then Malietoa Laupepa was made vice-king under Malietoa Talavou and, when the latter died in 1880, Malietoa Laupepa was proclaimed king once more. This new government was recognised by the German, American and British consuls in 1880. The disappointed Tui Atua Mata'afa, who had left the Sa Tupua side to join the Sa Malietoa (being related to both lineages), was not favoured as the king, as he had hoped, so he joined the opposing side who declared Tamasese as their king. Fighting recommenced but was contained by foreign naval intervention. A treaty signed aboard the US naval ship Lackawanna brought the two parties together in a new compromise, with Malietoa remaining as king and the youthful Tupua Tamasese as the vice-king.

The re-united government was not effective at the local level because local chiefs continued to regard the villages as independent identities and enforced and applied new laws to suit themselves. They were reluctant to pay taxes because they could not see what the money was needed for and suspected it was going into the hands of the foreigners. In particular the new government did not like the Germans, who had treated them without respect, and twice in 1884, they petitioned Queen Victoria to make Samoa a British protectorate. Malietoa also protested to the German Emperor regarding the convention that he had been forced to sign, which allowed a German-Samoan Council to prosecute Samoans who had committed offences against the Germans, without reference to other authorities in Samoa. When the German Consul, Theodore Weber (who headed Godeffroy & Sohn, the largest German plantation company), heard about the petitions to the Queen he retaliated by claiming ownership of the land at Mulinu'u where the government had its headquarters, and expelled them from the area. At the same time, he persuaded Tupua Tamasese and his supporters to form a rival government. A new German arrival, Eugen Brandeis, whom Stevenson identified as "a Bavarian captain of artillery, of a romantic and adventurous character",[4] was despatched by Weber to help them to organize. Brandeis was appointed prime minister of the rival government and set about training Tamasese's allies for war.

6. German economic interests

During the 1850s, J.C. Godeffroy & Sohn had acquired significant amounts of land as a result of the preceding wars, in which the people of the A'ana chiefdoms were driven from their land by the armies of other chiefdoms. This land was sold to the company which began rapidly expanding its planting and trading operations in Samoa.

In 1874, Steinberger visited Hamburg in Germany and made an agreement to act on behalf of Godeffroy & Sohn in exchange for their support for his efforts to negotiate a workable government in Samoa. Steinberger had agreed to try to accomplish four goals which would serve the interests of Godeffroy & Sohn. Firstly, he would obtain the consent of the Samoan government for the importation of indentured labour. Secondly, he would secure recognition for all German land claims. Thirdly, he would get the government to levy a tax on every Samoan chief to provide the government with 60 pounds of copra and 60 pounds of co-

---

4 *Ibid.*, 54.

conut fibre which the government would sell to Godeffroy & Sohn. The fourth item in the agreement was that Godeffroys would act as bankers to the Samoan Government.

Theodore Weber, the manager of this firm, was appointed German Consul. Godeffroy & Sohn was the biggest plantation interest in Samoa and Weber was frustrated at both Samoan and rival foreigners' restrictions on the expansion of their enterprises. Weber had pioneered the export of copra from Samoa. Previously locally processed coconut oil, which was prepared mainly by Samoans, who extracted the oil from grated coconut which had been left in the sun in old canoe hulls. By the time the oil reached Europe it had to be reprocessed before it could be used (for soap, cosmetics and medicines). Weber invented the method of drying the coconut meat which could then be exported in sacks and processed in Europe. The residue of the copra after the oil had been extracted was used as cattle feed, which added to the value of copra at that time. The fibre of the nut was also exported and used to make coarse mats and upholstery filling. To develop the industry the Germans needed more land and labour, and measures which would force the Samoans to grow and sell more coconuts. This provided the German company with a strong reason to press Germany to colonise Samoa.

By the 1890s the German plantations were extensively developed, as described by Stevenson writing in 1891:

> The total area in use is near ten thousand acres. Hedges of fragrant limes enclose, broad avenues intersect them. You shall walk for hours in parks of palm tree alleys, regular like soldiers on parade; in the recesses of the hills you may stumble on a mill house, toiling and trembling there, fathoms deep in superabundant forests. On the carpet of green sward, troops of horses and herds of handsome cattle may be seen to browse; and to one accustomed to the rough luxuriance of the tropics, the appearance is of fairyland. The managers, many of them German sea captains, are enthusiastic in their new employment. Experiment is constantly afoot; coffee and cacao, both of excellent quality are among the more recent outputs; and from one planation quantities of pineapples are send at a particular season to the Sydney markets. ... In these magnificent estates ... a fleet of ships must be remembered, and a strong staff of captains, supercargoes, overseers and clerks. These last mess together at a liberal board; the wages are high ... [and] ... seven or eight hundred imported [Melanesian] men and women toil for the company on contract of three or of five years.[5]

---

5 Ibid., 29–30.

7. The last Samoan government

In 1887, the forces of the rival Tamasese government attacked and defeated Malietoa and his allies, with the support of German warships. The Germans then deported Malietoa to the Marshall Islands. They hoped that in his absence, support for the government of Tupua Tamasese Titimaea would increase. However, Tamasese declared himself the holder of the four royal titles and also claimed the Malietoa title. This action antagonised many of his former supporters, including Mata'afa Iosefa who held the Tui Atua and who had a claim to the Malietoa title. Mata'afa raised support from the Malietoa factions with support from many Apia Europeans who acknowledged him as the rightful king. They supplied him with arms following which, he and his supporters went to war against Tamasese and his supporters.

The war of 1888 was probably the most savage since Samoa had opened up to foreigners. Each of the powers hurriedly sent for naval support as fighting spread through the Apia Municipality. These enforcements duly arrived, but were prevented from engaging in the action by the great hurricane of 1889. It sunk all but one of the ships. Three of the warships were American—the Trenton, the Vandalia and the Nipsic. Three were German—the Olga, the Adler and the Eber. The seventh warship was British, the Calliope. The American and German vessels were dashed to pieces against the shores and reefs of the harbour. Only the Calliope escaped, by getting out into the ocean beyond the force of the huge waves, which prevented the other ships from getting through the reef opening in time. Ninety two Germans and sixty three Americans lost their lives although many were saved by Samoans who risked their lives to swim out to the wrecked ships.

8. The Berlin Act and the Apia Municipality

The Berlin Act was passed by the three powers, German, Britain and the USA in 1889 to avoid war over Samoa. The provisions of the Act established a condominium or joint government by the representatives of the three powers over the Apia area, which became an internationally recognised foreign enclave (the Apia Municipality), governed by a joint council. The Act gave the Samoans very little power or recognition; it established a Supreme Court, to be presided over by a judge who was chosen by agreement between the three powers. In the event that they could not agree, the king of Sweden or Norway was to make the choice.

The great issue was to establish a Lands Commission to decide on land claims, which by that time exceed the acreage of the entire archipelago. The following table shows the results of the Land Commission of 1889.

Table 1. Results of the Land Commission of 1889

Nationality	Area claimed (acres)	Area confirmed by the Land Commission
German	134,419	75,000 (56%)
British	1,250,270	36,000 (3%)
American	302,746	21,000 (7%)
French	2,307	1, 3005 (7%)
Others	2,151	2,000 (95%)

Only eight percent or approximately 135,000 acres of the original land claims were confirmed. This represented less than 20 percent of the total area of Samoan land, but about 35 percent of land suitable for agricultural use. Along the north coast of Upolu from Apia to the western tip of the island, 60 percent of land which could be cultivated had been sold.

Although Mata'afa's side won the war he was not recognised as king by the three powers under the Berlin Act. This acknowledged Malietoa Laupepa as the rightful king. The Germans particularly objected to Mata'afa since he had thwarted their aspirations in the last war. Other Europeans in the Apia municipality regarded Mata'afa as the "rightful" king. Among other things, he had by that time been given the Malietoa title by the branch of the Sa Malietoa who did not support Malietoa Laupepa. They argued that since Mata'afa had won the war, and since he had all the correct genealogical connections, he should be the king. Stevenson wrote long letters in support of the Mata'afa side which were published in British newspapers. He also wrote a book in 1892 entitled *A Footnote to History* about the war.[6] But even if Mata'afa had been confirmed as the king, the task of reunification would still have been difficult because of the bitterness and desire for revenge by the Tupua supporters who had been defeated earlier by Mata'afa.

9. The final wars

The terms of the Berlin Act of 1889 offered little to the Samoan people and limited their independence. The explosive issue of the kingship remained unre-

---

6 *Ibid.*

solved and war was still imminent among the contenders. Mata'afa's closest allies were angry that he had not become king because when Tupua Tamasese Titimaea died in 1891, he had no rival from the Tupua side. Malietoa Laupepa, who had been brought back to Samoa in 1889, had said at first that Mata'afa should become king, but once he was among his supporters again they persuaded him to assert his own rights. So Mata'afa, the following year, began to disassociate himself from Malietoa Laupepa and began to gather military support for his right to become the king.

Hostilities broke out again in 1893 and Malietoa's supporters defeated those of Mata'afa. This time the consuls agreed to send Mata'afa into exile (the Germans in particular, had not forgiven Mata'afa's side for killing 17 German marines in the war of 1888). Tupua Tamasese Titimaea was succeeded by his son Tupua Tamasese Lealofi I. In 1898, Malietoa Laupepa died and the same year, Mata'afa, having meanwhile signed a pledge of allegiance to Malietoa Laupepa, was brought back from exile. With Malietoa Laupepa gone, Mata'afa may may well have expected to have been made king, but two factors intervened; first, Tupua Tamasese Leolofi I was contesting the office himself as the representative of the Sa Tupua and secondly, Malietoa Laupepa had been succeeded to the Malietoa title by his son, Malietoa Tanumafili I. The contest over the succession to the Malietoa title was taken to the Supreme Court. The Chief Justice decided in favour of Malietoa Tanumafili, a youth of nineteen years. Because the court had been established without consultation with the Samoans, they disregarded the verdict. Mata'afa and his supporters prepared for war. In January, 1899, they drove Malietoa Tanumafili's forces out of Apia, and established a de-facto government which was promptly recognized by all three consuls. British and American warships were involved, and the American shelling of Apia caused extensive damage to property.

In the same year, a joint commission was sent by the German, British and US government which ordered all armaments to be surrendered, and once again, declared Malietoa Tanumafili to be king but then decided to abolish the office of king altogether, with full political authority handed to the consuls. This arrangement preceded a new agreement between the three powers in December 1899. It resulted in Britain renouncing her claim to the Samoan islands enabling Germany and the United States to divided the archipelago between them. Germany took the main Western islands where their plantation interests were centered. America took the Eastern group because they wanted to maintain control of the Pago Pago harbour of Tutuila for a naval base.

10. German Samoa

The German annexation of Samoa was motivated by the interests of the plantation company Deutsche Handels and Plantagen Gesellschaft (D.H.P.G.) which had taken over the assets of Godeffroy & Sohn. Therefore, the new Governor of the Colony, Wilhelm Solf (formerly executive officer of the Apia Municipality in 1899) gave the interests of the company high priority in his administration. He soon became unpopular with the other settlers, including a number of German citizens, as he did not encourage smaller planters. Solf believed that planting was not profitable on a small scale and believed that the Europeans who tried to make their fortunes planting on a small scale would inevitably become poor and eventually, "go native". This in turn would lower the prestige of Europeans in Samoa. Solf also believed that small-scale planters were a bad influence on Samoans since they were likely to get involved in Samoan politics and cause trouble in order to get more land from the Samoans.

The D.H.P.G. was a very large operation. It was based in Germany and had branches in German New Guinea. The plantations were run by employees of the company and they could be dismissed and sent home if they caused trouble for the colonial administration. The large scale in which the company operated meant that the administration could maintain a balance between its operational needs and the welfare of the Samoans. The company brought in labour from overseas with the importation of indentured labour beginning in the 1880s. The right to import labour had been a source of disagreement between the Germans and other settlers and successive Samoan governments. Many missionaries, settlers and Samoan leaders opposed the idea. The European settlers were prejudiced against Chinese settlers and had persuaded the Malietoa Laupepa Government to forbid Chinese settlers to come to Samoa. This prejudice was common in the nineteenth century in the Australian and Californian gold fields, where Chinese immigrant miners were a threat because they worked hard and competed with Europeans.

But it was to prevent Samoans from being forced to work as labourers that Governor Soft decided to allow the continued importation of labourers for the D.H.P.G. plantations. In 1884, Germany had annexed north-eastern New Guinea and the Western Solomon Islands, giving German firms a privileged position from which to recruit Melanesian labour from those areas. From 1882, people in these areas were recruited extensively for the Samoan plantations. Recruits for D.H.P.G. were taken to the Duke of York Islands, where the company had a trading post and, from there travelled on a company ship, the Samoa, to work on plantations in German Samoa. The Melanesian recruits signed on in order to obtain foreign goods since they were paid in goods such as knives, axes, cloth and lamps after working for three years. Before 1900, guns and liquor were given as payment, along with other goods.

During the recruiting period, over 7,000 Melanesian workers were brought to Samoa. After 1900, D.H.P.G. also began to import Chinese labour. These labourers were available to other planters as well as D.H.P.G., but only the big company was allowed to employ Melanesians. During the period 1900 to 1914, Melanesian labourers were recruited mostly from Bougainville, in the North Solomons, from the Bismarck Archipelago of Papua New Guinea, and from Malaita in the Solomon Islands. The three main D.H.P.G. plantations were on the north coast of Upolu—at Mulifanua, Vaitele and Vailele. The company operated a store and central administration offices at Sogi in Apia. The Mulifanua estate was over 5,000 acres, divided into seven management units ranging from 50 to 800 acres. In 1906, the labour force consisted of 300 Melanesians and 16 Chinese. At Vailele, there were 130 Melanesians, and at Vaitele there were 130 Melanesians as well as 30 Chinese.

The Melanesians were under privileged compared to the Chinese, who began to arrive as indentured labour from 1903 onwards. After 1908, there was a Chinese consul to make sure that the Chinese were treated fairly and paid regularly. Before 1905, the Chinese were paid ten shillings a month and afterwards, twelve shillings a month, plus rations. Their quarters and working conditions were regularly inspected and a ward was set aside for them at the Apia hospital. In 1912, the legal status of the Chinese was changed from Native to European, meaning that they were given the legal privileges of Europeans. In contrast, Melanesians received no cash wages, were restricted entirely to D.H.P.G. employment, had no legal status as "native" or as "Europeans", and had no representatives or authorities to keep an eye on their living and working conditions. The only medical facility for them was a clinic at the D.H.P.G. headquarters in Apia. The German and other European overseers on the plantations were allowed to punish the Melanesians by beating them with whips and using other cruel methods.

Both the Chinese and Melanesians were forbidden to mix with Samoans. This was because of racial prejudices among Samoan leaders and Europeans. Because the Chinese had the freedom to work for any employer they chose, and to travel around without restrictions, they could easily ignore these rules and find Samoan wives. The Melanesians were cut away on the D.H.P.G. plantations and had less opportunity to mix with Samoans. It was not until the New Zealand administration began, after 1914, that Melanesians were able to marry Samoans, and even then it was a move that was officially disapproved. Nevertheless, intermarriage between Samoans and Melanesians, and Samoans and Chinese was quite common. In 1914, there were 877 Melanesian and 2,200 Chinese labourers in German Samoa.

Land acquisition was also controlled by giving preferential treatment to D.H.P.G. The company had control of the largest amount of alienated land, including some of the best agricultural land. When further land was required, or if dealings with the Samoans on land matters were necessary, the colonial administration conducted negotiations. Solf wanted to balance the economic interests of the colony by making Samoans plant coconuts. This, he believed, would make the Samoans more prosperous and enable them to pay taxes to the colonial administration, to offset administrative costs. It would also serve D.H.P.G. interests, because they could buy and export Samoan grown copra. Consequently, Samoan landholders were required to plant a minimum number of coconuts each year, and were fined if they did not. Copra was the major source of income for the colony. From 1900–1902, the average annual export of copra was just under 6,000 tons. From 1910–1912, it increased to 10,000 tons. Rising copra prices assisted the profitability of the crop; from 1900–1902 the average annual value was £63,500. This rose to £173,400 from 1910–1912. Cocoa planting began about 1900 and by 1910–1912 it had become the second most valuable crop, yielding about 600 tons and earning over £35,000. Rubber planting began and other tropical crops were under experimental development.

The dissatisfaction with Solf's economic policy among the smaller planters continued throughout his administration. His most outspoken opponent was Richard Deeken, a German who dreamed of transforming Samoa into a paradise of small plantations for German settlers. Deeken wrote a book which became very popular in Germany. It was full of romantic misrepresentations about Samoa; in particular, the supposed advantages for the small-scale settler. Deekens' trouble-making led to Solf's having to return to Germany to explain his administration's policy which was upheld by the colonial office, and a few years later Solf was promoted to the post of colonial secretary for the German empire. This suggests that Solf's economic policy of encouraging large capitalist enterprises and discouraging small scale settlement, was a model of German colonial policy.

11. The German administration

When Solf made his first speech to the Samoans after German annexation in 1900, he told them that he would govern them in accordance with Samoan custom. Samoans were soon to learn that Samoan custom was allowed only in Solf's administration when it aligned with the governor's plans. His first move was to settle the question of kingship. There was to be no Samoan king, only an Ali'i Sill or paramount chief. This office was given to Mata'afa Iosefa, who seemed to have the support of the majority of Samoans and was the eldest of the Sa Tupua and Sa Malietoa lineages. Solf soon made it clear that there was to be no recognition of other claims by chiefly factions. Solf wanted to abolish the four royal titles completely. There were to be no more opportunities for the king-making groups of orator-chiefs, such as Tumua and Pule, to bestow the titles and make their own kings. Instead, Solf offered recognition to the paramount titles of the Sa Tupua and Sa Malietoa which, in contemporary history, have been Tupua Tamasese (although the name of Tamasese is well known, it has historically been associated with the Tupua title), Mata'afa, Tuimaleali'ifano and Malietoa.

Another early action of the German administration was to disarm Samoans. By the end of 1901, 1,500 rifles had been collected. The Governor had an administrative staff and an advisory committee made up of three senior members of the administration and five members appointed from the local European community. The native administration was headed by Mata'afa. The role that Solf had allocated to him as the *Ali'i Sili* was that of an intermediary through whom the wishes and orders of the governor are made known to the Samoans. Associated with the *Ali'i Sili* was a governing council to represent all the districts of Samoa, with most of the appointees having been members of government in the 1890s. A subsidiary district administration was appointed by Solf who chose an influential chief from each district for these offices. Village representatives were also appointed, elected by, and from among the village council of chiefs but confirmation of their positions required the agreement of the governor. An important instrument of Solf's policy was the Lands and Titles Commission, but this was not established until 1903. The decisions of the 1889 Commission under the Berlin Act were upheld by the German administration.

There is evidence that Samoans accepted German rule initially with relief and co-operation. The civil wars of the late nineteenth century had been tragic and disruptive, and Samoans looked forward to a period of peace and security. Solf enjoyed the respect of the Samoans who, in the early days of his administration, referred to him as a "father". It is clear that Samoans did not understand that German annexation effectively stripped them of any real power, and it seems likely that they thought the Germans had established a protectorate, such as Britain had established over Tonga, which permitted internal self-government.

12. The dismantling of Samoan authority

The first indication that Solf intended to interfere with Samoan custom (and evidence of his understanding of significant Samoan customs) was in 1901. Mata'afa and his highest ranking kinsmen had prepared a traditional ceremony that confirms a new status or position, in this instance Mata'afa's appointment as *Ali'i Sili*. The ceremony took the form of distributing fine mats (Samoa's most important traditional valuable) which had been collected by Mata'afa's extended family, to all the important chiefs and orator groups of Samoa. When Solf heard of Mata'afa's plans he realized that this was an occasion on which many important expressions of traditional authority could be made, and one which might revive divisions among Samoans or create the impression that Mata'afa was the king. Accordingly, Solf instructed Mata'afa to hold the ceremony at Mulinu'u the seat of the government, instead of at Amaile, the seat of the Mata'afa title. No food was to be distributed and every district was to be given equal recognition in the number and quality of fine mats presented. Furthermore, Solf ordered that the parties from each district leave Mulinu'u as soon as they had received their gifts, without staying to see what other parties were being given. The ceremony went ahead according to Solf's orders, and Mata'afa made a speech declaring that his position as *Ali'i Sili* came from the German emperor. This was a new development for Samoan leaders since in the past, only Samoans could create a paramount chief. Furthermore, it was unheard of for a recognition ceremony to be held in such a manner, omitting the traditional recognition of the orator groups Tumua and Pule. By the second year of his administration, Solf had come into conflict with many members of the native administration and, his decisions clearly indicated that he was the ultimate authority in any matter that he chose to be involved in.

In February 1903, the German administration established the Lands and Titles Commission to adjudicate Samoan lands and titles disputes. There were no Samoans appointed to the Commission which was made up of the imperial judge, Dr E.E. Schultz, and two local European land surveyors. This new authority assumed responsibility for matters which had previously been the exclusive concern of Samoan villages, districts and family heads. However, a panel of Samoan advisers was appointed to the Commission from each administrative district.

By 1904, there was open antagonism towards Solf's administration from Samoans within, and outside the native government and by 1905, Solf had lost patience with them and he took actions which made it clear that Germany was to exercise all authority in the government of Samoa. Denouncing the orator groups

Tumua and Pule, Solf made it clear that he intended to give them no voice in government. He made changes to leaders of the native government and ordered them to stay in their villages instead of in the houses at the government's headquarters at Mulinu'u. From that time on, Solf called upon the Faipule to come to Mulinu'u only when he wanted to discuss something with them. The highest ranking chiefs of the native government remained at Mulinu'u where Solf could observe their activities. In 1912 when Mata'afa died, Governor Solf's successor, Dr Erich Schultz-Ewerth, abolished the position of *Ali'i Sili*, in accordance with long-term German policy to gradually remove all the traditional political institutions which gave the Samoans a basis for united action. Solf's plan was to proceed slowly in the destruction of the Samoan political system in order to avoid confrontation with its leaders. The office of *Ali'i Sili* was replaced by a new position Fautua or adviser. This was held jointly by Malietoa Tanumafili I and Tupua Tamasese Lealofi I. When they were appointed in 1913, they were required to swear an oath of allegiance to the German emperor. To complete the process by which Germany asserted supremacy, the Samoan national fa'alupega (national ceremonial address) which had previously honoured Tumua and Pule, the districts, and the paramount families of Samoa, was changed to honour the Kaiser of Germany and the officials of the administration in Samoa.

13. The 'Oloa Company

A source of discontent among Samoans was the drop in copra prices during the early 1900s which declined from nine cents a pound to five cents a pound. It was during this time that conflict between Solf and the independent planters was developing, and Solf's opponent Richard Deeken and his associates began to spread rumours that the German government was to blame for the decreasing prices.

At this point in Samoan history, people who were part-Europeans formed a significant interest group. A distinct social class, or sub-group of people of mixed race, can only arise when two populations, with marked differences in culture and physical appearance, meet on an unequal footing. A legally and socially defined "half-caste" group is therefore often the creation of a colonial situation. The separation of such a group from the two ethnic communities which created it, reflects the racial prejudices of eighteenth and nineteenth century Europeans. Part-Europeans, or "*Afakasi*", were the descendants of European settlers and their Samoan wives. Their emergence as a distinct social group in the early nineteenth century was the result of the Europeans' racist conviction, that persons of mixed blood were inferior to persons of "pure" European descent. Nevertheless, since the part-Europeans included sons and daughters of Samoa's wealthiest and most influential foreign settlers, they were legally classified as Europeans. This classification created an artificial barrier between children of mixed marriages and their maternal relatives, through legal distinctions between the rights of natives and the rights of Europeans.

By law, legitimately born offspring of foreigners (and this included Chinese) and Samoans succeeded to the legal status of their fathers. This legislation did not mean that the children of mixed marriages necessarily inherited their father's foreign nationality and in most cases, they did not. What it meant was that they were classified as resident aliens. Part-Samoans whose parents had not been married were classified as "natives". This was also the case if the European ancestry was on the mother's side. However, in 1903, the German Administration recognized that this placed many local-born people in social difficulties, since, as "natives", they could not buy liquor, enter a hotel, or inherit their father's property. Therefore, an ordinance was passed, permitting illegitimate part-Samoans, on application to the High Court, to be registered as resident aliens. Each case was considered on the grounds of whether the applicant lived as a European and possessed a certain percentage of foreign ancestry. Between 1903 and 1914, 391 persons applied for, and received, a change in legal status from 'native' to European, making them eligible for all foreign privileges, and exempt from all laws directed at Samoans. Since these rights were passed on to children, the law added a substantial number of families to the "local-born" community which, in 1903, numbered 599 and in 1910 the census recorded 1,033 part-Samoans registered as resident-aliens.

Division between Samoans and part-Samoans was probably an intentional creation of the German administration. Also, the participation of English and German-speaking part-Europeans in Samoan politics was discouraged by the German authorities. This became obvious when a part-European named Pullack promoted the idea of establishing a national trading company, to be owned by Samoan shareholders, which would buy copra from Samoan growers and export it. Pullack proposed that the capital to establish the company be raised in the same way that funds had been raised to pay compensation to consuls and naval officers in the nineteenth century; by each village contributing a set amount to a central fund. The idea appealed strongly to many members of the native government, since it seemed to suggest a means by which the Samoan Government could finance itself and even assert independence of German authority.

When Solf heard of the proposed Oloa Kamupani (trading company), as it came to be known, he opposed it and ordered the native government to give up the idea. Solf saw the proposal as a threat to the German administration and to the economic supremacy of European commercial interests in Samoa. He also believed that Samoans lacked the education and commercial knowledge to make the company a success. Samoan leaders decided to ignore Solf's prohibition, and representatives of Tumua and Pule spread the news, and gathered support for the company in villages throughout Samoa. While Solf was overseas, Schultz, the imperial judge and acting governor, tried to break up the movement by imprisoning two representatives of Pule, Malae'ulu and Namulau'ulu Pulai. These chiefs had been actively promoting the company, and Schultz arrested them for "disturbing the peace". Schultz also went on an official trip around Samoa to all the main villages, and tried to discredit the idea of the company and the actions of its promoters.

In January 1905, a group of members of the native government, including Tupua Tamasese, broke into the jail and released the two orators of Pule, after the German administration had denied Mata'afa's request that they be set free. But the sense of unity between Samoan leaders and the promoters of the company did not last, and factions for, and against, the company developed. This eventually led to the idea being abandoned.

14. The *Mau* of Pule

The failure of the 'Oloa movement did not stop Samoans from wanting to have a greater voice in governing the country. Namulau'ulu Lauaki Mamoe (whom shall be referred to as Lauaki), an orator chief of one of the traditional Pule districts of Savai'i, was a very important spokesman in Samoan politics and a member of the native government. By 1905, Lauaki articulated a number of objections to the German administration. Firstly, chiefs had lost the power to represent their families in the government of Samoa. In the days before the German administration, executive authority was shared among groups of orators and they had a voice in making the rules which governed the country. Secondly, it was wrong for a foreign authority to imprison and threaten Samoans. Thirdly, Lauaki felt that Samoans should take part in all aspects of national development, and not be excluded as they had been. Having heard about the British protectorate in Tonga, Lauaki declared that he wished for Britain to replace the German authorities in Samoa. The objection to German rule, expressed by Lauaki, came to be shared by many other chiefs, particularly among the *Pule* of Savai'i. A movement began which was known as the *Mau a Pule*, the Opinion of Pule. The supporters of the movement paid their taxes to the *Mau* instead of the government. According to an oral tradition from Savai'i, the first tax money collected by the *Mau a Pule* was used to buy horse-driven carts for Lauaki and Malietoa Tanumafili so they could be equal in dignity with the German administrators.

When Solf returned from overseas in 1908, having gone abroad to get married, Lauaki organized a big ceremony of welcome for the governor and his bride. He used the occasion to present a petition to Solf, complaining about the German administration. Lauaki was by then becoming impatient with Mata'afa Iosefa for allowing Solf to dictate to him, and considered transferring the support of Pule ware from Mata'afa to Malietoa and Tamasese as representatives of the Samoan Malo. The *Mau a Pule* was the first attempt by Samoans to reinstate their independence and assert their authority. In his petition to Solf, Lauaki demanded that German authorities show more respect to Mata'afa as he was the representative of the dignity of the Samoan people. The demand was for the titular heads of the two great lineages of Samoa to stay at Mulinu'u to assert the dignity of the Samoan government and for Mata'afa' s signature to appear beside that of Solf on important government papers. He also demanded that the German administration should be held accountable to the Samoan people for their expenditures. Also, Samoa should become fully independent as soon as possible. After travelling around the country to seek support for resistance to German authority, Lauaki finally decided to confront the governor. Davidson presents the following account of the motivation for Lauaki decision:

> Early in 1908 Lauaki Mamoe visited the Ali'i Sill at Mulinu'u. He found Mata'afa bitterly regretting his loss of power. 'I have wept,' he said, 'at the idea of Tolo and Laupu'e parading along the main road at Mulinu'u in their white coats, and neither advising nor consulting me about anything whatsoever. In the old days when the Faipule met at Mulinu'u it was I who had the power.[7]

In January 1909, when Lauaki was summoned by the governor to Mulinu'u, he set out with a fleet of canoes manned by his supporters from Savai'i, Apolima and Manono. They met their supporters from Tuamasaga who had gathered at Vaiusu, across the bay from Mulinu'u and sailed or rowed into the harbour in an impressive show of solidarity. When Solf could not persuade Lauaki to give up his opposition to German rule (in exchange for Solf's forgiveness for his rebellious challenge), Solf decided to punish him. On the arrival of German warships in Samoa, Lauaki and nine other chiefs were taken into custody. Accompanied by their families and a pastor, they were taken to the island of Saipan, in the Mariana Islands, which was also one of Germany's Pacific colonies. Solf

---

7 J. W. Davidson, *Samoa Mo Samoa: The Emergence of the Independent State of Western Samoa* (Melbourne: Oxford University press, 1967), 84.

thus brought about the end of the *Mau a Pule*. Namulau'ulu Lauaki Mamoe was the first leader of the Samoan independence movement, which was not to be successful for another fifty years. He died at sea, in 1915, aboard the ship which had been sent by the New Zealand authorities to bring him and his supporters home.

15. Conclusion

In 1914, a New Zealand military expedition seized control of the western part of the Samoa archipelago and established an interim administration based on the one established under German rule. Many of the institutions established by Germany still exist, notably the Land and Titles Court (formerly the Land and Titles Commission) and the modified traditional system of village government established under German administration. New Zealand's administration was bitterly opposed, but using passive resistance measures (the second *Mau*) by most of Samoa's leaders in the late 1920s and throughout the 1930s until a more inclusive system of government was introduced. Samoa became an independent country in 1962; the first of the Pacific Islands to do so.

The German administration of Samoa has been admired by many historians. It has been suggested governor Solf was a man ahead of his time, who ruled the Samoans fairly and wisely. In comparison with the governors of other colonies during this period, this claim is probably true. In some other parts of the world, colonial regimes were encouraging white settlers to grab land and use violence against native people who resisted. Solf protected Samoan land rights, prevented Samoans from being forced to labour on plantations, restricted white settlement of Samoa, and gave the country a period of peace and prosperity. This is why many old people heard about the German period as a good time in Samoan history. Indeed, in 1923, when Samoan leaders were becoming dissatisfied with the New Zealand administration, a telegram was sent to Solf while he was German ambassador to Japan, requesting him to return as governor once more.[8]

The alienation of land was under tragic circumstances at the time, but that land has been preserved to become a major asset of the Independent government of Samoa. Following Germany's defeat in World War I, the New Zealand occupation and administration of Samoa was formalised under a League of Nations Mandate in December 1920. The Samoa Act of 1921 transferred all freehold

---

[8] P. J. Hempenstall, *Pacific Islanders under German rule: A Study in the Meaning of Colonial Resistance* (Canberra: Australian National University Press, 1978), 68.

land held by German entities to the New Zealand administration. These former German plantations were managed by the New Zealand administration through the New Zealand Reparation Estates. Various parcels of land later became classified as government land and when Samoa gained independence in 1962, the large plantations became state property incorporated as the Western Samoa Trust Estates Corporation (WSTEC), now the Samoa Land Corporation (SLC). In the 1990s, the large landholdings of the Western Samoa Trusts Estates Corporation (WSTEC) were divided between two statuary corporations: STEC (renamed when Western Samoa was renamed Samoa) and the Samoa Land Corporation, and the Ministry of Natural Resources and Environment. This followed the financial collapse of former WSTEC and the government assuming responsibility for its multi-million SAT$ debt. Approximately 70 percent of WSTEC land was transferred to the government under the legislative provisions of the Samoa Trust Estates Corporation Reconstruction Act 1990. STEC retains 650 acres at Faleolo (Upolu) along with other smaller holdings on Upolu, and 1,200 acres in Savai'i.

Today there are three categories of land tenure in Samoa today—government land (mainly the former German holdings), freeheld or private owned land, and customary land. According to Ward and Ashcroft[9], government land constitutes approximately 15 per cent of all land, with 11 per cent under direct government management and four per cent under WSTEC/SLC management. Under New Zealand and the Independent State of Samoa, the plantations never recovered their former glory, but state ownership of these areas of former German land has provided the government with land for housing development, industries, tourist facilities, small-holder agricultural leases and government-owned agricultural industries, all contributing to modern Samoa's economic development.

Another remnant of the German period is the large and now somewhat derelict building on Beach Road in Apia known as 'the old court house' in reference to its last use before it was abandoned. The building is a pearl of Pacific colonial architecture. Built in 1901 it has successively served as the headquarters of three administrations, Germany, New Zealand and Samoa. It is now in the custody of a trust which has been trying for several years for find funds to restore it to its original condition, for use as a museum and cultural centre.

Finally there is the legacy of Germany in the genes and names in Samoa, where dozens of prominent Samoan families bear ancestral German names such as Keil, Schaffhausen, Brebner, Retzlaff and many more, including the first author of this paper, whose great grandfather was Emil Huch from Hamburg.

---

[9] R. Gerard Ward and Paul Ashcroft, *Samoa: Mapping the Diversity* (Suva Fiji: Institute of Pacific Studies and the National university of Samoa, 1998), 61–65.

Huch came to Samoa to work for Hedermanns trading company, and remained to become the operator of a successful coastal shipping business and founder of six more German-named families because all but one of his children by his first wife Sineva of Vaovai, married into other German-Samoan families. The second author is a granddaughter of Alfred Schoeffel from Württemberg, who was apprenticed to and later managed the same Pacific trading company when it became Hederman & Evers in Levuka, Fiji.

Works cited

Davidson, J.W. 1967. *Samoa Mo Samoa: The Emergence of the Independent State of Western Samoa.* Melbourne, Oxford University press.

Gilson, R.P. 1970. *Samoa: 1830–1900: The Politics of a Multi-cultural Community.* Melbourne, Oxford University Press.

Hempenstall, P.J. 1978. *Pacific Islanders under German rule: A Study in the Meaning of Colonial Resistance.* Canberra: Australian National University Press.

Ide, Henry C. 1899. "The Imbroglio in Samoa." *The North American Review*, Volume 168.

Kennedy, Paul M. 1974. *The Samoan Tangle: A Study in Anglo German Relations 1878–1900.* New York, Barnes and Noble.

Meleisea Malama, Penelope Schoeffel, et. al. 1987 *Lagaga: A short History of Samoa.* Institute of Pacific Studies (Much of this article has been abridged from our chapters in this book).

Stevenson, Robert Louis, 1967. *A Footnote to History: Eight Years of Trouble in Samoa.* London. Dawsons of Pall Mall [1892].

Ward, R. Gerard and Paul Ashcroft, 1998, *Samoa: Mapping the Diversity.* Suva Fiji, Institute of Pacific Studies and the National university of Samoa.

Craig Alan Volker
The legacy of the German language in Papua New Guinea

1. Introduction[1]

German colonial rule in the western Pacific began formally in 1884 when unbeknown to them, people in north-eastern New Guinea (Kaiser Wilhelmsland), the archipelago around the Bismarck Sea, and in the next year, almost all of neighboring Micronesia were proclaimed to be under German "protection". This act changed ways of living that had existed for tens of thousands of years and laid the foundation for what eventually became the modern state of Papua New Guinea. This proclamation was made in German, a language that was then unknown to Melanesians and Micronesians.

Today the German language is again mostly unknown to most Melanesians and only a few visible traces of any German colonial legacy remain. There are no old colonial buildings, no monuments outside of a few small and almost hidden cemeteries, and no German Clubs or public signs in German. In this century there has not even been a German embassy. But it is impossible to step out in New Ireland (the former "Neu-Mecklenburg"), for example, without being confronted by a twenty-first century reality that is in part a creation of German colonial rule. Species that were introduced by the Germans still retain their German name, from clover, *Klee* in both German and the local Nalik language to pineapples (German *Ananas* / Nalik *a nanas*). The best rural road in the country, the Bulominski Highway was started by and named after the last German governor of Neu-Mecklenburg and a mountain range is known as the Schleinitz Range. Locals have names such as Gertrud, Helga, Gustav, Guenther, and even Adolf and the language spoken by the locals—Tok Pisin, is one peppered with German words that became the lingua franca in German New Guinea because of widespread mobility under the Germans.

Shopping in Kavieng, the provincial capital founded by Germans as Käwieng, is popular, from where the island of New Hanover can be spotted on a clear day. The best prices are at Chinese shops, many of which are still owned

---

[1] Unless otherwise stated, information presented here comes from interviews and recordings made in Germany, Papua New Guinea, and Australia from 1979 to the present. I wish to thank the many people who so patiently answered questions and were willing to *tok stori*.

Klee (clover) garden in New Ireland (Neu-Mecklenburg)

by descendants of people brought out under Germans. At the other end of Neu-Mecklenburg/ New Ireland, cotton grows wild. It was part of an experiment that died with the Australian invasion.

In some villages it is difficult to acquire plots of land for gardening because of the large plantations surrounding the villages on land alienated from customary clan ownership by German colonial governors and which even today are controlled by foreigners.

The German colonial legacy is an ever–present background, but at the same time invisible and not part of conscious thought. The German legacy is rarely discussed and for most people not particularly controversial. Today the positive aspects of that time are usually emphasized, such as the beauty of the town of Rabaul (Simpsonhafen) before its destruction by volcanic eruption, the introduction of Christianity, and new technologies such as the wheel and iron tools. There is even a religious hymn giving praise for "living in a new day where we have wheels for travel, metal for tools, knowing the world knows us and we know the world". Negative attitudes towards colonialism are usually reserved for Australia, the more recent colonial master, with unfavorable comparisons often made between the slow pace of development in the Australian era

Bulominski Highway in New Ireland (Neu-Mecklenburg) (photo by Cláudio da Silva)

and the much greater development during the much shorter German era. Germany seems to have won the colonial popularity contest by losing its colony long before decolonialization could ever be even conceived of.

Language is the most palpable expression of culture, especially in Papua New Guinea, which with over 830 languages has more languages than any other country in the world. Since language is an important ethnic and cultural marker, this paper examines the visibility of the German language in Papua New Guinea in four historical periods, from 1884 to the present, using it as an indicator of the legacy of German colonialism, of the tenacity of this legacy, and of what Kößler has correctly called German colonial amnesia.[2]

---

[2] See Reinhart Kößler, "La fin d'une amnésie? L'Alemagne et son passé colonial depuis 2004," *Politique Africaine* 2, 102 (2006): 50–66.

2. The German language in the German colonial era (1884–1914)

2.1 German in government and business

Until 1899, German New Guinea was administered directly by the Neuguinea Compagnie, so that business rather than ideology governed language policies. Melanesian Pidgin English, the ancestor of today's Tok Pisin, developed on multi-ethnic sailing ships and spread quickly among "blackbirded" (indentured) Melanesian workers, who spoke many different languages and came together for the first time on plantations in both English and German colonies. Most German plantation and other commercial owners and employees already had a good command of English and found it much easier to use a pidginized English when speaking with indigenous and Asian people rather than trying to waste time and resources to teach them German. Some even argued against allowing indigenous people to learn German because it was such a useful secret language for Germans to use amongst themselves.[3] In addition, many prominent business people in the colony, most notably "Queen" Emma Forsayth-Coe, were non-Germans, speaking English or other languages and having no vested interest in what was for them a foreign language.[4] The situation was made even more complicated by the many Chinese and Malay speakers brought as artisans and craftsmen to the Bismarck Archipelago during this time.

Bureaucrats and jingoists in Berlin had a different opinion. In 1897, for example, the German Colonial Society lobbied the government to take over the colony and subsidize mission schools following a government curriculum that encouraged the learning and use of German.[5] German was, of course, the language of administration once the government set up a colonial administration in 1899. Increasing attempts were made to foster the German language among Chinese and Melanesians. Just before the colony was lost to the invading Australians,

---

3 Peter Mühlhäusler, "Tracing the roots of pidgin German," *Language and Communication* 41,1 (1984): 35.
4 See R. W. Robson, *Queen Emma: The Samoan-American Girl who founded an Empire in the 19th Century New Guinea* (Sydney/New York: Pacific Publications, 1973).
5 Heinrich Schnee, *Deutsches Kolonial-Lexikon* (Leipzig: Quelle & Meyer, 1920), 308. original print edition digitalized by the Stadt- und Universitätsbibliothek Frankfurt am Main, accessed May 1, 2007, www.ub.bildarchiv-dkg.uni-frankfurt.de/Bildprojekt/Lexikon/Standardframeseite.php.

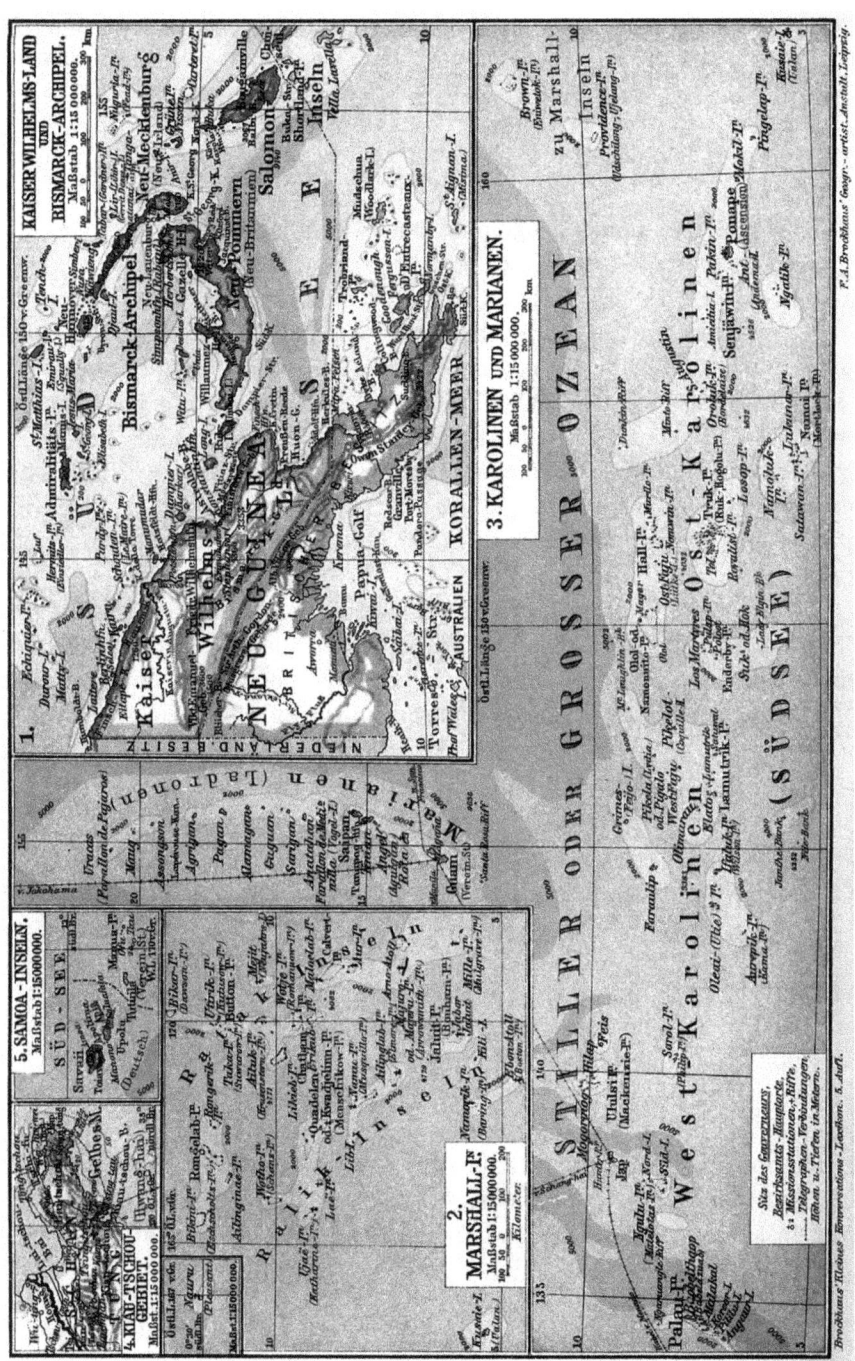

Map of German New Guinea

the colonial government was drafting legislation to expand German-language education in the areas under its control.⁶ This legislation was never enacted.

2.2 German names

During this period German geographic names were introduced throughout the island and coastal parts of the colony. In general these were used in places where there were no appropriate indigenous names. Often these words were used for large geographic entities that were too big to be a concept in the geographically small Melanesian cultures of the time, such as Neu-Pommern (today's New Britain) or Kaiser Wilhelmsland (the northern part of the island of New Guinea). At other times German was used for the names of rivers or mountain ranges spanning different language groups, each of which might have a different name for the same thing. Settlements and towns also tended to be given German names, even if there was an existing local name (such as Herbertshöhe for Kokopo).

At the same time that places were being given German names, German missionaries were baptizing an increasing number of Melanesians, often with new German names of saints or Bible personages. This followed a custom found in many Melanesian societies, where people are known by different names to different people, depending on their status or mother tongue, and where these names can be added to or changed with little or no ritual.

2.3 Education and access to the German language during the German colonial period.

From the very beginning, education was mostly in the hands of Christian missionaries, who saw their role as bringers of European civilization as much as of religious truth. According to the *Deutsches Kolonial-Lexikon*, when World War I began, there were 56 Protestant and 189 Catholic schools for indigenous students.⁷ Education was limited to basic literacy, religious instruction, and vocational training. It was usually in one of the languages chosen as regional lingua franca for missionary purposes. The medium of instruction was Kâte and Jabêm in Kaiser Wilhelmsland and Kuanua, (the language of the Tolai people

---

6 Mühlhäusler, "Tracing the roots of pidgin German," *art. cit.*, 34.
7 See Schnee, *Deutsches Kolonial-Lexikon, op. cit.*

of Neu-Pommern / New Britain) in the Bismarck Archipelago, but in a few schools, German was taught, especially to older students. The transfer of technology, new species, and religious training at these schools resulted in many loanwords from German into Tok Pisin and vernacular languages, many of which remain today, as with the examples of *Klee* and *a nanas* in Nalik.

There is evidence that in at least a couple of these schools, students used what Peter Mühlhäusler has called a pidgin German amongst themselves as a common language.[8] This does not seem to have been a systematic language, as there is much variation in the data he presents. It is more like the kind of German one sees in classes of German for foreigners, where students do not yet have a command of German structures.

In contrast to the many mission schools, the *Deutsches Kolonial-Lexikon* lists only two government schools for indigenous people in German New Guinea when World War I began, one in Simpsonshafen (Rabaul) and the other in Micronesia.[9] These seem to have been quite effective at teaching communicative German. In 1979 I met Mr ToUrapal, a Tolai elder who had attended the school as a boy and was still able to speak in German quite effortlessly.

2.4 German-speaking residents

During the first few years of the colony, when it was under the control of the Neuguinea Kompagnie, only a small number of Europeans came to the colony. At the time of its handover to the German government in 1899, there were only 400 white people in the colony. This grew to 1427 in 1913, of whom all but 400 were from Germany or other German-speaking countries.[10] Only one-quarter were female, and many of them nuns, so it is not surprising that many European had marriages or other relations with local women. In 1913 the government counted 281 "mixed-race" persons (*Mischlinge*)[11]. Of these many, but not all, would have been German-speaking and some were able to register themselves as German citizens. Many were educated in German at a Protestant school in Sat-

---

8 Mühlhäusler, "Tracing the roots of pidgin German," *art. cit.*, 35–36.
9 See Schnee, *Deutsches Kolonial-Lexikon, op. cit.*
10 *Ibid.*
11 Although possibly considered pejorative elsewhere, in Papua New Guinea mixed-race is normally used in English to describe persons with mixed heritage, including persons with two indigenous heritages. It is therefore used in this paper with this non-pejorative Papua New Guinean connotation.

telberg in Kaiser Wilhelmsland or at the Vunapope Catholic Mission near the colonial capital Herbertshöhe near Simpsonshafen (Rabaul).

2.4.1 The Unserdeutsch mixed-race children at Vunapope

The mixed-race children at Vunapope have proved to be a much more cohesive group than those at Sattelberg. Even today they remain a community, while the descendants of the Sattelberg children have been assimilated into Papua New Guinean or Australian society. The descendants of the Vunapope children are linked by Unserdeutsch (also known as Rabaul Creole German), the only known creole German to have arisen in the German colonial empire.

In 1898 the Vunapope Catholic Mission opened a school and "sanctuary" specifically for mixed-race children. Under the leadership of Bishop Coupé, an effort was made to use this to raise a critical mass of Catholic young people of the colony but isolated from indigenous culture who could form the nucleus of a Christian society in the Pacific.[12] Besides caring for abandoned children, the missionaries went to villages looking for mixed-race children to take to the orphanage so they could be given a European and Christian education and be kept away from the "vile habits" of their indigenous mothers (Janssen 1932:150, author's translation). Children in stable families were also brought to the school by their German fathers who wanted them to have a European education.

Although we do not know with any certainty how the creole developed, we do know that few of the children spoke German at home, and most of the ones old enough to speak already spoke Tok Pisin.[13] Adult children of the first generation interviewed in 1979 say their parents told them that the creole developed as the children played with language, replacing words in Tok Pisin sentences with German words as older children told stories to younger children in the evening. This may have been a way of circumventing the teachers' and dormitory supervisors' rules that the children were forbidden to speak anything except German or it may have been a way of relieving the stress of having to speak grammatical Standard German all day with teachers.

Examples of Unserdeutsch constructions are given in Appendix 2. Certainly, while most of the vocabulary of Unserdeutsch is German, many of the structures

---

[12] Horst Gründer et al., *Christliche Heilbotschaft und weltliche Macht. Studien zum Verhältnis von Mission und Kolonialismus. Gesammelte Aufsätze* (Münster: LIT Verlag, 2004), 114.
[13] Arnold Janssen, "Die Erziehungsanstalt für halbweisse Kinder," in *Pioniere der Südsee*, ed. Josef Hueskes (Hiltrup: Missionare Hlst. Herzen, 1932), 150.

show an obvious influence of Tok Pisin and the Austronesian languages of the area. For example, many speakers distinguish between "inclusive we" (you and me, Tok Pisin *yumi*) and "exclusive we" (we but not you, Tok Pisin *mipela*) made in Tok Pisin and Austronesian languages, as in the following two sentences, where *uns*, Standard German "us", is used for "inclusive we" and *wir*, Standard German "we", is used for "exclusive we":

1) Uns bis neben Saltzwasser.
   we:inclusive are next.to saltwater
   "We are next to the ocean."
   (Tok Pisin: Yumi klostu long solwara.)

2) Wir alle geht Rabaul.
   we:exclusive all go Rabaul
   "We (but not you) are going to Rabaul."
   (Tok Pisin: Mipela go long Rabaul.)

Word order is also similar to Tok Pisin, with strings of serial verbs and interrogatives usually at the end of a sentence, as the following example shows:

3) Du laufen geht wo?
   you run go where
   "Where are you running to?"
   (Tok Pisin: Yu ran i go we? Standard German: Wohin läufst du?)

At the same time some features of the language are undoubtedly the result of either imperfect second language learning or teasing others for poor language learning, as they are similar to the grammatically reduced forms of German used with guest workers in Germany or to the popular youth slang current now in Germany known as Kanak Sprak.[14]

In any case, Unserdeutsch quickly became the in-group language among the children, used in everyday situations when they were not with teachers. As the oldest of these pupils neared the end of their teen years, the nuns matched them up for marriage and most went to work as couples for the mission's many plantation, shipping, and other commercial outlets. The young couples usually spoke

---

[14] Kanaka is a pejorative word for indigenous people often used by the German nuns to their students speaking Tok Pisin or behaving in a Papua New Guinean way (*Kein Pidgin, ihr seid keine Kanaken!* "No Pidgin, you're not kanakas!"). It is therefore ironic that a way of speaking with reduced verbal and other marked grammatical features currently popular among German youth is called Kanak Sprak (see Füglein 2000), with Kanak becoming a synonym for "cool".

Unserdeutsch together, so their children grew up with Unserdeutsch as a first language, acquiring Standard German when they went to the Vunapope School, often as boarding students like their parents before them.

Older persons interviewed in 1979 and 1980 reported that Unserdeutsch played an important part in helping this small community establish an identity in the racially stratified society of colonial New Guinea. They had been denied any knowledge of their Melanesian heritage, although a few of them did maintain occasional contact with their indigenous extended families. At the same time, they were not allowed full entry into white society. The use of their own variety of German helped them to establish an identity that was of Melanesia but with German roots and a feeling that they were socially and educationally above the Melanesian masses. For this reason it was used as a symbol even by those who spoke and used Standard German fluently.

3. The German language in the interwar years (1921–1941)

In 1914 Australian troops invaded German New Guinea, proclaiming in poor Tok Pisin "God save him King". This de facto absorption of German New Guinea into Australia became official in 1921 with the legal announcement of what was now to be called the Territory of New Guinea as a League of Nations mandate under Australian administration.

3.1 German in government and business

Although the Australians changed little in the overall pattern of colonial administration, the language of government immediately became English. With the end of the war and the signing of the Versailles Treaty, most German plantation owners and business people were deported to Germany, with plantations usually being given to returned Australian veterans, who understandably had no interest in maintaining German as a language of business. Germans and their language no longer had a presence in public life outside of the missions.

3.2 German names

Of 39 prominent German geographic names in the Territory, 58% were changed to English or indigenous names.[15] In general, where there had once been an English name, such as New Britain and New Ireland, this was restored. Names associated with the German imperial family were usually changed to indigenous names (e.g., Kaiserin-Augustafluss to Sepik River and Friederich Wilhelmshafen to Madang), although the tallest mountain in the Territory, Mount Wilhelm, avoided being renamed. Surprisingly, the Bismarck Sea and Bismarck Archipelago were also left unchanged.

There was no objection to German personal names, however. As most Lutheran and Catholic missionaries were German, German baptismal and personal names remained popular.

3.3 Education and access to German in the interwar years

In spite of financial problems facing the Lutheran mission as a whole, German was still used at Sattelberg, where the Lutheran Church had a school for the children of missionaries, mixed-race children, and an occasional local child. As this was a centre of missionary activity and the home of training for Kâte-speaking church personnel, it can be assumed that German had a presence in this area that lasted until the Japanese invasion in 1941. But given the mission's strong emphasis on Kâte as the church's lingua franca and a medium of expression for the Melanesian *Volk*, there was no formal teaching of German.

The Vunapope School continued to teach German as a subject, but was required by the new Australian administration to adopt the official policy of using English as the medium of instruction in all other subjects. Former pupils interviewed in 1979 and 1980 reported that this policy was not always followed, as many of the teaching brothers and nuns could not express themselves well in English. There was also a shortage of textbooks in English, so even if the teacher spoke in English, often the textbook was an old one in German.

German remained an important language in the Vunapope Mission as a whole, as all missionaries came there from central Europe. Tolai choirs were taught to sing in German, especially at Christmas, but, as in Sattelberg, there

---

15 See Craig Alan Volker, "The German language in Papua New Guinea," in *Language in Papua New Guinea*, ed. Toru Okamura (Tokyo: Kuroshio, 2007), 107–125.

is no evidence that there was any attempt to teach indigenous persons communicative German.

3.4 German-speaking residents during the interwar years

After the Australian administration deported almost all non-missionary Germans, few had the means or desire to return to the Territory. By 1933, only 377 German citizens were in the Territory, all but 96 of them missionaries.[16] Even the German Club Rabaul had only 20 German members in 1932, far out-numbered by the more than 100 Australian members.[17] Without a critical mass of speakers, German was rarely heard outside of mission environments.

Among the mixed-race community on the mainland of New Guinea, some German fathers were successful in obtaining German citizenship for their mixed-race children and brought them to Germany. Children who were of only European ancestry tended to assimilate into the new Australian colonial society.

Lutheran mission personnel faced increasing hostility from the Australian administration in the 1930s as many of its workers became Nazi supporters, even founding a branch of the Nazi party in the New Guinea mainland coastal town of Finschhafen. With the outbreak of World War II in Europe and the Australian declaration of war against Germany, the Australian government deported German Lutheran missionaries and their families to Australia for internment.[18] Catholic missionaries, who had shown little or no interest in Nazi involvement, were left alone.

3.4.1 Unserdeutsch mixed-race community

The Unserdeutsch community remained more cohesive, helped by the fact that many families lived on isolated plantations on New Britain, coming together for special occasions with former schoolmates who were also Unserdeutsch speakers. Most continued to use Standard German in their contact with European staff at the Vunapope Mission. The period between the wars was probably the

---

16 See Reichsstelle für das Auswanderungswesen. Deutsche Evangelische Kirche, Evangelische Zentralarchiv Berlin. 5/2906 Neuguinea. 20.1.1936.
17 Christine Winter, *Looking after one's own: The Rise of Nationalism and the Politics of the Neuendettelsauer Mission in Germany, New Guinea and Australia (1922–1933)* (Frankfurt am Main: Peter Lang, Germanica Pacifica Volume 9, 2012), 180.
18 See *Ibid.*

time of the greatest stability for the language and its speakers. Racial barriers and acceptance into the ruling European society were, if anything, more difficult under Australian rule, causing the establishment of an intense social life within the mixed-race community itself. At the same time, accounts speak of the Australians permitting the missionaries to take any mixed-race children they found into their care, whether they were in a caring family relationship or not. One woman spoke of how her mother was found playing near her home on New Hanover by nuns, who simply bundled her into a car and took her to Vunapope on New Britain. This was in spite of her Chinese father and New Hanover mother being married and not consenting to her being taken. Her mother never saw her parents again. Actions such as this increased the number of children at the Vunapope orphanage, and as a result also increased the number of Unserdeutsch speakers.

4. German in the decades leading to Independence (1945–1975)

World War II brought modern violence to Papua New Guinea on a scale never before seen, as it experienced an often brutal Japanese occupation, American carpet bombings, and a bloody Australian counter invasion. It also brought a reappraisal in Australia of the importance of its northern neighbor and the debt owed by Australians to the "fuzzy wuzzy angels" who had supported Australian troops and helped prevent a Japanese invasion of Australia.

4.1 Education and access to the German language during the post-World War II years

In the aftermath of World War II, Australia joined the Territory of New Guinea, now a United Nations trusteeship, to its Territory of Papua under one administration. New areas of the country were opened to the outside world and school systems expanded significantly.

However, Papua New Guineans did not have renewed access to learning foreign languages other than English. After World War II, rebuilding the education system was part of an effort to tie Papua and New Guinea more closely to Australia[19], so there was little incentive to open up the world outside Australia to indigenous students. The education system remained rigidly divided along racial lines, so that while white (and sometimes mixed-race) children at the "A schools" following an Australian curriculum sometimes had the same opportunity to study German or French that their Australian counterparts had, the few Papua New Guinean children who attended post-secondary "T schools" for indigenous students were not given an option to study this or any other foreign language except English.

Two primary schools with boarding facilities were opened during this period that taught in German to the children of German-speaking expatriates, one operated in the Eastern Highlands by the Swiss Evangelical Brethren Mission and the other, the Kathrine Lehman Schule in the Wau highlands area of Morobe Province, operated by the Lutheran Church. Neither was open to indigenous children.

4.2 German-speaking residents after World War II

After World War II most Germans in Papua and New Guinea were missionaries. Although the German Catholic missionaries who survived the war years tended to stay back, they were often replaced by American and Australian staff after they had retired. The Lutheran Church rebuilt its mission and school system, expanding it far into the New Guinea Highlands region. It relied heavily on German staff. While the German language was not used in public, these German missionaries were very visible; in many areas they provided the only educational or health services available. In this way, although Papua New Guineans had little access to the German language, they often did develop a very positive attitude to the German people.

4.2.1 The Unserdeutsch community after World War II

After World War II, as the Vunapope Mission and schools were rebuilt, American nuns were brought in as teachers to reinforce English as the language of the school. Children were prohibited from speaking German either at school or in the dormitories, even with German staff. German was no longer offered as a subject and the teachers emphasized an Australian identity. Day scholars living near

---

19 Lyndon Megarrity, "Indigenous education in colonial Papua New Guinea: Australian government policy (1945–1975)," *History of Education Review* 34, 2 (2005): 43.

the school might still use German and Unserdeutsch at home, but this was strongly discouraged by teachers, who went to the pupils' homes to tell mixed-race parents not to speak German to their children any more. An indication of new attitudes of mixed-race confidence after the war can be seen in one respondent's story. After one such visit from a teacher, the respondent's mother was furious and said that as a German she did not have to do what "an uncultured Australian" asked her to do. The father of this family reacted by making his children speak Standard German instead of English at home. But given the lack of German instruction, even though this respondent and his siblings speak fluent Standard German as well as Unserdeutsch today, they are unable to read or write the language.

In the 1960s, mixed-race and Chinese residents of New Guinea were allowed to register as naturalized Australian citizens, thus ending the stateless status most had. This move allowed their children to be sent to Australia to attend boarding school at the government's expense, immersing them in an English-speaking environment with only one annual visit to their parents at Christmas. Understandably, this had a negative effect on their ability to retain Unserdeutsch. While this change in status opened up new avenues for these children, it still did not mean the abolition of racial barriers at home. One of these barriers was the inability to join social and sporting clubs. The Unserdeutsch community and their supporters, including a few white Australians, decided to form their own social club, the Ralum Club, in Kokopo (formerly Herbertshöhe), near Rabaul. This quickly became a meeting place where Unserdeutsch was often used amongst the emerging mixed-race middle class. This meant that even as their children in Australian boarding schools had fewer opportunities to speak Unserdeutsch, adult members of the community had more opportunities to socialize in the language.

5. German after Independence (1975 – 2016)

Papua New Guinea was granted independence peacefully from Australia in 1975 and has remained a democracy within the Commonwealth since then. In the constitution adopted at Independence, special mention was made in different sections of English, Tok Pisin, Hiri Motu, and, as a group, the many vernacular languages of the country. No mention was made of German or the German colonial period.

5.1 Ties with German-speaking countries

One year after Papua New Guinea achieved independence, both the Federal Republic of Germany[20] and Switzerland[21] established diplomatic relations with Papua New Guinea. This was followed in the following years by the German Democratic Republic in 1978[22] and Austria. Of these, the only one to open an embassy in Papua New Guinea was the Federal Republic of Germany, which it then closed in 2000. Today all these countries are represented only by honorary consuls and the European Delegation to Papua New Guinea, whose website states that the UK and France are the EU countries providing the most aid to Papua New Guinea.[23] Trade between Papua New Guinea and Germany is not significant; "there are currently no major German companies located in the country" according to the German Federal Foreign Office webpage for Papua New Guinea.[24]

Although the German ambassador in Australia is accredited to Papua New Guinea, ceremonial affairs are usually handled by the honorary consul, a long-time German resident of Port Moresby. This was so even at a ceremony marking the centenary of the 1914 Battle of Bita Paka near Rabaul, an event that resulted in the transfer of German New Guinea to Australian rule. There is therefore no significant governmental or commercial link between independent Papua New Guinea and its first colonial master.

5.2 German names today

Unlike many other countries achieving independence, Papua New Guinea did not rename geographic names inherited from the colonial era. This means that

---

20 See Auswärtiges Amt, "Papua Neuguinea," March 2015, accessed May 10, 2016, www.auswaertiges-amt.de/DE/Aussenpolitik/Laender/Laenderinfos/01-Nodes_Uebersichtsseiten/PapuaNeuguinea_node.html.
21 See Jean-Marc Crevoisier ed., "Bilaterale Beziehungen Schweiz–Papua-Neuguinea," *Eidgenössisches Departement für auswärtige Angelegenheiten*, accessed May 10, 2016, www.eda.admin.ch/eda/de/home/vertretungen-und-reisehinweise/papua-neuguinea/bilatereale-beziehungenschweizpapua-neuguinea.html.
22 Siegfried Bock, et al., eds., *DDR-Außenpolitik: Ein Überblick. Daten, Fakten, Personen (III)* (Berlin: LIT Verlag, 2010), 180.
23 See Delegation of the European Union to Papua New Guinea, "Papua New Guinea," accessed May 10, 2016, eeas.europa.eu/delegations/papua_new_guinea/index_en.htm.
24 See Auswärtiges Amt, "Papua Neuguinea," March 2015, accessed May 10, 2016, www.auswaertiges-amt.de/DE/Aussenpolitik/Laender/Laenderinfos/01-Nodes_Uebersichtsseiten/PapuaNeuguinea_node.html.

the German names that had not been changed by Australians at the end of World War I remained the same. The one exception is New Hanover, which in recent years has been referred to more often by its indigenous name Lavongai. On many maps today both names are mentioned. A list of significant geographic names of German origin and their current names is given in Appendix 1.

Even though German names have been retained, they have acquired a local significance, and their foreign origin is rarely given a thought. Almost every university has a "Bismarck Club", for example, but by this is meant a club for students from the Bismarck Archipelago, without any reference to the German politician. Similarly, for New Irelanders away from home, the Boluminski Highway is something to be nostalgic about, not a remembrance of German domination, but as something uniquely related to New Ireland. These names are an unconscious legacy of colonial rule, without any reference to outsiders or their language.

5.3 Education and access to German

For many years after independence, students could learn German at Lae International High School, a private school attended by both expatriates and wealthy Papua New Guineans. This was the only access indigenous Papua New Guineans had to the German language. When smaller student numbers required a downsizing in staff and curriculum offerings in 2003, German was dropped. At that time about twenty students were studying German, about half of them Papua New Guinea citizens. Since German is not taught at any other high schools or at the six universities in the country, there is now nowhere in Papua New Guinea where German can be learnt.

This contrasts sharply with neighboring Indonesia. The website of the German embassy there describes a vibrant cultural and educational scene with an active German Academic Exchange Service (DAAD), and a Goethe-Institute in Jakarta with a branch at a university elsewhere on Java offering many opportunities to learn German.[25] It states that about 27,000 Indonesians have studied in Germany since 1945, many with German scholarships. The corresponding number for Papua New Guinea would be much smaller. There is no Goethe Institute in Papua New Guinea, which is theoretically within the region of the Jakarta Goethe Institute, and no office organizing scholarships or information for Papua New Guineans wishing to study in Germany. There is no facility in the

---

25 www.jakarta.diplo.de/Vertretung/jakarta/de/07_20Kultur/0-Kultur.html.

country for applying for German student visas, which in recent years have become very difficult and expensive to get.[26] The German language is therefore inaccessible to Papua New Guinean students and has no presence in their academic planning.

Education in German for expatriate children has also almost completely disappeared. In the 1990s, crime levels on the New Guinea mainland, especially in Morobe Province, worsened in the midst of serious economic problems. Due of this and also because of a localization policy aimed at replacing foreign mission workers with Papua New Guineans, the number of foreign mission staff declined. As a result, the Lutheran Kathrine Lehman Schule for the children of German Lutheran missionaries in Wau closed in the 1990s.

Of the two schools teaching in German for the children of missionary families after World War II, only the Swiss Evangelical Brethren Mission school remains open. The mission has a policy to keep its school open as long as any of its workers are in the country with children. It usually has less than a dozen students at any time, only a few of whom are from the Swiss mission itself and none of whom is indigenous.

5.4 The Unserdeutsch and other German-Melanesian communities after Independence

Like other mixed-race and Chinese residents of New Britain, many members of the Unserdeutsch community became worried about possible violence in the months leading up to Independence. While that did not happen, most did choose to retain Australian citizenship rather than opt for Papua New Guinean citizenship at Independence. In many cases their children, having gone to school or university in Australia, had already decided to stay and make a new life there. Increasingly, more moved to Australia until today there are less than a dozen speakers of Unserdeutsch in Papua New Guinea itself.

In Australia, most speakers and their families live in or around the Brisbane-Gold Coast area in south-eastern Queensland, although there are smaller groups in Cairns and Sydney. Today not more than 120 persons speak the language, the youngest of whom are in their fifties, as English has become the dominant home language of all but one household. With increased social mobility and much

---

[26] Applicants must appear in person at the German consulate in Sydney for fingerprinting and an interview, but to do this they must first obtain an expensive Australian visa, which is normally not given to persons travelling to Australia to apply for a visa to a third country.

Unserdeutsch reunion in Brisbane with German New Guinea flag

more relaxed attitudes about racial categories in both Papua New Guinea and Australia, most younger and middle-aged persons have married out of their community and are well integrated into either Papua New Guinean or Australian society. Among the youngest generation in Australia, nostalgia is more likely to be expressed towards Papua New Guinea than to Germany. Some who have grown up in Australia even speak Tok Pisin because of their friendships with other Papua New Guineans there. In Brisbane the community meets once a year for a community picnic. As a result of visits by linguists associated with the University of Augsburg documenting the language and history of the community since 2014, there has recently been a renewed interest in the Unserdeutsch language by its speakers in Australia and an awareness of its unique position as the only recorded creole language with a German base. A Facebook group for Unserdeutsch speakers has become popular in the community, including among younger persons who no longer speak the language.

In Papua New Guinea itself Unserdeutsch has become the first Papua New Guinean language to become moribund through emigration to another country, as there are too few speakers distributed over too many areas to constitute a critical mass to keep the language alive in the country. A few individuals keep a German or Unserdeutsch identity through family ties and Facebook connections to friends and family in Australia, but this is not enough to keep a language or community alive. When asked how he practices speaking German when there is no one left on his island to speak Unserdeutsch to, one of these few speakers left said he speaks with his flowers every morning, as no person on his island will be able to understand what he says.

In this respect they are like other groups of Papua New Guineans with German heritage. While several individuals from other mixed-race communities are active politically or professionally, their Australian and middle-class Papua New Guinean identities are stronger than any German heritage. Certainly, there is no public awareness of a German community in Papua New Guinea. The only real awareness of a German-Melanesian connection is among older Unserdeutsch speakers living in Australia, who are, as one speaker said, "the last drops of Germany in the Pacific Ocean".

6. Conclusion

In 1884, German became the official language of a colony that, together with British Papua, eventually became the Independent State of Papua New Guinea. German colonization was short, but had a lasting effect on the people of this part of Melanesia.

Many of the foundations of this modern nation state come from Germans and their colonial empire, and many basic modern structures and social patterns come from the German *guttaim bipo*. Many customs, in fact, are still even called by their German names, like the colorful arches of flowers (*Bogen*) at the entrances to Lutheran churches during church festivals. Names of German origin, such as Boluminski Highway, Mount Hagen Town, and Mount Wilhelm, are thought of as local names and a focus for local pride, not nostalgia for, or even memory of, the time of the German colonisers. The invisibility of the German language and culture is symptomatic of the almost non-existent engagement by Germany itself with Papua New Guinea today. Tok Pisin and Chinese, not German, are the linguistic legacies of German colonial rule.

In Papua New Guinea today, German has same position it had in 1883, the year before the German colonial rule started. It is the language of a few foreign sojourners, learned by their partners and the occasional Papua New Guinean person coming to Europe. As in 1883, it is no longer a language of Papua New Guinea, and Germany itself is faraway, exotic, and inaccessible. The strongest nostalgia for the German engagement in Papua New Guinea is in Australia, the country that took the colony away from Germany, among the small Unserdeutsch community, German-Melanesians who have nearly all left the country their great-grandfathers tried to colonize.

**Appendix 1 Major geographic names of German origin
(German data from Dotlan (2005), Moran (2004), and Schnee (1920))**

German name	modern name	changed?
Adelbertgebirge	Adelbert Range (Madang Province)	no
Alexishafen	Alexishafen (Madang Province)	no
Berlinhafen	Aitape (East Sepik Province)	yes
Binnenhafen	Binnen (Madang Town)	no
Bismarkarchipel	Bismarck Archipelago	no
Bismarkgebirge	Bismarck Range (Eastern Highlands Province)	no
Dallmannhafen	Vanimo (Sandaun Province)	yes
Finschhafen	Finschhafen (Morobe Province)	no
Französische Inseln	Vitu Islands	yes
Friedrich Wilhelmshafen	Madang Town	yes
Hansemannküste	Sepik coast (northern New Guinea coast)	yes
Hagenberg, Hagengebirge	Mt Hagen	no
Hatzfeldhafen	Hatzfeldhaven (Madang Province)	no
Herbertshöhe	Kokopo	yes
Kaiserin-Augustafluss	Sepik River	yes
Kaiser Wilhelmsland	northeastern New Guinea Island	yes
Konstantinhafen	Erimba (Madang Province)	yes
Neuhannover	New Hannover (New Ireland Province) (also known as Lavongai)	no
Neulauenberg (Neu-Lauenberg)	Duke of York Islands (East New Britain)	yes
Neumecklenburg (Neu-Mecklenburg)	New Ireland	yes
Neupommern (Neu-Pommern)	New Britain	yes
Ottilienfluss	Ramu River	yes
Potsdamhafen	Gabun? (Madang Province)	yes
Preussen-Reede	Lae	yes
Sattelberg	Sattelberg (Moroibe Province)	no

Schleinitzgebirge	Schleinitz Range (New Ireland Province)	no
Schouten-Inseln	Schouten Islands	no
Schradergebirge	Schrader Range (Madang Province)	no
Seeadlerhafen	Lorengau (Manus Province)	yes
Simpsonhafen	Rabaul Town (East New Britain Province)	yes
	Blanche Harbour	yes
St. Matthias-Inseln	St. Matthias Islands (New Ireland Province)	no
Stephansort	Bogadjim (Madang Province)	yes
Stoschberg	Suilik? (New Ireland Province)	yes
Varzinberg	Vunakokar (East New Britain Province)	yes
Weberhafen	Nonga (East New Britain Province)	yes
Wilhelmsberg	Mt Wilhelm (Simbu Province)	no
Willaumezhalbinsel	Willaimez Peninsula (West New Britain)	no

Translations of German geographic terms:

Archipel = archipelago
Berg = mountain
Binnen = inner
Fluss = river
Französische = French
Gebirge = mountain range
Hafen = habor
Halbinsel = peninsula
Insel(n) = island(s)
Kaiser = emperor
Kaiserin = empress
Küste = coast
Neu = new
Ort = place
Preussen = Prussia
Reede = road

Appendix 2 Representative examples of Rabaul Creole German sentences and phrases

1 | Schtor | wo | alle | Boi | komm.
 | Store | where | plural | indigenous. man | come

"Store where the indigenous men go."

Alle = Tok Pisin plural marker *ol*
Schtor and *Boi* from English "store" and "boy"

2 | Maria | is | mehr | klein | denn | Des.
 | Maria | is | more | small | than | Des.

"Maria is smaller than Des."

mehr + *denn* = English "more" + "than"
cf Standard German comparative with adjective + -er: kleiner

3 Mein   Bein   is   wie   ein
   Hols.
   my   leg   is   like   a
   wood
   My leg has fallen asleep. / My leg has pins and needles.
   from a Tok Pisin idiom

4 I   war   gegangen   fi   such.
   I   was   gone   for   search
   I went looking for them.

fi, from Standard German *für* "for", as complementizer, analogous to early Melanesian Pidgin *fo*
cf Standard German *um* (direct object) + *zu* + verb

5 Haus fi   Tom. De   Stov fi   wir is   gel.
   house for   Tom. The   stove for   we is   yellow.
   Tom's house. Our stove is yellow

fi, from Standard German *für* "for", as possessive
cf Standard German *von* "of"
Stov from English "stove"
Gel, from Standard German *gelb*, with consonant cluster simplification

6 Maski,   i-un-du   / uns   geht   Flantage.
   Never.mind   I-and-you   / we.exclusive   go   plantation
   Never mind, we (including you) / we (excluding you) will go to the plantation.

Tok Pisin inclusive / exclusive "we" distinction, cf Tok Pisin *yumi* / *mipela*
Maski from Tok Pisin
Flantage from Standard German *Pflantage* with consonant cluster simplification

7 Du   laufen   geht   wo?
   You   run   go   where
   Where are you running?

Tok Pisin-like serial verb construction, (Tok Pisin *ran i go we*)
As in Tok Pisin and English no distinction between locative and directional where,
cf Standard German *wo* "where at" and *wohin* "where to"

8 De   Chicken war   gestohlen bei alle   Raskol.
  The   chicken was   stolen   by   plural criminal

The chicken was stolen by the criminals.

English-like passive: copula + participle + *by* + agent,
cf Standard German *werden* "become" + *von* "from" + agent + participle
Chicken from English,
Raskol from Tok Pisin *raskol* and PNG English *rascal* "criminal"
alle = Tok Pisin plural marker *ol*

Works cited

Auswärtiges Amt, "Papua Neuguinea." www.auswaertiges-amt.de/DE/Aussenpolitik/Laender/Laenderinfos/01-Nodes_Uebersichtsseiten/PapuaNeuguinea_node.html. March 2015 (accessed 10 May 2016).

Bock, Siegfried, Ingrid Muth, and Hermann Schwiesau, eds. *DDR-Außenpolitik: Ein Überblick. Daten, Fakten, Personen (III)*. Berlin: LIT Verlag. 2010.

Crevoisier, Jean-Marc, ed., "Bilaterale Beziehungen Schweiz–Papua-Neuguinea." *Eidgenössisches Departement für auswärtige Angelegenheiten*. www.eda.admin.ch/eda/de/home/vertretungen-und-reisehinweise/papua-neuguinea/bilatereale-beziehungenschweizpapua-neuguinea.html (accessed 10 May 2016).

Delegation of the European Union to Papua New Guinea, "Papua New Guinea." eeas.europa.eu/delegations/papua_new_guinea/index_en.htm (accessed 10 May 2016).

Dotlan, G., "Frontline18: Die deutschen Kolonien – Neuguinea und die Inseln des Stillen Ozeans." www.frontline18.com/history/326/.2005 (accessed 1 May 2007).

Füglein, Rosemarie. "Kanak Sprak. Eine ethnolinguistische Untersuchung eines Sprachphänomens im Deutschen". Magisterarbeit. Universität Bamberg, 2000.

Gründer, Horst et al. *Christliche Heilbotschaft und weltliche Macht. Studien zum Verhältnis von Mission und Kolonialismus. Gesammelte Aufsätze*. Münster: LIT Verlag. 2004.

Janssen, Arnold. "Die Erziehungsanstalt für halbweisse Kinder." In *Pioniere der Südsee*, edited by Josef Hueskes, 150–155. Hiltrup: Missionare Hlst. Herzen, 1932.

Kößler, Reinhart. "La fin d'une amnésie? L'Alemagne et son passé colonial depuis 2004." *Politique Africaine* 2.102 (2006): 50–66.

Megarrity, Lyndon. "Indigenous education in colonial Papua New Guinea: Australian government policy (1945–1975)." *History of Education Review* 34.2 (2005): 41–58.

Moran, Michael. *Beyond the Coral Sea*. London: Harper Collins. 2003.

Mühlhäusler, Peter. "Tracing the roots of pidgin German". *Language and Communication* 41.1 (1984): 27–57.

Mühlhäusler, Peter. "Die deutsche Sprache im Pazifik." In *Die deutsche Südsee 1884–1914. Ein Handbuch*, edited by Hermann J. Hiery, 239–260. Paderhorn: Schöningh, 2001.

Reichsstelle für das Auswanderungswesen. Deutsche Evangelische Kirche, Evangelische Zentralarchiv Berlin. 5/2906 Neuguinea. 20.1.1936.

Robson, R. W. *Queen Emma: The Samoan-American Girl who founded an Empire in the 19th Century New Guinea*. Sydney / New York: Pacific Publications. 1973.

Schnee, Heinrich. *Deutsches Kolonial-Lexikon*. Leipzig: Quelle & Meyer. 1920. Original print edition digitalized by the Stadt- und Universitätsbibliothek Frankfurt am Main, www.ub.bildarchiv-dkg.uni-frankfurt.de/Bildprojekt/Lexikon/Standardframeseite.php (accessed 1 May 2007).

Volker, Craig Alan. "The German language in Papua New Guinea." In *Language in Papua New Guinea*, edited by Toru Okamura, 107–125. Tokyo: Kuroshio, 2007.

Winter, Christine. *Looking after one's own: The Rise of Nationalism and the Politics of the Neuendettelsauer Mission in Germany, New Guinea and Australia (1922–1933)*. Frankfurt am Main: Peter Lang. Germanica Pacifica Volume 9. 2012.

www.ingramcontent.com/pod-product-compliance
Lightning Source LLC
Chambersburg PA
CBHW070612170426
43200CB00012B/2671